Hipbillies

Ⓞzarks Studies
EDITED BY BROOKS BLEVINS

OTHER TITLES IN THIS SERIES

The Literature of the Ozarks:
An Anthology

Down on Mahans Creek:
A History of an Ozarks Neighborhood

Hipbillies

Deep Revolution
in the Arkansas Ozarks

Jared M. Phillips

The University of Arkansas Press
Fayetteville
2019

ISBN: 978-1-68226-089-0 (cloth)
ISBN: 978-1-68226-090-6 (paper)
eISBN: 978-1-61075-659-4

23   22   21   20   5   4   3

Designed by Liz Lester

♾ The paper used in this publication meets
the minimum requirements of the American
National Standard for Permanence of Paper
for Printed Library Materials Z39.48-1984.

Library of Congress Cataloging-in-Publication Data

Names: Phillips, Jared M., 1982–   author.
Title: Hipbillies : deep revolution in the Arkansas Ozarks /
    Jared M. Phillips.
Other titles: Hipbillies, deep revolution in the Arkansas Ozarks
Description: Fayetteville, AR : The University of Arkansas Press, [2019] |
    Includes bibliographical references and index. |
Identifiers: LCCN 2018037826 (print) | LCCN 2018046874 (ebook) |
    ISBN 9781610756594 (electronic) | ISBN 9781682260890 (cloth :
    alk. paper) | ISBN 9781682260906 (pbk. : alk. paper)
Subjects: LCSH: Ozark Mountains Region—History—20th century. |
    Counterculture—Arkansas—History. | Counterculture—Ozark
    Mountain Region—History. | Hippies—Arkansas—History. |
    Hippies—Ozark Mountains—History. | Jeffords, Edd. | Ozark
    Institute. | Arkansas—Civilization. | Arkansas—Politics and
    government—20th century. | Urban-rural migration—United States—
    History. | Self-reliant living—Arkansas—History.
Classification: LCC F417.O9 (ebook) | LCC F417.O9 P55 2019 (print) |
    DDC 305.5/6807671—dc23
    LC record available at https://lccn.loc.gov/2018037826

CONTENTS

I Was a Teenage Hipbilly

As I read an advance manuscript for Jared Phillip's *Hipbillies*, I kept going back to Elvira and the pig creep.

Elvira was a Hampshire sow, black with a white bellyband, on the communal farm I lived on in Ava, Missouri. This was in 1970, back when I was a teenage hipbilly. The pig creep was to be her winter shelter, and I had taken on the task of its construction.

I certainly would have proudly owned the witty self-definition *hipbilly* had I heard it at the time, but I didn't, not until decades later. We alternative types—and here I must confess that every time I refer to this looser-than-loose affiliation as "we," I cringe a little—usually used the word *freaks*, nonpejoratively, to describe ourselves.

But closer to what I think I considered myself might've been "a fugitive from injustice," in the words of a rock 'n' roll song of the period ("What about Me?" by Quicksilver Messenger Service). I think a lot of those who were part of the broader back to the land countercultural movement unfolding across the country in that era saw themselves as this kind of fugitive, a point Phillips makes clearly as he takes apart the widespread disgust, horror, and despair, among a certain subset of young people (predominantly white, middle class, educated) when we gazed at our country. We saw an unjust war, systemic racism and injustice, ecologically rash policies, a class-divided consumerist society undergirded by a shortsighted, powerful, threatening military-industrial complex.

Yet, as Phillips points out, we were also disillusioned by its opposition. Taking-it-to-the-streets political action had proved so ineffective at bringing change.

Back to the land represented a third choice. It was a movement that was idealistic, recurrent in America, full of "old beliefs about human community" and "anchored by a renewed belief in the power of the environment" (as Phillips puts it). It was contradictory, independent, somewhat hopeful. It promised hard work, meaning, and the chance to live a different life . . . and maybe save the planet, or a little piece of it.

This movement was not monolithic. Yet there were some universals, and Phillips finds them.

In *Hipbillies,* I see myself—at least partially. I'm here directly, quoted a few times. I'm here indirectly, as part of the movement he describes. I was, after all, a "Yankee [who] had left the big city and headed for the hills."

That brings me, sort of, to Elvira.

Part of my disgust with the system as a whole was with industrialized food systems that despoiled both human health and the planet. By the time I got to the Ozarks, I was already thinking about food in ways that wound up informing a good chunk of my life's work: that one should be thoughtful about what one ate, should not be alienated from one's food. If one was going to eat meat, one should accept, up close, slaughter, and should be reverent, holistic, logical, with no disgust at eating organ meat and with no preference for eating some kinds of animals and not others. I am the rare vegetarian who has helped (in her nonvegetarian past) butcher goats, lambs, chickens; who has skinned, cleaned, and eaten squirrel, groundhog, and snapping turtle; and who has prepared and eaten animal livers, kidneys, hearts, brains, and thymus glands (sweetbreads).

In the life I had growing up, far from Ava, Missouri, I had eaten sweetbreads with my father at Sardi's, a storied white-tablecloth restaurant in New York City's theater district, epicenter of my father's professional world, where he was greeted by name. There, tall men in special black suits with white shirts would lean down asking him, "And who's this young lady?" And I, in my velvet party dress with the white lace collar, would be introduced.

But what I'd learned as the daughter of a show business biographer was of little relevance as a teenager aspiring to self-sufficiency in the Ozarks, except as a source of shame. New York, celebrity: it looked to me then like such irrelevance, decadence, ego, folly, hubris. The world was falling apart, trembling on the brink of ecocide! Who cared if your caricature hung on the wall of Sardi's?

Which was how I found myself attempting to build a pig creep in the Ozarks.

I had taken care of Elvira when she was a piglet. We were fond of each other. She would trot over at the sound of my footsteps without even being called and rub her head with its pointed ears affectionately against my knee. "Pigs," the man I was then coupled with told me, "are as smart as dogs." In contrast to mine, his skill set—growing up on a farm in Spur, Texas—was useful. *He* had nothing to be ashamed of. All of us considered him the authority on matters of rural life, though, being antiauthoritarian, none of us would have said so.

When I scratched Elvira behind her ears, she would give a delighted little squeal and push her snout against me, her version of what a dog or cat does when indicating it appreciates the attention and wants more. Still, I was prepared for the fact that one day she would be part of breakfasts and pots of beans.

But black-eyes and bacon would be next fall. Right now it was *this* fall. Winter was coming. Elvira would need a shelter, called by our Texan a pig creep.

"I want to build it," I said. "Myself. As much as possible."

For again, there they are, in Phillips's explorations: The currents of feminism and I-can-by-God-do-anything ran through my sensibilities; while Elvira was an actual pig, I was plenty pigheaded and as bristly. I was also an utterly unhandy seventeen-year-old, ashamed of having grown up in a family where you all but called an electrician if you wanted to change a lightbulb. I had to prove that I was of use, now and after the revolution. That I could rely on myself, and my comrades could rely on me, in ways closer to the ground zero of real survival than my velvet-party-dress upbringing.

This also made me eager to learn from my native Ozark neighbors, who clearly had more of what I considered real-world experience than I did.

In those days, many farmers had old falling-down barns and outbuildings and would allow hipbillies to come tear them down, as long as we carried off all the old wood. That was of course what we wanted. Both parties thought they were getting the better deal. The farmer had gotten rid of an eyesore, a fire hazard, hadn't had to pay to have it torn down and hauled off. The alternative types had gotten thousands of board feet of wood, free. This kind of exchange often started the social ecology and mutual respect between natives and back to the landers. It added to what Phillips calls "an air of possibility" in the Ozarks.

Our group having torn down such a barn, we had plenty of wood: white oak, not just hardwood but *very* hard wood, dense, weathered. It could become yurts, toolsheds, smokehouses (we'd also need to build one before Elvira's eventual slaughter). I would use it to build the pig creep.

Fall is busy for those who aspire to self-sufficiency. The last of the garden's yield has to be picked, put up, or dried. (Our most successful crop, that first year, was turnips. I had never been fond of turnips, but by the end of our first winter at the farm I developed a loathing for them that's never left me).

Between chores, I would go off to work on Elvira's pig creep.

Every day, Elvira grew larger. And because it was fall, every day grew shorter.

Elvira's pen—large, shaded with oaks providing plenty of the acorns she loved—was uphill from the nondescript forties-era farmhouse we shared, with its assortment of cars and pickups decorated with muddy prints—of not only the farm's cats' and dogs' paws but of the hooves of goats who also enjoyed clambering up and down the vehicles. (Phillips is right about the omnipresent goats.) The pen was bordered with a low single-strand electric fence. Once I got past the terrifying idea of barely visible electrified wire, it was easy to step over it.

The Texan built the frame for the pig creep, this being beyond my nonexistent carpentry skills. All I had to do was hammer the boards, which I had handsawed: back and forth, a sixteenth of an inch gained at a time, boring work, and hard. My hands blistered, then callused; probably my upper body never looked better. Then I carried the boards up the hill and stacked them in the pen, near the frame.

After stepping over the electric wire each afternoon, I'd be greeted by Elvira, who on hearing my footsteps, came trotting up with happy enthusiasm, vocalizing joyfully on a rising squeal of "EeeeeEEEEEEE, eeeeeeEEEEEEE, eeeeeeeEEEE!" I'd scratch her behind her ears—something that grew less pleasant after small insects began living on her tough skin in the forest of her bristles, and the Texan rubbed her down with motor oil to kill them. And then, to work.

Elvira had no interest in the creep. She wanted to play. When I stopped scratching her and walked over to the boards, boards I soon hated on sight, she would follow me hopefully, asking, "EeeeEEEE?" meaning, "Aren't we going to play some more?"

"No, Elvira, I have to build your house for the winter."

Her response was to nudge me, with increasing firmness. "Don't you remember how much fun it is to play? Come on! Put that stuff down! We can play!"

Pushing away a sow who wants to play is not easy. In fact, when you weigh 115 pounds or so, and she weighs double that, not even possible. As I'd select boards and begin to place them, kneeling on the ground to do the floor, I'd periodically be nudged, hard.

I'd place the nail, hold it, raise the hammer, swing. Most of the time, the nail would simply not penetrate. Nine times out of ten it would bend, defeated by the density of the oak. Oh, the frustration at being unable to do this, at wasting a resource (nails), at hammering fruitlessly while nudged by a gigantic, friendly sow.

Now, if I had to build a pig creep today, I'd ask for help. I'd use an electric drill and premake the holes (but we didn't use power tools). I would Google "nails," "weathered oak," and "pig creep" (no computers, Internet, or Google).

One gray November afternoon, when it was spitting cold rain and there was only an hour of daylight left, I went grimly to the pen. The floor was done, and I was working my way up the walls. I had to hold the boards up while attempting to hammer in the nails.

I had in one nail of the four each board required when Elvira gave me a nudge that knocked me off my feet into the leaves and icy mud, a kind of choppy stew macerated by Elvira's hooves. I lay on the ground, cold drizzle falling. Elvira, motor oiled, nudged my face gently, slightly anxious about me, it seemed. I got back up, lifted the iron-hard board, hanging by one nail, wedged my hip against it to hold in place, got another worthless nail, placed it, lifted the hammer, and swung again.

At that precise moment Elvira gave another nudge. I missed the nail altogether and brought the hammer, which I had been swinging with all the fury, frustration and unhappiness in my confused heart, on my thumb. Elvira nudged me a second time, hard, and I was back down on the ground again, cold, wet, muddy, leaves sticking to me, a large, anxious, long-lashed, oiled sow looking down at me, hopeful that I might yet get up and play. My throbbing thumb, which hurt so much I momentarily could not breathe, was already swelling.

I left the farm not long after that, before Elvira was slaughtered. About a year later, I made my way to Eureka Springs, where I gradually became part of a community, not a commune. There I gardened, preserved, and made friends with my neighbors (hip and straight) but did not try for self-sufficiency.

A few years later, Edd Jeffords, mentioned at length in *Hipbillies*, arrived. Corduroy-jacketed, pipe-smoking, he struck me as a conceited, smug, egotistical blowhard who was milking the system. What gave *him* the right to pontificate on "Ozarks in-migration" and back-to-the-landism? I couldn't imagine that *he* would ever be willing to roll in the mud to build a pig creep!

Of course, I had no more right than he, and Phillips's fair and documented portrait of the man and his endeavors made me reconsider my view.

But I got along all right with banker John Cross, also mentioned. Yes, he was an odious and controlling racist, but you knew where you stood with him, unlike Jeffords. (When Cross told me, "If we get any more hippies, we'll have to get out the white sheets," I replied, "Why not tie-dye them, John? White is so dull.")

I started the *Down Home*, mentioned by Phillips, after the *Times-Echo* began promulgating the utterly ridiculous story of the alleged upcoming planned hippie ballot-box takeover (*Planned?* Are you kidding?). I think the *Down Home* lasted ten months.

I was a month past my eighteenth birthday when I moved to Eureka Springs. I grew up there, gradually. I became more middle-of-the-road. I married. I opened an inn and restaurant called Dairy Hollow House, which was built around local, seasonal organic food. I wrote a few cookbooks about such food, one of which won a James Beard Award.

It was indeed to my surprise that I found myself, as Jared says, "a pillar of the community." Eventually, after being widowed, I left that community only to return sixteen years later to Fayetteville. As in the line from *The Godfather,* I felt of the Arkansas Ozarks that "they pull me back in."

But many of those one might loosely call my brothers and sisters in this movement never left. Just yesterday I shopped at Fayetteville's burgeoning, cheerful, friendly, extraordinarily diverse farmer's market, and saw many of them. The stand from Foothold Farm, in Jasper, Arkansas, featured tomatoes. (Thirty-six varieties! Most heirlooms!) It's one of many businesses created over time by aging hipbillies—and all of us still alive from that time *are* aging.

But was I, or were any of us, actually "neopioneers", engaging in acts of "deep revolution"? And if I was, or we were, were any of those acts effective? What makes a person a "true utopian revolutionary," anyway?

Trying to answer this had me scratching my head, as I considered Phillips's thoughtful take as an historian, an academic, a researcher par excellence, a fifth-generation Ozarker, who also wants, as he says, "to see the world remade." As he believes, partially correctly, that we, the original back to the landers, did.

Now, my particular life in this era is slightly outside Jared's described parameters. "Communes are left out," he writes, "because they are hefty enough to deserve a full study of their own. The same is true for the back to the land community in the Missouri Ozarks." Well, during the time of the pig creep, when I was a hardcore back to the lander, I lived in a commune in southwest Missouri.

Yet, as I said, there I am too in the taking back of childbirth from the system. While I never had a child of my own, I wrote a picture book (*Wind Rose,* 1976) loosely based on a friend who did, with the help of a midwife and the baby's father. And I did join the fight against 2,4,5 T. (My letters to SWEPCO are in the archives in the University of Arkansas Special Collections, as are the letters from two SWEPCO executives I once served tea to. Another story.)

As Phillips says, the stories are not finished yet. Sometimes you just have to be willing to roll in the mud to get at the truth. Some questions are not meant to be answered or are not, perhaps, answerable. But Jared Phillips has well and truly, respectfully and thoughtfully, begun here.

Crescent Dragonwagon

ACKNOWLEDGMENTS

To write anything requires the accruing of debts so large as to be beyond repayment—large enough, in fact, that I have considered asking friends in the classics how one goes about hiring Atlas to carry the load.

First and foremost, my thanks go out to the back to the landers (BTLs) themselves. I am loath to try and name them all here—some wish to be anonymous, some would be mortified, and some had already passed on before I learned their stories. But most of all, to list you all and thank you for trusting me with your stories would take another book in and of itself. This book would not exist had you all not believed in a better world and then gone out and built it. Nor would it exist had you all not taken time out of busy farming and work schedules to share your lives with me—something for which I am eternally grateful. I hope that this work will help begin paying the debt I owe you all.

That being said, I would like to thank a few of you in particular: Bob Billig, Guy Ames, and the late Frank Egan, who unexpectedly passed away as this book was going to press. Between you three, you read just about everything I wrote or heard every thought I had in my head. You made countless introductions, corrected my misperceptions, sharpened my thinking, and on the whole pushed me not to just understand the times but (unintentionally perhaps) to begin seeing how to embody the lessons of the hipbillies in my own life. Mostly, you tolerated the inane questioning of a young historian caught in wistful wishing that he had been there, living on the homestead one hill over. For that, I thank you.

Another large dose of thanks goes out to the kind staff at the Shiloh Museum of Ozark History in Springdale. In particular, I am grateful to Allyn Lord, Marie Demeroukas, and Susan Young. I will never forget the day I walked in rather innocently asking about hippies and you all, in separate conversations, said I was in over my head (or something to that effect). How right you were! And though she is no longer at the Shiloh

Museum, I also owe April Griffith thanks as well. Had I not heard her story about the Ozark Mountain Folk Fair on the Arkansas Public Radio station KUAF, I may not have gotten off my couch and started this project. To the folks at the University of Arkansas Libraries, in particular the special collections staff (current and past)—Joshua Youngblood, Tim Nutt, Geoffrey Stark, and others—thanks! You all helped me track down random publications, memoirs, newspapers, and more needed for the skeleton of the book. The indefatigable Interlibrary Loan Department at the University of Arkansas Libraries, in particular Robyn Young, also deserve more than a simple mention for the work done tracking down long-lost articles and publications about communes and hippies everywhere.

The Department of History at the University of Arkansas, the training ground I came through, deserves a greater mention than I am able to put here. Randall Woods, Patrick Williams, Mike Pierce, Robert Finlay, Trish Starks, Lynda Coon, and Kathy Sloan not only taught me the craft of the historian but listened patiently as I began this project, provided sage advice on writing, creating the book, and more. Thanks to you all. A further debt is also owed to Patrick Williams and the staff (and reviewers) at the *Arkansas Historical Quarterly* who published an early portion of the research and now are stuck with having longhairs gracing a cover of the *AHQ* forever. Justin Nolan, Joshua Lockyer, and Brian Campbell, anthropologists extraordinaire, thanks! Brooks Blevins, up north in the wilds of Missouri State University, the grand master of Ozark history, thanks for allowing me to ask impertinent questions and for sharpening my understanding of the Ozarks in general, but of the region at midcentury in particular. Brooks also deserves a healthy dose of thanks for shepherding this book from a rambling proposal into something almost readable. Thanks also go out to the organizers and participants of the Ozarks Symposium in West Plains—Phil Howerton, especially—for a rousing conference and discussions that continue to deepen my understanding of the Ozarks.

Another measure of thanks also goes out to The Thacher School in California, where the bulk of the book was written while I was an Anacapa Fellow. To Rod Jacobsen, Sarah DelVecchio, Michael Mulligan, Blossom Pidduck, the late Marvin Shagam, Bonnie LaForge, and everyone else there—thanks very much for allowing me, and my family, to be a part of your amazing community.

Thanks to the residents of the little office in Old Main: Jason McCollum, Bianca Rowlett, and Mike McCoy. The encouragement and heckling I received at the hands of you lot are a large measure of the reason this book came about. Thanks to you all.

The folks at the University of Arkansas Press are an exceptional group to work with. D. S. Cunningham and Mike Bieker took a chance on this half-cocked idea, burdened two exceptional reviewers who provided sage comments that made the manuscript far stronger, and tortured their editorial staff with my writing. Crescent Dragonwagon should be thanked here as well—she, in the midst of moving back to the Ozarks—kindly read the manuscript and agreed to write a forward for it. My gratitude! Obviously, the book would not be here were it not for you all—my thanks for that! Keep the fires of Ozark history burning.

Finally, to my wife and sons. I do not think there can ever be enough acknowledgment of the price that families pay for a spouse to write a book. My oldest son endured many an afternoon or weekend when I was gone on an interview, stuffed away in my office writing, transcribing interviews, or at a conference. To Cass—thanks for understanding and for being gracious. This book has been the better part of your early life, and I hope one day you read it and see in these BTLs the wonder and power that I do. My youngest son, Ben, came into this world just as this book was winding down, and as such he did not have to make as many sacrifices, though his life seems like it will be shaped by it in ways yet unforeseen. The biggest thanks, though, goes to my wife, Lindi. Through graduate school and beyond, she stood beside me as I stumbled around trying to figure out what it was I really wanted to say as a scholar—and I think she always knew but was, as is her way, kind enough to wait for me to catch up. She has also lived out the legacy of the deep revolution, joining in the community of midwives in the region that exists thanks to the hipbillies. Indeed, she graciously reminded me that I probably ought to talk about midwives in this book. Lindi, I feel like in many ways this book has become a map for the road we are walking along. Thank you for being patient with me, for tolerating my never-ending jabbering about hippies, and for being okay with the insane stacks of notes that would pile up on my desk and occasionally spill out into the house.

I am sure I've forgotten people and groups—and for that, I am sorry. It was unintentional.

I know it can never be enough of a repayment, but this book is for Lindi, the love of my life and the star I set my course by.

PREFACE

It's early and cold. The sun is just popping over the ridge to the east of our farm; during the wee hours, frost has settled on the cows that wait impatiently, breath steaming, for the morning hay and for the ice to be broken. The momma cows and their new calves have an other-worldly appearance in the hazy half-light, hair askew and tinged with ice. While I finish feeding and go about the rest of the morning's chores, I'm reminded of the stories I have pulled together and tried to understand in this book. The 1970s, it seems, was the coldest decade on record in the Ozarks (or so I'm told by natives and hippies alike). While they didn't always have cows to feed in the early mornings, folks like Cindy Arsaga did have to navigate life in the rural Ozarks, a life that had little similarity with the ones they left behind. Indeed, the general unpreparedness of the back to the landers (BTLs)—they had canvas tents on platforms tucked into the trees in the holler—prompted a neighbor to rescue them. Not fully a local himself, Glenn Haught ordered Cindy Arsaga and her companions into his house for the winter so he wouldn't have to watch them freeze, and along the way, he inaugurated them into the grand Ozark tradition of making do with what other people have either written off or romanticized into nonsense. Kind of like feeding cows—it seems simple, romantic, and supremely self-reliant. Rarely is it that easy.

This is not a simple history, at least not in the way that might be usual. The back to the land movement is a living and breathing thing, something that never really ended despite the arbitrary dates of 1968–1982 that I have assigned to it in this study. The movement is still very much alive; indeed, my family is, in our own way, part of a fourth readily identifiable generation of BTLs in the country, following—in some cases quite literally—in the footsteps of the generations that have gone before us. That closeness has often made the process of research and writing this book more engaging and more personal than other subjects I've worked on in my brief career as a historian—and has often challenged my ability to maintain scholarly objectivity. That personal part is really how this project found its start: I grew up in a home replete with mentions of *Mother Earth News* and self-sufficiency; later, my next-door neighbors (and landlord) for several years were part of the back to the land movement here in the Ozarks, and the parents of some of our good friends were also veterans of the movement in one form or another. As fifth-generation Ozarker (in the old sense—these days Logan County doesn't get counted much as an Ozark place, much to my grandfather's surprise, I'm sure), I became curious about why all these Yankees had left the big city and headed for the hills in the 1960s and 1970s—and I was also curious about why it seemed like there were so many bad stories floating around about them. And so, like any hot-headed do-gooder, I decided to find out and got far more than I bargained for.

The process of finding out has paralleled the journey I have taken over the course of my life, and most recently in my family's attempts at breaking free of the corporate structures of American society. Like the people discussed in this book, I read Gary Snyder and Jack Kerouac at far too young an age. Like those folks, I grew up in a middle-class family; wandered the world; and rejected, regained, and remade much of the ethos I grew up with, arriving at a system of thought and belief oddly similar to what I discovered in the memories and lives of this older generation of hipbillies. Like them, I want to see the world remade, and like them, I am not so sure it can happen through marching in the streets or changing whoever might be in political power. And so this book has emerged, a history of a critical and fascinating moment in American life and certainly in the life of my beloved Ozarks. But it might also be guilty of presentism, as it is also an attempt to understand the lineage I now live within, to understand the mistakes made, the lessons learned, what battles have already been won, which ones cannot be, and more.

Another element that makes this more than a simple history is the fact that so many members of the back to the land community are still alive—and often incredulous that anybody has bothered to look past the absurd stereotypes trotted out with disturbing regularity over the years by our state's rather dubious news outlets.[1] The stories I have collected here are not finished, unlike archived letters or diaries from centuries past. The lives these people set out to live have not yet concluded— they are still active farmers, teachers, activists, and professionals in the Ozarks and beyond. This book will become rapidly outdated simply due to the fact that the lives of its subjects will keep going.

As such this manuscript is not meant to answer all the questions and tell all the stories; indeed, that would be impossible. Rather, it is structured largely as a beginning to the story, an overlong introduction, if you will. In brief, I argue that the back to the landers (BTLs) in the Ozarks were true utopian revolutionaries—purveyors of what I have termed a "deep revolution" rooted in a sophisticated and profoundly American philosophy—and had, by and large, the wherewithal to achieve their goals. While they often are portrayed as permanently unorganized, disconnected, *Big Lebowski*-esque caricatures, in truth they fit well into the Ozarks—after all, as one BTL in Madison County remarked, "To live here in the Ozarks, you've got to be a bit strange." They worked hard, became pillars in their communities (much to their surprise), and succeeded in creating the pieces of a new America. Thus, a study of the back to the landers, or country hippies, in the Ozarks necessarily becomes a study of America at the same time, and as such this book weaves in national figures and conversations, though they are rooted as deeply in the Ozarks as they are in California or the Maine woods.

While some scholars are only now beginning to treat the cultural revolutions of the 1960s and 1970s with any serious thought, in most cases the story of the hippies in tents learning to farm is told as a delightful afterthought—that is certainly the case in local memory. This story, then, weaves in and out of the Ozarks, highlighting how the movement in Arkansas (and Missouri, discussed to a lesser degree here) was not isolated; indeed, it was far more intertwined with the national counterculture than previously thought. Despite the effort here to peel back the layers of nostalgia and inject the BTL story into the historiography, there are topics that are not deeply plumbed in this book. Most conspicuously, communes and marijuana production are left out, not because they are unimportant but because they are hefty enough topics to deserve full studies of their own. The same is true for the back to the land community in the Missouri Ozarks. While I make mention of Missouri, I devote little time to pulling at those threads. The region is much larger than the Arkansas Ozarks, and while it contains many similarities to the Arkansas side, there are substantial differences as well. This, too, is an area in need of further study. Despite these caveats, I have no doubt made errors and omissions which I take full credit for. As to whether or not I succeed in what I set out to do here, well, that is up to you as the reader.

Hipbillies

INTRODUCTION

———

A Place Outside of Time

It's a land of incomparable beauty,
of infinite charm, of limitless opportunities. . .

—William R. Lighton,
"The Story of an Arkansas Farm"

THE AMERICAN DREAM, America itself even, was bogus. At least, that is what a young beatnik believed in a landmark poem read during San Francisco's 1955 Gallery Six gathering. The moment looked something like this, at least according to Jack Kerouac's fictionalized version:

> Everyone was there. It was a mad night. And I was the one who got things jumping by . . . coming back with three huge gallon jugs of California Burgundy and getting all piffed so that by eleven o'clock when Alvah Goldbrook was wailing, wailing his poem "Wail" drunk with arms outspread everybody was yelling "Go! Go! Go!"[1]

The poet was ostensibly Allen Ginsberg reading "Howl," a scathing and joyous call to bring down the "establishment." The beatniks, represented in full force in San Francisco that night, were part of a growing challenge to America's status quo, a general refutation of a life defined by gray flannel suits and Eisenhower's domesticity. Ginsburg's poem challenged and tore down the facade of Cold War conformity throughout the nation. The "best minds" of a generation were "destroyed by madness" and "burning for the ancient heavenly connection to the starry dynamo in the machinery of night" as they tried to understand the "shocks of hospitals and jails and wars."[2]

Picture, then, that you are at one of the "endings" of the mythic sixties, trying to evaluate the past decade via Ginsberg's prophetic declarations in "Howl." No matter which ending you pick, be it the death of Dr. King, the 1968 election, or the ubiquitous riots of the early 1970s, just imagine it: you had protested, sat in, loved in, tuned in, dropped out, and suddenly it was over. Nixon had won, and the law-and-order status quo resumed control of American life and left the Age of Aquarius sitting on the side of the road, tired and rejected, with an inexplicable urge to get a haircut and buy a suit. Like a bad dream, the revolution was over, and the nation simply needed to shake it off—or at least this is what popular memory often argues.[3] Casting the story in such a reductionist way, however, only furthers problematic depictions of the American Century's midpoint and diminishes the lasting impact of the cultural revolution that back to the landers (BTLs) and others ushered in.[4]

As scholars have shown, the 1970s—dubbed the polyester decade, known for disco and an ascendant narcissism—was also the age when the revolutions of the 1960s achieved greater success.[5] The 1970s, then, were a period of deep revolution more important in the scope of American life than previously understood. It was an age in which revolutionaries dug deeper into America's vision of itself than ever before and, along the way, recreated the pioneer spirit and wrestled it into relevance as folks from burned out Haight-Ashburians to Exxon engineers left the mainstream and headed for the hills.

This "deep revolution," as it is termed here, was an effort by a select group of the counterculture to remake America in its image, but not through street protests and violence. Rather, the urge to change the world was rooted in old beliefs about human community and how such a community could return "home." Along the way, the BTLs hoped to stitch back together a nation coming apart at the seams. This was not a group of burned out druggies seeking a place to lounge about in the sun and recover from the street battles of previous years. Rather, going back to the land was an intentional act by a group disillusioned with the *methods*, not the *vision*, of revolution. Indeed, the failure of the political protests had brought to the fore questions about humanity, spirituality, and nature.[6] These questions, while not new in American life, found an urgency in the lives of deep revolutionaries as they birthed a collective desire to recalibrate American culture and society at the individual and local level. To achieve this, these quiet renegades went "back to the land" in order to live out a pragmatic utopianism. This dream was anchored by a renewed belief in the power of the environment, thanks in part to the writings of Thoreau, Aldo Leopold, Rachel Carson, and more.[7]

A key component of the deep revolution was to leave behind the stagnant world of Cold War consumption and return "home" to nature. The natural world the revolutionaries sought to reconnect with, however, was embattled thanks to the rise of the nuclear age, the surging use of pesticides and herbicides, and a rapidly expanding population. Later than Thoreau would have liked, perhaps, the BTL were afraid of becoming the "tools of their tools" and sought to return to a more ecological existence that used appropriate technology, to borrow a phrase from the revolution.[8] Thus, while these people were indeed rejecting broad swaths of American life, they also appropriated the tools of modern America that might help reset the world and create a true, lasting revolution. The deep revolution was indeed successful, as evidenced by today's growing consumer turn toward organic and slow foods, localized economies, alternative energy, and other acts of reconnection with community and place.[9] By examining the response of the back to the landers in the Ozarks to America's perceived slide into chaos, scholars gain a clearer picture of how the deep revolution served to provide idealistic yet feasible answers to the nation's problems. To see how this occurred, we can examine how America "lost" itself in the confusion of the 1960s and then found the path that restored hope, at least in the minds of the country hippies that came to the Ozarks.

From the end of World War II through the 1960s, America was not the golden age often described by popular memory. To be sure, while there were indeed great advances in the nation's standard of living, global stature, and more, there were deep problems roiling just below the surface. After all, the civil rights movement began a new era of struggle in the wake of the *Brown* decision; likewise, feminists renewed their efforts, and a host of figures from the Beats to fundamentalists continued a slow revolt to reshape the nation. These reactions, part of the long tradition of American protest movements, were mighty challenges to the paradox of stability and uncertainty presented by Cold War affluence.[10] The promise of material stability, evidenced by rising wages, home owner-ship, and education, was under threat of nuclear destruction as Cold War tensions ebbed and flowed, finally coming to a head with the twin crises of the Cuban Missile Crisis (1962) and the proxy war in Vietnam (1954–1975). Such events created a cognitive dissonance that could not be reconciled by the simple acceptance of a *Leave It to Beaver* world cleansed of global strife, racial conflict, and social upheaval.

That vision of the world, though, was part of the problem for the emerging counterculture. The "movement" was always a minority in the nation, and as scholars have pointed out, the counterculture tended to reflect its location. Indeed, when the counterculture is discussed, commentators are quick to note *which* counterculture they mean: civil rights, women's rights, hippies, or something different. It was, according to Terry Anderson, a movement in a constant state of definition, never settling on one particular vision other than being against the "establish-ment" in some fashion.[11] Perhaps this is, in part, why commentators at the time, like Theodore Roszak, likened the counterculture to an invasion of the centaurs—the traditional standards and structures of American life appeared to be under a relentless attack from all sides by the hippies and protestors.[12]

This perception of attack is not without merit. Indeed, the coun-terculture, as historians now show with greater nuance, was a critique of the promise made by the American dream.[13] That ideal was always in flux, and by the mid-twentieth century it was precariously balanced between the poles of prosperity and security. What this meant in prac-ticality depended on intersections of class, race, gender, and geogra-phy as well as the idealization of the American dream by pop culture. Underlying the drive to achieve material prosperity, measured by con-sumptive power, were the real fears spawned by the Cold War. While nothing as all-consuming as a world war emerged between 1945 and 1980, the decades following America's deployment of nuclear weapons in Japan saw a growing global fear of atomic death as the superpowers built arsenals capable of destroying their enemies many times over. This idea of "mutually assured destruction," loved by the Eisenhower White House, served as a powerful catalyst to America's perception of itself as the leader of the free world and a place where its citizens were able to advance themselves in the nation's new prosperity.[14] In such an environment, it is not surprising that thousands of young folks left Dallas and Chicago and New Orleans and headed for the "safety" of the Ozark Mountains.

Just what were these urban refugees to be called? At the time, many either adopted or were given the appellative "back to the lander." But what might that be? For our purposes, a general definition of a back to the lander (BTL is useful: a BTL is a person who left an urban center and headed to a rural area for a life of "homesteading." Homesteading, a shifting idea, was generally accepted as living an "off-grid" existence founded on partial to complete self-sufficiency; BTLs were, in short, neopioneers. This was a remarkable cultural shift in that the BTLs were young people (between late teens and early thirties), were generally white and middle class, and had at least some exposure to collegiate studies.[15] As such, they were unfamiliar with homesteading skills but were eager to work hard and learn from publications and local expertise.[16] Most BTLs intended to stay on the land indefinitely, though this dream often evolved in relation to the demands of life in the hills. To gauge the success of these revolutionaries by their ability to stay in perpetuity on the land unduly limits any attempt to understand the movement, however. Rather, it is more useful to suggest that a BTL was someone who stayed on the land a minimum of one year; however the Ozarks, at least, boasted a stronger retention rate than that suggested by much of the existing scholarship and by memory.

Prior attempts at defining the movement have rarely produced results any more nuanced than this, often because they lack a concerted effort to understand the intellectual lineage of the BTL movement and provide statistical data, however basic.[17] Thus, the questions of how to define the back to the land era and whether or not it succeeded have long presented a challenge for scholars. The few scholars who have tried to address this have often left behind more questions than answers, leaving a gap in understanding the counterculture. This problem has also impeded any sustained discussion of the long tradition of back to the land movements in American life.[18]

As such, detailed study of one population of back to the landers, or "hipbillies" as they termed themselves in the Ozarks, gives greater depth to the discussion. Guy Ames was one such refugee. In 1969, he was seventeen and had just graduated high school in Dallas, Texas. In many ways, his life was a typical expression of the national dream: he came from a stable, middle class family that had long been involved in the country's armed forces. The America Ames knew was one similar to much of stereotypical Middle America: a place defined by tight-knit nuclear families in new suburbs, who were depicted on nightly shows like *The Dick Van Dyke Show* (1961–1966) and who were situated firmly within the Cold War diplomatic and domestic narratives. In much of the South, visions of poodle skirts and "I Like Ike" buttons had not quite faded, and while chaos was on the nightly news, people rested comfortably in their homes, content in the belief that the hippies were elsewhere.

Through the counterculture's many forms, though, these assumptions were called into question. As thousands of young people like Ames came of age, they questioned the rhetoric surrounding America's global dominance. During the end of his high school career and his preparation for college life, Ames realized that the United States might not be the cowboy in white ready to save the world through democracy. As he read through the counterculture's growing catalog—voices like Jack Kerouac, Ken Kesey, and others—Ames developed an understanding of how he fit in to the movement. By 1970, at school in Commerce, Texas, he became a member of the antiwar movement as he began "waking up" to what was happening in the world around him.[19] Initially, this came from having read and seen "enough."[20] Instead of America as the cowboy saving the world from communism, his reading and his teachers in college pushed him to shift his views.[21] Ames credits the success of this shift in perspective, in part, to two things: his family and the first essay he had to write as a freshman in college (on whether or not the American Revolution was actually a revolution, which opened his eyes to the fact that "old, rich white guys were in charge then and are in charge now," and that maybe something should change).[22] As a result of these influences, Ames began a quick move into the counterculture, becoming as he put it, "disaffected" from the mainstream of American life.[23]

Ames was not abnormal, at least for Middle America where the counterculture arrived late. On the coasts, however, the counterculture was unrecognizable to its early self, as the Summer of Love (1967) gave way to the chaos of Altamont Free Festival.[24] The bedlam experienced at Altamont was not merely a symptom of the hedonistic excesses often attributed to the drug and alcohol use of the counterculture at the time—though, to be sure, that was partly responsible. After all, portions of the stereotypes of hippies and hipbillies were correct: nudity was normal, and open sexuality (at least compared to square society) and drug use were seen as the new standard. Such open confrontation with the moral standards of the American dream only served to highlight the divides in American life. By 1970, the nation was on fire as Nixon escalated parts of the war in Vietnam. Indeed, the conflict in Vietnam, at least for young students like Ames, "radicalized a huge part of our generation" and convinced the growing numbers of BTLs that the promise of the status quo was wanting.[25]

The world inhabited by the American middle class by the early 1970s was one no longer filled with the surety of New Deal liberalism but instead dominated by uncertainty at home and abroad, at least in the minds of the country's vocal counterculture and conservative movements. Nixon's new Republican coalition and the back to the landers both argued that the nation was changed and changing; it was no longer the nation they had been promised—and indeed, the promise itself might be the problem. In part, they all were right. Where the 1950s and 1960s saw the creation of the vast majority of America's middle class, stagflation, evidenced by a faltering American economy and global market insecurities, threatened to unravel the successes of New Deal liberalism and the Great Society. For the first time in history, on the nightly news, Americans watched as minorities claimed their place at the table. And to top it off, the 1960s and 1970s birthed the revolt of the middle class's own children who claimed that the world created for them was one built of cages, not freedom.[26] The counterculture's claims that their society was not free were not unique to them, to be sure, but they were singularly situated to provide a critique of American life just as those with the most to lose were desperately trying to maintain it. While those on the Left tried to create, in the words of Herbert Marcuse, a world that allowed the "free development of human needs and faculties," those on the Right believed they were holding the world together as it disintegrated and their children rejected the life they had built on assembly lines across the nation.[27]

Indeed, the assembly line no longer promised the socioeconomic stability it once did. During the 1968 election, Nixon had made much of his silent majority, that group of Americans who quietly went to work and to church, paid their taxes, and did not break the law.[28] Nixon, though, did not actively pursue policies in the best interest of his prime constituents. Instead of creating a domestic agenda focused on stabilizing or improving wages and working conditions for the "two-fisted . . . men, not softies" of America, President Nixon opted to shift the rhetoric, appealing to the morality of the blue-collar and middle-class worker.[29] In so doing, Nixon moved the discussion of class away from New Deal liberalism and rebuilt it on cultural fractures, allowing fear and insecurity to take a renewed prominence in discussions about American political and social life.[30] This discussion served as a distraction from the problems associated with Nixon's New Federalism and his odd combination of liberal and conservative efforts that harmed much of the previous quarter-century's socioeconomic gains. The end result of these policies was the forging of white, working-class men into a group that angrily sought to establish bulwarks against the encroaching tide of minorities, women, hippies, and homosexuals.[31]

Building such a safe-haven was perhaps easier to do in the nation's heartland, as it seemed the chaos was confined to the coasts. In truth, no region was immune to the counterculture, though this phenomenon has been little tracked by scholars. As the protests and participants in the counterculture moved into the nation's interior, they changed to a quieter form of protest. Thus, the middle-class, Middle America revolutionary often reflected the region, or in the case country hippies, a perception of a given region (plus a vision of "country life").[32] Some scholars have tried to further explain the counterculture in flyover country, as Jeffery Turner did with *Sitting In and Speaking Out* and Beth Bailey did with *Sex in the Heartland*. Together these books highlight how the Midwest and the South, while often neglected by discussions of the counterculture writ large, deserve more attention. Indeed, the South was the initial hub of civil rights protest, and while efforts to expand the franchise did not always attract white supporters, it served to plant the seed for more general protest into the student populations across the region. While the South was less active than the coasts, according to Turner's work, some 36 percent of Southern universities experienced demonstrations against the war or in favor of civil rights in the 1967–1968 academic year.[33] Likewise, Bailey's work highlights how the sexual revolution was already well on its way before the 1960s, and that this was the case in the heartland just like anywhere else. In Lawrence, Kansas, Bailey finds that the "battles of the sexual revolution were most widely engaged and most visible" for residents of the state and region.[34] And just as the student protests documented by Turner were reflective of the Southern culture they emerged from, so too was the revolution Bailey discusses—Lawrence, as she points out, never had the bath house culture of Haight-Ashbury, for instance, but neither did most of Middle and Southern America.

Thus, while riots did not occur in the area, the Arkansas Ozarks were not immune to the shifting national mood and the growth of protest movements. The region, and the state, had gone through an economic restructuring as its large agriculture industry was forced to reinvent itself, leaving behind small farmers as the new Big Ag era declared by secretary of agriculture Earl Butz emerged. Although Secretary Butz oversaw the creation of the new agricultural future of the nation, in truth the process of consolidation had begun earlier during the New Deal.[35] This process, championed by Butz's belief in the "trend in modern agriculture toward bigness, toward well-capitalized and heavily mechanized units," encouraged an agriculture system that rewarded farmers willing to take on increasing amounts of debt and grow "fencerow to fencerow," pushing out smaller family farms.[36] As some small farmers sold out, their land was often consolidated into ever-expanding farms—or turned into subdivisions for incoming retirees and tourists.[37]

In the face of this brave new world, farmers in the Ozarks, as elsewhere, often sought off-farm employment in the developing tourist havens along the newly created lakes or at retirement settlements like Horseshoe Bend. Such communities challenged the Ozarks to understand how to deal with incoming retirees, a group who, despite their alleged desire to return to the America of yore, had little regard for the traditions of the region—a debate hipbillies walked blindly into.[38] As places like Horseshoe Bend and Cherokee Village attracted retirees from across the Midwest, the new construction and service industries built to service them profited from the death of small farms as the population that inspired bucolic images of rural life transitioned away from agriculture, in part to facilitate the new arrivals.[39] Midwestern retirees, although they brought money, also brought preconceptions, both about the Ozarks and about back to the landers migrating into the region. The problems of the nation came to the hills as retirement communities were populated by people seeking what they hoped would be a reprieve from the social chaos of the preceding years. Indeed, the chasm between Nixon's silent majority and the reformulated counter-culture was at times deeply felt in communities like Eureka Springs as people like Ames moved in and rubbed shoulders with retirees and "town" Ozarkers intent on holding on to the economic boom tourists and retired plumbers brought with them. In the words of *Rolling Stone* reporter Donald Katz who traveled through the region in the late 1970s:

> The roads up at the Missouri border are cluttered with large signs announcing the entrances to instantaneous walled villages whose names end with words like Acres, Hills, Estates, and City. These are little insulated islands of white middle-class affluence nestled in relatively untouched rural beauty, each complete with its own police department, medical clinic, restaurants—and no Arkansans. The appeal to the elderly retirees from Illinois or Pennsylvania who account for half of the Ozark population boom is, according to one Eureka Springs resident, 'fresh air, clean water, low taxes, and no crime'—'crime' being a delicate euphemism for which several retirees were quite ready to substitute 'Negroes.' [40]

This debate between "counterculture" and "squares," then, was not new to the area. The cultural battles that began during the 1960s and continued, though rarely with the storied fervor of popular mythology, during the 1970s were a reformulation of the decades-old fight between advocates of tradition and modernity, perhaps made most famous by the Scopes Trial in 1925. There, at the beginning of the American Century, the battle lines between the forces of tradition and moder-nity were sharply drawn for Americans.[41] While the battle seemingly paused during the Great Depression and the war years, it was rejoined with gusto as American society imploded during the Johnson and Nixon years. Ironically, perhaps, by the mid-twentieth century, the children of the universities sought not an America filled with the promise of technology and secular ideas, but rather a complex modernity-infused traditionalism.[42]

Faced by these contradictions and conflicts, Guy Ames and others like him searched out how to reframe the coastal revolution in ways that made sense in their context. Along the way, Ames read a review of the 1970 reprint of *Living the Good Life* by Helen Nearing and Scott Nearing, the figureheads of the burgeoning back-to-the-land movement. Reading the Nearings' work "really fired me up," Ames recalled, "and I thought, my God, there's a different way!"[43] The Nearings' work and life showed Ames and others that they could break free of the American machine and define life on their own terms. Almost immediately, Ames sought out the longhairs on his college campus, met a girl, and together they discussed moving to the land.[44] Like other folks, after travelling up through Maine and into the Appalachians, Ames and his girlfriend ended up in the Ozarks where they decided to buy land near Pyatt, Arkansas, in Marion County.[45]

What sort of Arkansas did Ames and his friends encounter? Arkansas, at once a state so traditional that time had apparently forgotten it, was also a state belatedly clutching after the prosperity of postwar America. In many ways, Arkansas—and especially the Ozarks—was at the edge of the country's vision, prompting the question *What was Arkansas in America?* More particularly, *What were the Arkansas Ozarks to America, in the years prior to the full corporatization of Tyson and Walmart or the political visibility of the Clintons?* Some basic answers are useful for locating the state and the Ozarks within the national consciousness.

In 1965, for instance, famed naturalist Edwin Way Teale published the final volume of his series, *The American Seasons,* a Pulitzer Prize winning work that marked the culmination of nearly seventy-five thousand miles of travel to document the nation's four seasons.[46] Telling, perhaps, of the nation's perception of the region are his brief observations of the Ozarks in this last volume:

> At Fort Smith we turned north. The road we followed rose and fell along the western edge of the Ozarks, then climbed among these ancient and picturesque mountains, older than the Rockies. At times, we rode lofty ridges with mountain vistas, blue-tinted, spreading away on either hand. We were in a land of "yarb doctors" and "ridge runners" where local superstitions abounded. Among the curious ideas about winter that have been handed down from generation to generation in the Ozarks is the belief that there will be as many frosts in May as there are thunderclaps in February.[47]

Guy King Ames, Medicine Wheel Commune near the Buffalo River.
Courtesy Guy King Ames.

This quaintly dismissive vision of the Ozarks was not uncommon at the time, as Blevins has ably shown. Like Appalachia, the Ozarks helped to "expel, or at least soften, any doubts that depression-era and Cold War Americans might harbor concerning the innate goodness of science and 'progress.'"[48] Such an effort resulted in a new kind of Ozarker: the outlander.

In large measure, the Ozarks, and the state, were no longer agricultural, at least in the old way. According to Blevins, between 1940 and 1965, the "largest outmigration in Ozark history" occurred, resulting in the unprecedented loss of half of Ozark farms.[49] Because the Ozarks had not mechanized in substantive ways until the mid-1960s, the region inadvertently preserved traditional methods, an element attractive to the "outlander Ozarker" like Ames and the retirees.[50] Agriculture, though key to the region, moved to the background as the Ozarks rebuilt after high rates of outmigration and the transition of farmland into retirement communities. By the end of the 1970s, largely as a result of tourism and the influx of in-migrants, the area's economy had stabilized enough to stem the flow of out-migrants, even prompting some Arkansans to return.[51] Although the nature of farm labor had lessened and changed, the regional economy saw improvements from the establishment of retirement communities, potentially the new face of the hills.[52]

The Ozarks, thanks to the combination of travel writing, increased interest in folklore, and the out-migration of hill folk during the 1940s, 1950s, and 1960s, loomed large in the national consciousness. In particular, the popular influence of writers like Otto Rayburn (*Ozark Country*, 1941) and Vance Randolph (*Ozark Superstitions*, 1947; *The Ozarks*, 1931) served to solidify the image of the hill country, creating in part the motivation for retirees and BTLs to find their way to the area.[53] Many of these newcomers concentrated in the westernmost counties (Washington and Benton, primarily, with some bleed over into Madison, Boone, and Marion Counties), while the eastern counties were the "dowdy stepsister."[54] This was partly thanks to the legacy of decades of "cultural" tourism into the region. In the nation's mind, the Arkansas Ozarks no longer represented real people or places but had become a sort of "hillbilly Neverland" where nostalgic visions of what America had been remained. It was as if the Ozarks was a living museum of American hillbilly life waiting to be consumed—an idea not lost on the back-to-the-land movement that sought a place where they could learn traditional methods for self-sufficiency.[55] Though often associated with Appalachia due to environmental and cultural similarities, the Ozarks were indeed a distinct area, especially in the minds of the counterculture. Where Appalachia became known for its poverty and despair, the Ozarks presented a different vision of life in the hardscrabble hills. While the region was not as scarred by the desperate cycles of poverty found in upland communities further east like Appalachia, the Arkansas Ozarks remained entrenched in a fictionalized version of the past, à la Otto Rayburn's *Ozark Country*.[56]

This is not to say there were not more realistic visions of what life in the Ozarks might entail, especially for the back-to-the-land movement. The neo-homesteader life embraced with gusto in the 1960s and 1970s was, as Joe Neal noted in *The Grapevine* in 1977, not new to Arkansas's (and Missouri's) hill country.[57] Given the region's climate, geology, and culture, the style of farming that dominated the uplands for generations lived between the margins of subsistence agriculture and small-scale cash-crop systems. While the tractor had slowly changed that, agricultural concerns in the region had remained modest compared to those in the Plains states. This, paired with general perceptions of the Arkansas hills as a place where traditional folk cultures lived in opposition to the breakneck acquisition of modernity on the coasts, lent the Ozarks an air of possibility to folks wanting to live in greater connection to the natural world. Indeed, by the 1970s, local commentators like Neal noted that in-migrants were, in many ways, in line with their predecessors, "dreaming the purest dreamings [sic] . . . a time-honored occupation in the mountains—and it is clearly preferable to the confusing futility spawned en masse when human beings get pushed like rats into the cage of anonymous urban sprawl."[58]

One of the more widely known proponents of leaving the "anonymous urban sprawl" for the Arkansas countryside was William Lighton, a journalist, author, and screenwriter.[59] Lighton rose to national prominence by writing about the San Francisco earthquake in 1906. Following this, he and his wife combed the nation for a small farm, ultimately settling on Arkansas, and bought a farm just outside the sleepy college town of Fayetteville in Washington County in 1908.[60] Lighton detailed his family's efforts, first in a series of articles for *The Saturday Evening Post*, and then in the book, *Happy Hollow Farm* (1915). The Happy Hollow stories catapulted Lighton to fame and reaffirmed the Ozarks' place at the center of national attention for its traditional livelihoods and bucolic settings, where it remained for the next several decades. Lighton detailed how he and his wife had searched for security for their children, earnestly questing for a home that, as he said, would "slowly fill with kindly associations and gentle memories; a place that would endure not for a day but for generations, growing and gaining all the time in richness and grace."[61] After a period of time they decided it was too expensive and came to a region "where the materials for homemaking may be got without sapping one's life out in the process:" the Ozarks.[62] Describing their new homestead with a rapturous joy, Lighton noted that the work of establishing a home never finished; indeed, finishing it was not the point. Foreshadowing the deep revolution, Lighton put it this way:

We shall never finish. That's the beauty of it. If we live and work at it for a million years we shan't be in the least danger of the horrid melancholy of having our occupation gone . . . A lifetime might be spent on any one of a hundred nooks and beauty spots, doing things to it, fixing it up . . . There, as we see it, is the secret of happiness, the lure of continual achievement in something worth doing, and not the stodgy satisfaction of final accomplishment.[63]

Others followed closely on Lighton's heels. Howard and Charlie May Simon were just such a couple. Howard Simon was a noted illustrator, and Charlie May Simon was rapidly becoming an acclaimed children's author with roots in the Arkansas highlands.[64] The Simons, in part looking for adventure, moved from the glitz and glamour of New York to Arkansas, purchasing sixty acres in Perry County where they, with the help of their neighbors, established a relatively profitable homesteading life, supported by their writing and illustrations.[65] After building a small cabin, learning to rive shingles, and making comic mistakes when planting their first garden, the Simons recorded a life that gave them plenty of time for reading or taking walks as well as maintaining their homestead—the image offered by counterculture icons like the Nearings. The Simons also offered a word of potential warning to any who followed them: the experience of going back to the land "has really proven nothing except that, whatever the cause of this world economic disturbance, the remedy is not back to the soil, to the simple life of our forefathers, in spite of what theorists sitting on easy chairs in warm houses may say."[66] Their experience, though, is most certainly a reflection of their particular context. The Simons, like many back to the land authors from the end of the nineteenth century through the 1980s, supported themselves thanks to their well-known off-farm writing. Indeed, by and large, authors like the Simons and the Lightons in the Ozarks or Helen and Scott Nearing of New England subsidized their homesteading efforts in various ways (as would later icons to the back to the land movement like Wendell Berry and Gary Snyder). They were thereby freed to enjoy larger amounts of leisure time than most, all the while projecting a particular vision of life on the land at odds with reality.[67]

The Simons were not the only ones who migrated to the Ozarks during the Depression and World War II years. Don West and his family, chronicled in his *Broadside to the Sun*, moved to a remote hollow in Winslow, southern Washington County.[68] Though the book moves between novel and memoir, West's account provides a more realistic portrayal of life as a back to the lander in the 1940s Arkansas Ozarks. West and his family eked out a gradually improving existence aided by locals who, among other things, showed the novice farmer West how to fix the teeth on his chisel plow. While West and his family did not stay forever on the homestead, the experience and publication of the book kept the Ozarks at the forefront of American consciousness throughout the war and immediate post-war years.[69] West's work neatly portrayed Ozark hospitality and culture as the 1940s wound to a close while also articulating how his perception of an era of small-scale community had long since faded: "What had once been good was now bad. Subsistence farming was out of date; riches were in store for the man who would give up his Jersey cows and his brood mare, his dog and his banjo."[70]

Though hard to gauge the impact such early experiences had on the generation that came in the 1970s, it is fair to say that as people like Guy Ames came of age, they did so in an America that knew the Ozarks. This knowledge, while deeply colored by stereotypes, contained within it bits of reality: the guarded friendliness of the region's inhabitants, the reality of hard work, and the value of community. This knowledge came to the nation largely from the continued presence in American popular culture of Arkansas and its hill folk. As Blevins noted, by the 1940s Arkansas occupied a well-defined space in American life, a push-pull relationship between the competing images of "Arkansas" and "Arkansaw." Thanks to the imagery of Lum n' Abner, by the end of the Second World War, millions of Americans were familiar with the "Arkansaw" image, a picture often inseparable from other stereotypes of the upland South.[71] The hillbilly of the Ozarks came to represent a subset of American life passed over by the manic drive to modernize in the post-war era, and it seemed to some outsiders that this was fine with rural Arkansans.[72]

While problematic, these stereotypes were still strong in the 1960s and 1970s and were capitalized on by Ozarkers intent on drawing in investment and tourist revenue. While these efforts were often organized by investment groups, city improvement associations, or local politicians, the emerging counterculture in Arkansas's hill country also took part in maintaining the "Arkansaw" image as a way to entice BTLs as the 1970s moved along. Not only this, but the articles and ads that appeared in the new burst of guerilla print material served as a connecting point, a Siren call to a wounded and wandering generation. *Mother Earth News* (often reduced to a simple *"Mother"* by those in the know), which first hit the shelves in 1970, or *Communities*, founded in 1972, regularly featured the Ozarks until the mid 1980s. These stories ranged from cautionary to Edenic in their description of the place—often at the same time. For example, in the May 1975 issue, Paul Durand character-ized living in the Ozarks in this way:

> The Ozarks is (or are) a beautiful wild region of several hundred square miles . . . mainly a land of low rolling hills covered with oaks and other types of trees. Summers are hot, winters are mild and short, and spring and fall are wonderful. Relatively few people live in the district. Towns are small and far apart, farms tend to be limited in cultivated area, and the majority of land holdings are just virgin forest, left idle and untouched for the most part. This is, in fact, one of the last sections of real "country" left in the US.[73]

This picture of the region was something the local community had struggled to preserve, albeit in different ways. In 1972, after a long cam-paign led by Dr. Neil Compton and aided by famed artist Thomas Hart Benton, the Buffalo River was declared the nation's first national river.[74] Such an action indeed preserved a large section of wild and scenic space and served to draw further attention to the Ozarks as a place where life continued in harmony with the natural world.

It was not just the increasing environmental recognition, though, or the mythic image the region held that brought the Ozarks to the coun-terculture's attention. By the end of the 1960s, as hipbillies tried to find a way to reinvigorate the revolution, the Arkansas hill country offered a sort of "cultural salvation through the worship of a traditional way of life supposedly maintained in conscious tradition."[75] The members of the back to the land movement, essentializing and essentialized to be sure, saw the land and its people as a community where they could learn and grow as they lived out their lives and built the world they had been promised.[76] In coming to the Ozarks, Ames and the other BTLs found a place where the deep revolution could grow. To do so required a strong philosophy, sense of self, and a vision for what life should be, beyond the chaos found at the close of the 1960s. They needed a philosophy of deep revolution, and here they were able fit the pieces together and go back to the land.

CHAPTER 1

The Making of a Hipbilly

We tried to change the world. And we got Nixon.

—"T"

THE TRADITIONAL PICTURE of a pioneer might include a covered wagon, perhaps a few children running alongside, crossing the grassy prairie of the American West. Those pioneers of yore were armed with a belief in Manifest Destiny and the hope of achieving self-sufficiency in a new, wild land. Pioneers in the 1960s and 1970s, however, eschewed the covered wagons for "Volkswagens, pickup trucks and sports cars."[1] The new settlers in the Ozarks were fortified not by Manifest Destiny but by an equally revolutionary philosophy, born of the ashes of protests and riots in places as far flung as San Francisco or Greenwich Village. They were, at least in the minds of native Ozarkers, "hippies," and there were more "coming in every week," with their "hair long and their hands soft."[2]

These hipbillies were similar to Edwin Teale in that they knew little about the region. They differed in one important way, though. Where Teale saw the Ozarks as a quaint relic, the incoming hippies—though naive—saw in the Ozarks a place where they could "reduce the complexities of life to the traditional struggle of man against nature," a response to the social revolutions that began throughout America during the 1960s.[3] This generation of the BTL movement, lasting from roughly 1965 into the early 1980s, has been little addressed by scholars.

This lack of detailed attention can be, in part, attributed to a benign disregard for this group of young revolutionaries' intentions and where-withal to homestead the rocky hills of the region.[4]

Just as the conversation about back to the landers nationally offers little beyond surface level discussions of the movement, the same is true in the Ozarks. Blevins's discussion of the country hippies, in his masterful work *Hill Folks*, provides the most relevant conversation for our purposes. Blevins divides them into three groups: the general counterculture (described simply as "hippies"), urban escapists, and a disenchanted youth drawn to the area due to its promise of preserved traditional livelihoods.[5] Definitions like this, also found in the works of Jacobs and Brown, provide those interested in the back to the land movement of the 1960s and 1970s with only a partial, external foundation for discussing the community that emerged in the Ozarks.[6] As a result, there is little clarification given as to why people adopted this lifestyle, how they interacted with local communities, and how they lived out their lives in relation to the national counterculture.

It is useful, then, to understand more fully who moved into the Arkansas hill country and went back to the land. (See table 1.) The stories compiled for this work were gathered via interviews conducted by the author and questionnaires returned to the author, and through newspaper archives, unpublished memoirs, and stories collected by members of the back to the land community. As such, the stories span the late-1960s through the early 1980s and cover experiences from the western, central, and eastern portions of the Arkansas Ozarks. From these sources, a picture of the group appeared relatively quickly, starting with their ages: nearly all of the BTLs moved to the region in their early-to mid-twenties, with a few who were younger and older.[7] Reflecting the high rate of college attendance during the time, 75 percent had completed an undergraduate degree by the time they moved to the Ozarks, and 92 percent of the respondents came from urban areas such as Los Angeles or New York. Nearly all were white, from middle-class families, and had little practical knowledge of how to live "on the land."

Hipbillies coming to the Ozarks were part of the same general population of young people that created more well-known places, like Black Bear Commune in northern California or The Farm in Tennessee. Indeed, this might be part of the problem in addressing the regional— and national—back to the land experiences. The common assumption

TABLE 1. Brief Summary of Ozark Back-to-the-Land Population

NUMBER OF STORIES	URBAN MIGRANT	RURAL MIGRANT	POST-SECONDARY EDUCATION*	AVERAGE TIME ON LAND**
40	37 (92.5%)	3 (7%)	30 (75%)	14.60 years

*Post-secondary education includes any education beyond high school.

**In some cases, time on land was not ascertainable, and as such was not included in the average. Eleven families/individuals (30.56 percent) are still on the land and several others exceeded the average time on the land. It should also be noted that this statistic is reflective of self-selection—mostly those interviewed were back to the landers still in the area, though this figure is adjusted somewhat to reflect the stories of those who did not remain in the area or on the land as long as the average suggests.

that country hippies were bereft of ideological fortitude and a work ethic, built in part by the stereotypes portrayed in pop culture and the media at the time, was attached to groups such as those. Such an assumption, however, is belied by an in-depth examination of the group. Though some scholars, such as Dona Brown, have recently attempted to provide a corrective by noting that the movement was not isolated to the 1960s, her assertion that the BTLs should be associated "with the end of that era" or with "the beginning of the next" does not go far enough.[8] By making such assumptions, Brown—like others writing about the back to the land community—unwittingly assumes that there was not a philosophy, a revolutionary intent, behind the back to the land movement in the 1960s and 1970s. Though commentators assumed a lackadaisical air presided throughout the BTL world, this is indeed far from the truth.[9] The fact of the matter is that back to the landers from 1965 through the early 1980s were not only decidedly a unique addition to the tradition of self-sufficient agrarianism in America but were far more ideologically organized and successful than popular culture holds and previous scholarship argues.

Probing deeper into the motivations of the young neopioneers is admittedly difficult. Indeed, there are no simple reasons as to why people came to the Ozarks in particular.[10] In order to understand and provide a broad framework of the push and pull factors that drew people to the Ozarks, we can briefly look at the story of two families for general trends in Arkansas' BTL community, as well as the foundations of the deep revolution. In 1974 Bob Billig and his wife moved to the region from New York City, where he had been a teacher.[11] After visiting places in Ohio and in the Appalachians, they finally settled in near Pettigrew in Madison County and were instrumental in founding the Headwaters School (a free school established by the BTL community in Madison County as a supplement to the rural education system and to provide community networking). The Billigs moved to the country, as Bob put it, in a wave of disillusionment and despair—it was "a mark of desperation that we left anyhow."[12] This feeling of angst pushed Billig and his wife to try and "find an alternative narrative for our lives, preferably closer to the earth."[13] In part, their search was for a connected, rooted home and community in a world that seemed to have lost these things. Upon their arrival, Bob and his wife found exactly this. A few weeks after they arrived in Huntsville they

> journeyed south to Pettigrew to meet [the contact person] that brought us here and were immediately invited to go to a local swimming hole. We piled into the open back of his pickup truck and bounced down miles of dirt road . . . We were greeted by a scene that changed our lives: 30–40 naked hippies, with children, playing in the water and socializing on the river banks. We said to each other, "We've found a home."[14]

Others, like Joel and Sherri Davidson, who also lived in Madison County near Pettigrew, expanded on this idea. (Indeed, the Davidsons were part of the initial conversations surrounding the Headwaters School and the Upper Friley Organization.) The Davidsons brought a distinctly utopian tone with them as they set up shop outside of Pettigrew. The Davidsons, like the Billigs, moved in part to get away from prevailing society and from a government Joel saw as repressive, with the hope of unplugging from the mainstream of an increasingly consumptive culture.[15] Citing Henry David Thoreau as a key influence, Joel wanted to live a more deliberate life and no longer be mired in "quiet desperation."[16] Davidson wanted to focus not on living "cheaply" or "dearly" but rather on an existence that allowed him to "transact some private business with the fewest obstacles," that is, to practice revolution.[17] Indeed, by joining the back to the land movement, Davidson saw himself not as part of an alternative culture, but as exiting a "dominant culture" that was simply a "thin veneer of civilization," and a rapidly failing one at that.[18] For Davidson, like many, creating a localized utopia in the Ozarks seemed to be the answer to society's ills.[19]

While not all the individuals or families who moved from the cities to the hills consciously possessed a vehement philosophical or revolutionary bent, when examined as a group it becomes readily apparent that instead of a movement bereft of goals or purpose beyond fleeing the 1960s, back to the landers at large and in the Ozarks in particular held a deceptively simple vision paired with attainable goals. The back to the land community possessed a belief in a deep revolution that maintained the dreams of the political fights of the 1960s but linked those dreams with the emerging deep ecological consciousness of writers like Gary Snyder or Wendell Berry. As a result, the group believed the world could be remade. Instead of street protests and violence, the deep revolution could only be achieved via a sociocultural reset rooted in a reconnection with the natural world. While utopian, this vision readily afforded measures of success at the individual and community levels.

The back to the land movement, then, was an effort to rebuild society, as BTL member Crescent Dragonwagon told Ruth Weinstein, a fellow hipbilly who conducted a series of interviews throughout the community in the early 1990s. In 1970 Dragonwagon and her partner moved to the Ozarks, where she hoped they might "build a new society from the ashes of the old, building a collective, cooperative society instead of one founded on Social Darwinism."[20] Dropping out of American life at large was part of how this would happen. Others interviewed by Weinstein voiced the same view. "B," an anonymous voice, put it this way:

> The solution to the problem with the government—as perceived by the back-to-the-landers—was to withdraw and form, alternative cultures, alternative economies . . . In one sense you could be an isolationist/activist, in that you are actually doing the kinds of change that you advocate for others . . . But anyway what we were doing at that time was trying to demonstrate that attitude, to accept a more cooperative way of living, to realize that we could do with less, be happy with less."[21]

The sentiment was repeated throughout the rest of Weinstein's interviews and matches with the interviews recorded for this study as well. "J" and "T" agreed with the impulse to drop out and intentionally isolate themselves but noted that there was also an impulse for changing society at large.[22] "J" argued that while the BTL community lived isolated existences to a degree, they were not completely "disconnected from society. I think a lot of people's initial thing was to totally drop out. I think in the long run that everybody wanted to make some kind of change at the same time."[23] This impulse for a different kind of change was readily understood as a result of the 1960s chaos. "N," reflecting both on the aftermath of the stunted revolutions of previous years and the prevailing mood of the 1970s, argued, "We were looking for social change, to create that society, because we weren't happy with the one that was out there."[24] What was out there? "We came out of the sixties where we fought politically. We went to demonstrations. We tried to change the world. And we got Nixon. I mean I think that's why we left and why other people our age left."[25] As they left the cities, the drive to institute social change did not diminish, rather it evolved into a sophisticated ecological consciousness befitting the grand American intellectual traditions represented by Thoreau and others. Central to the urge to move back to the countryside was the neopioneers' overarching desire to not simply remove themselves from the main of American life but to begin building a new world, at least at the individual and community levels. Key to this was a rejection of the consumption-driven lifestyle dominating the United States at the end of the 1960s.[26]

As David Shi has aptly shown, in the wake of World War II, American consumers and marketers and manufacturers developed a relationship wherein the producers demanded Americans buy more and more to believe that not only was infinite economic growth possible but "essential," and that hedonism based on consumption should be the name of the game—and the American public was happy to comply.[27] The counterculture as a whole, and the BTLs specifically, had a different understanding of how the world operated. While not rejecting everything the system had built—food stamps and welfare were often a part of the early days of the back to the land experience—country hippies advocated a way of life that was a far-reaching shift from mindless materialism, reviving "a radical transcendentalism that called for revolutionary change in consciousness."[28] So while political protests and radical demonstrations were without moral suasion by 1968 and 1969, hipbillies felt that "to restore meaning in America required a revolutionary change in the individual perception, a dramatic transformation in the way people viewed themselves and the world."[29]

Though young and jaded, these advocates of deep revolution did not wander completely blind into the wilderness with axes and acid. America has had a longstanding affair with notions of self-sufficiency. Rarely, however, do they succeed in breaking into the national consciousness with the lasting power on popular culture that the neopioneers had. As the events of the early 1970s once again placed these ideas at the forefront, figures like Aldo Leopold, Helen and Scott Nearing, and others became patron saints to a generation that eschewed organized religions for Eastern-flavored mysticism aided by generous doses of weed, acid, and booze.[30] While the country hippies may have lacked a thorough historical context for their movement, they were often familiar with at least one or two of these figures. Combined with longstanding counterculture prophets such as Gary Snyder and relatively new sages like Wendell Berry, these voices served as guides for the nascent communes, couples, and individuals in their quest to live a life of simplicity joined with the mysteries of the natural world.[31] Indeed, it may be that only by delving into the intellectual and mystical life of the country hippies can the appeal of the back to the land moment be fully understood.

While Thoreau had set the model, as it were, for critiquing urban life, by the 1920s his ideas seemed to need refinement. This update came through Ralph Borsodi's writings, which served as a major influence on the trajectory of modern back to the landers.[32] Borsodi, founder of the School of Living and one of the central agrarian theorists of the twentieth century, came of age as a writer in New York just before and during the Great Depression. His writing was strongly influenced by his father's work with Bolton Hall on the iconic *A Little Land and a Living,* a book that "played an important part in the back to the land movement that took place during the banking panic of 1907." [33] Throughout his life Borsodi "aimed at creating a systematic economic theory of decentralization, one including a compelling integration of home production into calculations of economic gain."[34] Like his father and Hall, Borsodi's work focused on resurrecting small-scale agrarian community and the establishment of the rural peasantry rather than the large-scale homesteads of the American West.[35] Foreshadowing the slow food movement and many of the arguments used by the counterculture to explain their move to the land, Borsodi believed that such a lifestyle was the best way to introduce the next generation to all the facts of life. Sexuality, birth, and death all had ready examples on the homestead.[36]

The key writings that enshrined Borsodi in the back to the land consciousness were *This Ugly Civilization* (1929), *Flight from the City* (1933), and *Prosperity and Security* (1938). Together, these works advocated a rejection of status quo economics and social structure and the creation of a world built around a new—yet old—system. "This is an ugly civilization," Borsodi declared, "It is a civilization of noise, smoke, smells, and crowds—of people content to live amidst the throbbing of its machines; the smoke and smells of its factories; the crowds and the discomforts of the cities of which it proudly boasts."[37] Not only did these material factors create ugliness, but so too did the "persistent failure [of America] to concern itself about whether the work men do, and the things they produce, and above all the way they live, create the comfort and understanding essential" for humanity to truly thrive.[38] For Borsodi, removing the ugliness required reorienting Western society, an existence rooted in an agrarian community.[39] Throughout his works, Borsodi argued in language that looked ahead to the BTLs of the 1970s, boldly stating that not all technology should be rejected, but that it should be employed at correct scale.[40] This early call for appropriate technology, among his other arguments, served as the grafting point between the 1920s and the reappearance of Scott and Helen Nearing.

Scott Nearing's impulse to live off the land began in 1905 when, at the age of twenty-two, he built his first house and planted his first garden according to "organic" principles, quickly establishing a reputation for stonework and gardening in Arden, Delaware.[41] By 1915 Nearing, with his new wife Helen, decided to begin homesteading, as it "provided a means of subsisting without requiring a paycheck from a capitalist institution to which one had to be ideologically beholden."[42] The Nearings sought to be free of the reigning economic crisis of the time, the Great Depression, hoping to become as "independent as possible of the commodity and labor markets."[43] Most directly for the back to the landers in the Ozarks, the couple strove to live in a way that "liberate[d] and dissociate[d]" themselves "from the cruder forms of exploitation: the plunder of the planet; the slavery of man and beast; the slaughter of men in war, and of animals for food."[44] For the Nearings, "simplicity should take the place of multiplicity, complexity and confusion."[45]

While their efforts at crafting an example that "solv[ed] the problem of living" did not always succeed, Helen was confident that she and Scott had shown that

> no family group possessing a normal share of vigor, energy, pur-
> pose, imagination and determination need continue to wear the
> yoke of a competitive, acquisitive, predatory culture . . . the family
> can live with nature, make themselves a living that will preserve
> and enhance their efficiency, and give them leisure in which they
> can do their bit to make the world a better place.[46]

In the same vein as the Nearings was Aldo Leopold, who quietly rose to the front of debates about enlightened ecological conscious-ness in twentieth-century America. Leopold, best known for the post-humous publication of his seminal *A Sand County Almanac*, articulated what he called the "land ethic."[47] *A Sand County Almanac* was the culmi-nation of years of work and thought brought on by Leopold's constant exposure to the natural world and the demands placed on it by modern society. He came to understand, according to environmental philoso-pher Max Oelschlaeger, that in contrast to the modern scientific systems "the human species, when viewed from an ecological (and temporal) perspective, is a part of nature."[48] Concluding *A Sand County Almanac*, Leopold's essay "The Land Ethic" became a clarion call for responsible interaction between human society and the natural world. For Leopold, holding true to such an idea allowed for the "boundaries of the [human] community" to be expanded, thereby allowing the inclusion of "soils, waters, plants, and animals, or collectively: the land."[49] Such an expan-sion of relationships led to a weighty obligation for humanity. While the land ethic "cannot prevent the alteration, management, and use" of nat-ural resources, it "does affirm their right to continued existence, and, at least in spots, their continual existence in a natural state."[50] This marked a monumental shift in how many in the twentieth century viewed their environment, changing the vision of society's relationship with the land from that of "conqueror" to "plain member and citizen of it. It implies respect for his fellow-members, and also respect for the community as such."[51]

While Leopold was hardly an avid member of the emerging post-war counterculture, his work echoed throughout the writing of the beatniks and the new agrarians like Wendell Berry, many of whom felt the ideals of the land ethic heralded a return to a better way for human society. While the land ethic was in part an intellectual affair, for Leopold it was also an "emotional process."[52] The present problem of land care stemmed from the wrong attitude, one that needed to be replaced by a "gentler" criterion rooted in a "biocentric perspective" that was "inherently synoptic and organismic rather than reductionistic and mechanistic" with humans as parts of the "community of life."[53] The problem stemmed from the West's blind acceptance of a cultural overlay on nature based on an "'Abrahamic concept of the land' [that] was upsetting the integrity and stability of natural ecosystems."[54] For Leopold, the Beats, and others, the structure of this overlay— government, Judeo-Christianity, economics, and more—must be rebuilt with the emotional power of Leopold and his land ethic.[55]

But who would tear down the structure? Leopold died of a heart attack in 1948, Borsodi was an aging revolutionary, and the Nearings were busy in New England. At the end of the 1940s, a group of literary and social rebels known as the beatniks dismantled some of these structures. While many of the beatniks—from Jack Kerouac to Allen Ginsberg—extolled the virtues and power of wild places, few articulated this vision so well, so consistently, and with such impact on the American ecological imagination as Gary Snyder.[56] Snyder began writing in the throes of the 1950s youth revolt, and in so doing he joined the main beat generation figures while studying at the University of California, Berkeley. After studying Zen Buddhism in Japan for several years, Snyder continued writing as he established his small Sierra Nevada homestead, Kitkidizzie, living life as a BTL but also as an elder voice in the counterculture. The life Snyder built in the Sierra Nevadas was at first blush an overly romantic vision of what the back-to-the-land dream promised; in reality for Snyder,

> the return to marginal farmland on the part of longhairs is not some nostalgic replay of the nineteenth century. Here is a generation of white people finally ready to learn from the Elders. How to live on the continent as though our children, and on down, for many ages, will still be here (not on the moon). Loving and protecting this soil, these trees, these wolves. Natives of Turtle Island . . . Those who have already sensed these necessities and have begun, whether in the country or the city, to "grow with less," are the only counterculture that counts.[57]

Turtle Island, a collection of poems and loosely constructed essays for which Snyder would win the Pulitzer in 1975, further illustrated his thoughts on humanity's interaction with the land. Decrying the "war against the earth" as the American military poured poisons from planes "Across Asia first/and next North America," Snyder presented a vision in which nature and humanity worked in harmony.[58] The collection, catapulted Snyder to national recognition, lending weight and power to back to the land ideals. Understanding and forming a right relationship with the natural world was, for Snyder, crucial to the success of human existence. Utilizing lessons drawn from Zen Buddhism and Daoism, that relationship began when man slowed enough to be amazed once again by the world around him. A love of learning how to live within nature drove Snyder's spiritual and physical life, an existence marked by a mistrust of Western structures that pushed aside the wisdom of Native Americans and Eastern traditions. He called for the restoration of primitivism, which would allow human society to embark on a "quiet revolution" that might "transform the way in which the earth's peoples interact with the land and among themselves."[59]

Though mainly a poet during the 1950s and 1960s, Snyder's work translated the ecologically based vision of society espoused by the likes of the Nearings and Leopold while also paving the way for his friendship with Kentucky native Wendell Berry.[60] At the same time that Snyder was working on his epic poetry collection and formulated the essays that formed *The Practice of the Wild* (1990), Berry made a splash as a leading agrarian voice, serving to link Leopold and Snyder's work while infusing within it a broader appreciation for the value of a working community's relationship to the natural world. Like Snyder, Berry pushed the discussion of the land ethic further by arguing first in his poetry, then in fiction and essays, that humanity and the natural world should operate in membership with one another.

Berry and Snyder were more closely linked than many understood at the time, building a friendship and collective influence that lasted for decades. Growing up, Berry worked on the farms of friends and family, attended the University of Kentucky, and graduated with a master's in English in 1957. He and his new wife Tanja then moved to California where Berry took part in Wallace Stegner's prestigious writing group at Stanford.[61] In 1964 Berry returned to the hills of his childhood, where he remained to work and write about the world as it could be, much as his friend Snyder was doing in the mountains of California. The friendship between Berry and Snyder was based in part on their mutual respect for each other's work—Berry had begun reading Snyder's writing in *Poetry* magazine while on the West Coast. In 1960, a few years after the publication of *Riprap*, Berry published his first novel, *Nathan Coulter*, introducing the world to the membership of Port William, a fictional community that deepened over time as stories, novels, and poems expanded the world and philosophy Berry articulated for his readers. By the 1970s, the two men had embarked on a friendship, and in the process sharpened each other's thoughts and writings as they discussed the problem of living well in a place.[62]

The idea of membership, in short, was Berry's summation of what was wrong with the world and what was needed to restore it. In his first novel, named for the main character, Berry gives the story of Nathan Coulter and his wanderings through Port William to his readers. Along the way Berry charts life in a bygone era replete with horse and mule teams, smallholder farmers, and self-sufficient towns with minimal connections to the outside, modernizing world. As Nathan and his brother transition to their grandparents' house after the death of their mother, the rhythm of work done well begins to mold and chart Nathan's life— that and the good-timing nature of his uncle, Burley Coulter. Work on and in the land "sheltered" them; work bound the community together when barns burned, people aged, and—eventually—war came.[63]

Berry's fiction and poetry, though, were not the only ways he shared his vision for life. *The Long-Legged House* (1969) and *The Unsettling of America* (1977) highlighted the destruction of rural American communities and advocated a manner in which they could be rebuilt. Arguing that the modern practices of agriculture as espoused by the Nixon administration were akin to that of a strip miner, Berry provided a view of human community based on the need to remain connected to the land and to work. Berry believed then (and now) that for the natural world to be truly protected, humanity must have a right working relationship with it, a sort of "kindly use," as he defined it.[64] Kindly use, though, was not unspecific, nor was it determined by the behemoths of agriculture sanctioned by large corporations. Rather, "kindly use depends upon intimate knowledge, the most sensitive responsiveness and responsibility."[65] For Berry, without intimate knowledge of place, the kind of knowledge a married couple has of each other, the essential facets of life and the world were in danger of destruction.

Following on the heels of these writers would be another seminal, though by no means final, thinker. In 1973 E. F. Schumacher published his iconic *Small is Beautiful: Economics as if People Mattered*, which was reprinted in 1975 with Theodore Roszak, noted counterculture intellectual, providing the introduction. Schumacher's book served as an introduction for many back to the landers to the decentralist ideas that attracted advocates for an agrarian, self-sufficient life, like the Nearings or Berry. Decentralists, emerging around figures like Ralph Borsodi, took some of their inspiration from the Southern Agrarians, who defended traditional agricultural life in the South as a way to combat the technocratic and wasteful vision of modernity espoused by large industry in America.[66] Borsodi and others argued for an "economic democracy" that centered around a vision of a nation where all were intimately connected to meaningful production and saw themselves "as the defenders of small-scale independent proprietors against their chief enemy, monopoly capitalism."[67]

Using a language familiar to fans of Snyder and other counterculture authors, Schumacher argued that humanity was "estranged from reality and inclined to treat as valueless everything that we have not made ourselves."[68] Building on the work of the previous two decades, Schumacher articulated in terms readily understood by members of the Aquarian Revolution that "Spaceship Earth" was in need not of more consumer-driven economics but instead of "Buddhist economics." This system, rooted in a practical application of the Eightfold Path, offered a middle way that established balance between "materialist heedlessness and traditionalist immobility" and allowed it to be "recommended even to those who believe that economic growth is more important than any spiritual or religious values."[69] The book became a classic and sat on store shelves beside the works of the Nearings and other major voices that advocated a new revolution.

What emerges from a close reading of these figures is a philosophy of rural redemption rather than Roszak's "invasion of the centaurs," that is, that the rural areas of America offered a place in which the counterculture could live out the deep revolution.[70] Deep revolution was built on appropriate scale and had to begin with the individual learning to act in concert with the land and local economies of scale. This philosophy was not arrived at only through books, however. It was a hardscrabble system, forged through work and in the ecstasies of post-industrial excess—an "open" vision of sexuality paired with the consciousness-bending impact of acid. Indeed, it may be said this rather work-a-day philosophy was not countercultural in the long run. It was instead the most American of philosophies, a syncretic creation born out of the pragmatic and mystical, as if Jefferson and Thoreau had been modulated by chemical dreams.

Indeed, chemical dreams were significant for much of the BTLs' outlook. Discussions of drugs and their relationship to the counterculture are often either demurely dismissive or excessively nostalgic, making any estimate of their impact on the community difficult. Despite this, understanding the role LSD played in the community helps illustrate how their philosophy was enacted in real life. But it is important to note at the outset that drugs were not the end-all for hipbillies. Marijuana, for many, was the main drug of choice, as "altering one's consciousness . . . probably inspired hopes of a higher consciousness."[71] While marijuana use was often approached in the same vein as alcohol consumption, LSD was something that was gradually left by the wayside, both for practical and spiritual reasons. The practical note is easy to understand—if one must work hard all day and every day in order to secure food, tripping on acid all the time was a serious impediment to survival. On the spiritual note, the reasons for leaving LSD behind are often vague.

This vagueness stems in part from the nature of LSD in general. LSD (lysergic acid diethylamide) was created in 1938 by Dr. Albert Hoffman. During the course of his work, Hoffman arrived at the most potent man-made hallucinogenic at the time.[72] For the purposes of the counterculture, LSD was a tool: the "psychedelics," a term coined in 1957 as a result of the growing popularity of LSD, had long been used by traditions the counterculture admired and sought to emulate.[73] During the 1950s, LSD and other psychedelics enjoyed widespread use and commentary by the likes of Henry Luce, founder of *Time* and *Life*. In May 1957, *Life* published an article about the experience of using "divine mushrooms" (or magic mushrooms).[74] The article was read by none other than Dr. Timothy Leary, a young psychologist whose widely known work had led to an appointment at Harvard University. Not long after reading the article, Leary ate some magic mushrooms while on vacation in Mexico and suddenly had "the deepest religious experience of my life. I discovered that beauty, revelation, sensuality, the cellular history of the past, God, the Devil—all lie inside my body, outside my mind."[75] Of particular interest to Leary was the impact psychedelics had on religious life. In one particular experiment, Leary and his research team attempted to understand if the transcendental experiences described by those under the influence of LSD or mushrooms were akin to those discussed by mystics. In the aftermath of the "Miracle at Marsh Chapel" experiment, in which participants did not know whether or not they had been given any sort of psychedelics, the team "concluded that the experiences described by those who had taken the drug were 'indistinguishable from, if not identical with' the classical mystical experience."[76]

The religio-mystical experience produced by LSD and other psychedelics translated, at least for back to the landers in the Arkansas Ozarks, into what one member called the "Ozark mystic vision," a sense of "complete interconnectedness with the universe, the natural world."[77] Members of the BTL community who experienced this vision often felt they had no choice but to live on and work the land in order to establish the deep revolution. Indeed, the deliberate usage of LSD in part allowed for the role of the imagination in one's life as a tool to be recovered and reemployed. By using this tool, the gateway to the universe was opened and the old structures of the "overlaid culture" that Leopold bemoaned, the beats railed against, and the urban revolutions of the 1960s assailed was peeled away and cast aside once and for all, as if Adam and Eve had cast off their animal skins and ran, dancing and singing, back into the garden as they returned humanity to its rightful place in harmony with nature.

While no single issue discussed above pushed or pulled most hipbillies to the Ozarks, in combination, the desire to recreate community, expanded consciousness, and the social upheaval of the previous decade created a powerful moment. Thus, hipbillies moved to the Ozarks thanks to a general discomfiture with prevailing society and a desire to create a more perfect world—a world in which the "man in the grey flannel suit" of the previous decades gave way to "true" human relationships;

a world where humanity lived, to borrow author Berry's phrasing, in "membership" with the land, thereby living within the "land ethic" of Aldo Leopold. Billig, Davidson, Ames, and others sought more than a radical removal of themselves from society, but also the rekindling of human community, something akin the agrarian village that Borsodi aspired to in his writing during the 1930s. This idea, bolstered by the growing power of the environmental movement, allowed the BTLs to build a utopia rooted in the social and environmental justice dreamed of by the 1960s revolutionaries.[78] Instead of piecemeal policies and protests, the back to the landers created a deep revolution; one so deep it needed to begin in the very dirt humanity came from. Only by beginning there could the individual be "revolutionized" enough to change communities and, ultimately, the nation and the world.

This rejection of the status quo was unique not simply because of the desire to leave the urban world and head for the hills, but because it occurred at a time when the nation had achieved the greatest levels of prosperity and ease it had ever seen. The "American Dream" ceased to be ephemeral as an increase in private home ownership, appliances for easy living, television, the automobile, and dramatic increases in real wages allowed the average American to experience a lifestyle that far outpaced any previous generation. Though often written off, the revolution offered by hipbillies was far more in line with traditional American ideals (especially when placed in juxtaposition with the new consumerism) and far more powerful than previously described. The Cold War's vision of American power rested on the maintenance, in part, of a consumerist status quo, but this vision of prosperity was increasingly critiqued, loudly in protests but also quietly as the cost of the nation's prosperity was counted. Environmental degradation, the loss of human community, and a blind drive toward the acquisition of wealth created an impulse for the deep revolution, prompting a new generation of Americans to go "back to the land" as they attempted to find for themselves the promise of Borsodi, Berry, and Snyder.

CHAPTER 2

Pioneers in an Age of Plenty

We didn't know shit.

—Guy King Ames

There is a good life here [but] not an easy one.

—Jory Sherman

THE BTL QUEST, however philosophical it might have been, was fundamentally based on living well in a place. To do so required not just revolutionary ideals, but also a great deal of alternative education and work on the part of the young in-migrants. The fastest teacher was experience, both their own and that of others. Following closely behind this was education via copious reading of *Mother Earth News*, the *Whole Earth Catalog*, *Organic Gardening*, and the ever-present guerilla presses of the Ozarks. The printed word served as a crucial source of knowledge and contacts needed for survival as urbanites moved to the hills. Though the daily in and out of a neopioneer is quickly described—chores, chores, and more chores—the manner in which homesteads operated is not easily fathomed by those outside the movement. For scholars of back to the landers, though, the recorded experiences and publications are a foggy window by which the idealism can be measured against the reality of the Ozarks.

To a degree, all the efforts at living on the land were the same: long days of work building houses, fences, sheds, and more. Longer days tilling, planting, weeding, and harvesting. Cold, snow-bound evenings and impassably muddy roads dominate many stories, as do evenings and days spent working side-by-side with friends. Within the general struggle to homestead, though, were differences, often a function of place and community. To help illustrate these differences, snippets from two families serve to show these varying aspects of the homesteading life.[1] Bill and Anne Williams and Richard and Wendy Neidhardt moved to their Ozark locales in 1976 and 1973, respectively, beginning the tedious process of finding a piece of land and setting foot into Teale's land of yarb doctors and ridge runners.

In 1973 the Neidhart family moved to the small town of Fox in Stone County, farther east in the Arkansas uplands. Like many, they were drawn to the region in part thanks to the cheap land as they paid only $2,200 for twenty acres.[2] Their first weeks in the state were consumed with battling an ever-increasing amount of mud, a typical complaint of many at the time, though Wendy noted that "our land is beautiful" despite the relative inaccessibility and lack of buildings.[3] Wendy staying at home with her and Richard's three children, described how locals had told them that the winter of 1973 was the worst since 1917, "which means chiefly that it rains one hell of a lot and there is mud everywhere."[4] She went on to explain that

> too much mud has been everywhere since we got here—which has slowed progress on the land since the road only exists in good weather and then just barely. But all that will be repaired someday —and we will have a thriving homestead in no time in spite of all the difficulties involved in living on the land. The 1st [sic] logs are up on our cabin—the garden land is turned and cleared and we have a tool shed—ugly but serviceable. How proud we feel of our small accomplishments![5]

The The Neidhardts had gone in on the land together with another couple both to help defray the costs and to distribute some of the labor, but this quickly became tough as both families were living in a small house together, with the wives and children often stuck at the house while the men were out on the land attempting to build the needed structures. Wendy told her mother in March 1973, that she and Grace (the other wife) were "homestead widows," as the men were "twenty miles away" working.[6]

Life on the land—or life trying to get to the land—remained an adventure for both families in Stone County (and hipbillies across the Ozarks). Life for Wendy in the early days was tough and "lonely," as Richard spent several days away either out on their land with their partner or doing odd jobs to help pay the bills.[7] The little farmhouse they rented was cramped and full of problems. Compounding this, life was more expensive than they had thought, preventing them from being able to buy meat regularly and enjoy a diverse diet.[8] These hardships, though, served as fuel for the dream of living on the land, and by the end of March 1973, things began to look up. Thanks to the above-average rainfall, they hoped for a bountiful garden, and they moved from the cramped and problematic farmhouse to one closer to their land, which prompted Wendy to hope to "see our menfolk 2 or 3 times a week instead of once a week" and that the new place would "be a good introduction to country life" as it had electricity and running water but no hot water and only a wood stove for cooking.[9]

Experience—like Wendy Neidhardt learning to cook on a wood stove—was a steady tutor for many things, but the problems faced by hipbillies were also addressed in the emerging back to the land "database" of information that proved critical information for the deep revolution's success. Questions about power production, water use, and how to pull together folk customs regarding planting with scientific evidence were pervasive as neopioneers established a new life. For many newcomers, local Ozark knowledge was the first course of action. Old-timers brought lessons on gardening, dealing with goats, working fields, and even economic survival. In part, this knowledge was readily shared because of the hipbillies' desire to work. Work was a common language throughout the dwindling old Ozark communities, and as such enabled many cultural bridges to be built.[10]

The Williamses moved from Texas to Madison County in 1976, settling on a piece of land outside Huntsville. While they were waiting to have a road cleared—a common issue many BTLs faced—Anne borrowed some garden space from a friend and began the first of many Ozark gardens as she planted early spring staples: onions, carrots, greens, potatoes, and more in April.[11] As they began life on the farm, Bill and

Anne also took time to get connected throughout the area. That same April, they went into Fayetteville and joined the nascent food co-op (what would ultimately become Ozark Natural Foods) and met other hippies in the area. As these connections grew, the Williamses quickly became part of several of the small countercultural communities popping up throughout the Arkansas Ozarks, from seed blessing groups to beekeepers to environmental activists—all while dodging the rain and trying to get the rest of the spring crops planted.[12] The Williamses also quickly became known among locals before they had even been on the land two months: they were part of "neighborhood" efforts to round up cattle that had gotten out of a nearby pasture, assistance that was greatly appreciated by Ozark natives in the area.

All of this activity was done before Bill and Anne had finished their house or even had electricity extended out onto their land—which would happen, after much negotiation with the power company, in early May 1976. As the Williamses settled into the area during the spring and summer of 1976, they began to receive regular visits from folks they met on their outings across the region, linking them into the broader network of the counterculture in the area as they made friends with Albert Skiles, now a noted architect, and others.

The life documented by Anne in her diary shows how she and Bill slipped into the life of Madison County—they had good relationships with the locals they knew and met and grew more connected with the BTL community across the Ozarks. It also shows how the back to the land community tried to operate. Day in and day out, the Williamses worked hard—moved logs, cleared springs, built a house, helped neighbors. But they also took time to enjoy the Ozarks—while most of Anne's notes about a day's work ended with a simple "full day" or "hard day," several times a week there were notes of dinners with friends, swimming in the river midafternoon, and more. The quality of life promised by the materialist American dream—if only you could find the money to buy things—was, for the Williamses, unnecessary. They found satisfaction not by purchasing but by living within the simple rhythms of agrarian life as they became integrated into the Ozarks.

In many cases, answers that melded the traditional world with the growing technological world were found in publications that ranged from flashy catalogs to home-printed newsletters. These items were part of a broad national shift in how the press was understood by America's youth, foreshadowing the impact of the internet and social media. Underground press offerings had been a part of the American experience for generations, popping up whenever there seemed to be an issue or cause ignored by mainstream news outlets. Such presses advocated for issues "so radical that the establishment press was not willing to provide a forum for the discussion," in the words of Rodger Streitmatter.[13] It was a tradition littered with august names: Upton Sinclair, Ida Tarbell, and others, all of whom took on the pressing issues of the day. While the form and presentation of the 1960s and 1970s counterculture presses was different than that of earlier generations, the topics approached were much the same: gender, the environment, or economics.[14]

The counterculture took advantage of a revolution in typesetting—by the 1960s, "cold" setting had become common and was easily used at home. This technique was well received by the do-it-yourself attitude of America's counterculture: anyone with a typewriter and access to a copy machine could create and distribute a magazine or newsletter for a fraction of the cost of a decade before.[15] While underground efforts to challenge the focus of the establishment papers had existed for centuries, the iteration they took in the 1960s were part and parcel with the rest of the revolution. Building on the counterculture's "fervent belief in freedom of expression, and their staunch advocacy of both a politically radical and counterculture lifestyle," experimental typography and unconventional presentation became the norm, and along the way they "gave shape to an alternative media culture as much informed by the space age, television, the computer era, and socialism as by the holy trinity of the sixties underground: sex, drugs, and rock 'n' roll."[16] Despite the impact, these publications were often criticized for the seemingly haphazard visual, writing, and layout style they used.[17] This perception was often misplaced, as art scholar Gwen Allen points out. Rather than seeing publications like *RAT* or *Fuck You* as hastily drawn and printed while under the influence of LSD or other chemicals, Allen astutely argues that the editors and writers in these magazines "in fact strategically employed a range of sophisticated visual practices that parallel those utilized by artists during this period," thereby "questioning the rational basis of modern communication itself, envisioning the printed page as a very different kind of interface—one that was deeply antiauthoritarian in nature."[18]

This assessment holds true for key national back to the lander publications like the *Whole Earth Catalog* and *Mother Earth News*. Perhaps more than any other pairing of publications, these two represented the ethos and aims of the entire back to the land movement, highlighting its connection to other portions of the counterculture as well. Paired with local creations, *Whole Earth Catalog* and *Mother Earth News* helped entice, place, and guide urban refugees as they searched for a way to live out the deep revolution in the aftermath of the 1960s—and often there was a discussion of the Ozarks in publications like the ubiquitous *Mother Earth News*, solidifying in the national consciousness the idea of the Ozarks as a countercultural haven. But before *Mother Earth News* there had to be a *Whole Earth Catalog*.

Stewart Brand created the *Whole Earth Catalog* in 1966 after listening to a lecture by R. Buckminster Fuller, an early proponent of environmentalism.[19] Brand, after the talk, returned home, took LSD, and thought about Fuller's comment that we as humans had never seen the world from space, which meant we as a race had an incorrect perception of the universe.[20] Brand resolved to convince NASA to take a picture to put earth into perspective for humanity, succeeding in 1967. The picture of the "blue marble" became famous across the world and was the cover image for Brand's next venture, the *Whole Earth Catalog*. Subtitled *Access to Tools*, the catalog envisioned a new way of living and organizing information—the catalog itself was a tool, just as much as the items discussed within its pages.

First published in the fall of 1968, the catalog ran sporadically throughout the 1970s and 1980s, and it was based on the premise that "a love of the earth and a love of technology could coexist, that hippies should make common cause with engineers."[21] Brand's work highlighted all sorts of things, but much of *Whole Earth Catalog* focused on access to information needed to survive outside of the urban context— details on tool selection and constructing solar arrays were paired with poetry, stories, and essays extolling the virtues of breaking free from mainstream society and creating a world with a proper perspective on humanity's place on the planet. Brand envisioned the catalog not as a drop in a bucket full of competing voices but as the vanguard, a trendsetter not just for hippies but, hopefully, all of American life.[22] In a large measure, Brand succeeded in achieving this—as the *Catalog* grew in physical size from sixty-odd pages in 1968 to over four hundred by 1972, so too did readers. (Indeed, Dennis Sanders, a hipbilly in southern Washington County was quick to bring out his well-used copy of the first *Whole Earth Catalog*, noting that this was akin to the Bible for back to the landers throughout the Ozarks.)[23] At the beginning of the *Whole Earth Catalog's* life, it claimed some fifteen thousand subscribers; by the time Brand was awarded a National Book Award in 1973, readership of *Whole Earth Catalog* had jumped to over one million, earning Brand and the *Catalog* "countercultural celebrity and acceptance among the East coast publishing establishment."[24]

The vision the *Catalog* claimed was ideally suited for adherents of the deep revolution:

> We are as gods and might as well get used to it. So far, remotely done power and glory—as via government, big business, formal education, church—has succeeded to the point where gross defects obscure actual gains. In response to this dilemma and to these gains a realm of intimate, personal power is developing—power of the individual to conduct his own education, find his own inspiration, shape his own environment, and share his adventure with whoever is interested. Tools that aid this process are sought and promoted by the WHOLE EARTH CATALOG.[25]

It was, in Brand's conception, an "evaluation and access device," a sort of proto-Wikipedia that discussed useful tools that were readily available by mail.[26] Complete with a code that let the reader know if something was still readily available and useful, the *Catalog* provided book reviews, tutorials, and more. It also offered introductions to various iconic ideas of the era, like geodesic domes. In its discussion of the Lama Foundation's *The Dome Cookbook*, the *Catalog* noted that domes reflected an ideal society, where "intelligent" load sharing was part not just of architectural design but of good human relationships.[27] Domes were not just something that appeared in communes outside of Berkeley: the Ozarks had their own "Dome People," a loose cooperative of families that resided in Washington County during the bulk of the 1970s. David Pride and others set up shop in Weedy Rough, or

"Domeland," in Hazel Valley, near where the Sanders lived (and close to the old stomping grounds of Don West). Domeland was made up of about two dozen folks who bought 120 acres in late 1970. The goal was to create an "experimental community" that hoped to show "a better way to do things."[28] When Pride and his companions bought their land, *Domebook* quickly became the guide for building shelters out on the land.[29]

Mother Earth News followed in the same vein as the *Domebooks* and the *Whole Earth Catalog* but with more specific discussions of daily life out on the land. Like many early back to the lander presses, *Mother Earth News* was started in 1970 by John and Jane Shuttleworth on a shoestring budget.[30] Like the *Whole Earth Catalog*, *Mother Earth News* held discussions of tools, techniques, and books that were seen as essential to a revolutionary life but focused on specific issues that the movement faced. As such, *Mother Earth News* opted for a regular publication schedule, sending out magazines filled with commentary, advice, questions, and more every month to readers across the nation.

Mother Earth News, even though it was national magazine, did not ignore the Ozarks. The region was often mentioned, starring in at least nine feature articles between 1972 and 1986, and was discussed more briefly dozens of times in between. The stories ranged in attitude about the region, as Durand's article discussed in the introduction illustrated. Though Durand characterized the Ozarks "as a beautiful wild region of several hundred square miles," he cautioned that if you loved your children, don't subject them to the schools.[31] Durand went further, stating that in-migrants must be prepared for grueling work on poor land, unless you were already wealthy. According to Durand, even if you did find moderately good land, there were no good roads, no good jobs, and no "satisfactory social experiences."[32] Not all the pieces in *Mother Earth News* presented such a negative picture, however. Indeed, when the Arkansas Ozarks were discussed in *Mother Earth News* during the 1970s and 1980s, the region was by and large described in positive terms, though with sage bits of advice about life in the hills.[33]

Comment's like Paul Durand's were not met with a great deal of enthusiasm from other Ozark country hippies. Mary Jo Frolick, for example, provided a terse response to Durand. Noting that he had bad-mouthed "friends, neighbors and my mountains," Frolick castigated

Durand for arriving in the Ozarks with "a head stuffed (over-stuffed?) with book learning" about how "he was going to teach these hillbillies a thing or two."[34] In so doing, Durand had done precisely what many moving into the Ozarks tried to avoid; namely, he broke "every social grace of the hills" and expected the locals to "love him for it."[35] Indeed, anywhere Durand found "ignorance," she found "intelligence."[36] Frolick concluded her rebuttal, noting it "makes my blood boil when people move to the mountains and then complain because things are not easy like they are in the cities . . . Mountain living has always been beautiful but hard and I don't expect it to change much."[37]

Negative comments aside, the articles in *Mother Earth News* underlined that hard work was needed to survive while also reminding readers of the gentler side of the Ozarks. For example, in the September/October 1973 issue, Myrtle Cress (who described herself as having been "a city gal, schoolmarm [nationally honored], farmer's wife, farmer, mother, VISTA teacher" before being a homesteader) offered a simple list of things to make pioneering easier, chief of which were a large "black iron kettle" and stirring paddle as "you'll have dozens of uses for this tool besides making hominy, rendering fat for food or soap, and heating the laundry water."[38] This discussion of useful tools and techniques extended beyond pots—one Ozark homesteader wrote in to discuss how he and his wife purchased a tiller for their garden and the many uses it had beyond the garden. In the March/April 1975 issue, Monte Burch discussed how his Troy-Bilt tiller helped break open garden sections on their eighty-five-acre hill farm but also was used to begin postholes and holes to transplant fruit trees. The tiller had, in Burch's eyes, no end of practical uses.[39]

Other equipment advice dealt with things inside the home, like old-fashioned cook stoves. In 1971 B. Touchstone Hardaway wrote in and gave a long, exultant piece on the virtues of wood-burning stoves in the kitchen. After noting that she was "semi-old fashioned," Hardaway described how "the idea of a wood-burning cookstove had sort of eased into my mind over the years even though I knew absolutely nothing about using one."[40] Acknowledging the difficulties—using the stove could be a "real hair shirt"—Hardaway concluded that "if you're able to slow your pace," you will be rewarded by "the wonderful smell of wood smoke, apples in your cheeks" and a "jim-dandy supply of wood."[41]

Other articles, like Tom Hodge's in 1979, featured advice on adapting stereotypical New England projects to the Ozarks, such as his maple sugaring operation.[42]

The BTL movement in the Ozarks was not just discussed in the national underground media; hipbillies also created their own. While some, like Streitmatter, argue that the South had only one or two visible markers of underground press, like *Kudzu* in Mississippi, in truth the Ozarks held more than its fair share of home-published newsletters and papers.[43] Like their big city kin, Ozark guerilla presses aimed to take apart the establishment and offered lessons on how to live as longhairs in the hills.[44] One of the earliest hipbilly-focused publications was the *Ozark Access Catalog (OAC)*.[45] The *OAC* was the brainchild of Edd Jeffords, an Ozark returnee and active part of the counterculture scene in Eureka Springs in Carroll County. Jeffords, following Stewart Brand's *Whole Earth Catalog*, designed the *OAC* to be "a tool for regional reference and information." In so doing, he hoped the *OAC* would give "to potential new residents accurate information about the region."[46] Though it would be short-lived—only four issues were printed—its reach was impressive. By the summer of 1973, after its second issue, the *OAC* had twelve hundred regular subscribers and printed and distributed some thirty thousand copies.[47]

Like many of the guerilla presses that popped up during the counterculture's heyday, the *OAC* operated based on feedback from readers, either in the form of comments, or just general ideas.[48] This was quickly evident, as letters and article responses appeared in the issues following April 1973. Like *Whole Earth Catalog*, the first issue published set the stage for people arriving in the Ozark hill country with topical articles on issues from how to buy land to native crafts and folklore, as well as how to apply old technology to new problems, such as wind power or solar heating.[49] Working to counter the idea that the Ozarks were cut off from everything presented by folks like Durand, the *OAC's* first volume quickly noted that "despite a euphoric feeling of remoteness that can accompany life in the rural Ozark mountains, there is scarcely a spot further than 50 miles from the nearest large trade center."[50] The first volume also pointed out that the perceived rurality of the Ozarks allowed for something that was hard to come by elsewhere: "Land still is inexpensive and easily available in the Ozark regions," though this was

Ozark Access Catalog

April '73

1⁰⁰

Ozark Access Catalog.
Courtesy Special Collections, University of Arkansas Libraries, Fayetteville.

sure to change as rising prices and the influx of land developers made finding good land more difficult.[51] Not only did the *OAC* staff note the general Ozark region was a good place to look for affordable land, but they also recommended two realtors that had developed a reputation for working well with young in-migrants, Jim Diggs in Eureka Springs and Jim Rice in Mountain View.[52]

Such knowledge of realtors was crucial as the Ozarks was experiencing a minor land rush. As retirees flocked to the state in greater numbers than the BTLs, in many cases land prices in the region began to climb—though they still remained cheaper than California. In such conditions, things got muddled. In 1972, when Cindy Davidson and a group of folks from Little Rock moved up to Madison County they inadvertently got mixed up in such an issue. Initially, they thought they had purchased eighty acres of cheap land that ran back off the road. What had actually happened, it turned out, was that the parcel had been split into two forty-acre sections, with only forty acres that had road access. Davidson and her group's piece lay *behind* the front forty acres without a road to get into it.[53] Thus, advice on reputable land agents like the *OAC* provided was invaluable.

Jeffords and his staff, attempting to temper the exuberance of would-be back to the landers, noted that the best way to understand what was happening with land prices would be to live in the Ozarks for a little while before purchasing a farm. "That's the only way to really learn about local conditions, prices and values. Its [*sic*] also important to become familiar with the local customs and peculiarities of the people who'll be your neighbors and fellow citizens."[54] Doing so would introduce one to the local farmers, who were "honest, but sharp from years of horse-trading," as well as help one become sure of what was wanted in a homestead, especially as the "country and the elements have beaten lots of city-bred, back to the land enthusiasts. In the mountains you're dealing with harsh realities, and they say that if you make it through that first winter you can stay as long as you like."[55]

The remaining issues of the *Ozark Access Catalog* provided information on everything from the mundane to the exciting—articles on fence building coexisted with discussions about bluegrass music (not just old-timey music). But the real meat of the catalog were the letters. In the second volume, as people wrote in from across the region, the *OAC* saw requests for information on splitting shingles and finding wooden barrels, and answers to questions about cover crops and inoculants.[56] The last issues followed suit, but with a readership that expanded beyond the Ozarks—Riley Richard from Cameron, Louisiana, wrote in to tell how he was moving to eighty acres in Searcy County and how he was "glad to see a local magazine that will maybe help me from making mistakes."[57] The *OAC* even pulled in an older crowd—eighty-three-year-old Lydia Holland from Texarkana, Texas, wrote in for the third issue to say that the *OAC* was "most interesting."[58] Joel Davidson, the soon-to-be founder of the *Living in the Ozarks Newsletter*, wrote in to propose a gathering of people to learn about shelter building, solar technology, and more.[59] By the fourth issue, the *OAC* received requests from Peace Corps members as far away as Africa for a subscription—provided air rates could be determined.[60]

Perhaps one of the more illuminating letters came from Richard and Marlene in the final volume of the *OAC*. The couple had homesteaded outside of Lebanon, Missouri, on twenty acres for a little over a year at the time they wrote the letter. Their cabin burned down while they were away from the property—the cause of the fire was "unknown"—and they had moved into a twelve-by-twenty-two-foot tent in the meantime.[61] They hauled their water from the Osage River, about three quarters of a mile from the farm—but only if rain had not muddied the water. As if hauling water were not hard enough, they were having a hard time gardening: "We planted a fairly large garden this spring but every thing [*sic*] came up in miniature—something like those Japanese gardens where all the plants are four to six inches high with fully mature fruit."[62] The lesson, according to the young couple, was "quite clear. The soil suits such plants and grasses as are found growing abundantly in it but will not provide the nutrition needed by those garden vegetables which require a richer, sweeter soil."[63] To create such a soil, they invested in rabbits for manure for their garden while also digging in leaf compost to help aid in soil fertility and retention—in line with the recommendations of Helen and Scott Nearing. Instead of the goats many BTLs had, Richard and Marlene opted for hogs—two runts and two healthy ones. In this, they offered advice for other homesteaders—buy runts as "they are a very good investment as they are usually the smallest pigs in the litter and have the same growth potential as the others . . . Most of the pig farmers like to find steady buyers for these."[64] They also invested in a large chicken flock to capitalize on high egg prices, and began a long-term building project to replace their cabin. They summed up their first year in the Ozark hills rather poetically:

> You can only get out of the land and living what you put in them. Thought, imagination, and action are the force-tools which we have available for use in our daily lives. When these are reinforced by love or enthusiasm results are certain. These result [sic] when coupled with good communications with God and neighbors creates or brings about successful living.[65]

More common than high-reaching pieces like the *OAC* were publications like *Living in the Ozarks Newsletter (LION)* from Madison County.[66] *LION* was started in 1974 by Joel and Sheri Davidson outside Pettigrew. The newsletter was like many of the other publications emerging at the time—it functioned as a sort of proto-internet, a meeting ground for people looking for information and connections to aid the back-to-the-land life in the region. "To many of us here in the Ozarks," wrote Davidson, life is about "slowing down, enjoying, living a life of peace and love. But before any real relaxing can happen, a lot of work needs doing," work that needs to "be done with soul so that they don't make a robot out of you."[67] Arguing that modern life had become "fragmented and disconnected," Davidson believed *LION* was a "vehicle to facilitate communications between people in the Ozarks so that they can get the help they need to make their personal dream come true."[68] This was done through the letters and articles in the newsletter and also by organizing workshops and get-togethers. The goal was to foster community, for in the end community was what this whole endeavor was about. "All of us who want the feeling of community have discovered that to get that feeling you need people. They are the basic ingredient. But how do you find people who you would want to get together with, be it your neighbors or water brothers and sisters or anywhere in between? We will try to help."[69] And so *LION* did.

The issues, ranging from twice a month to every two months, contained articles, letters, and commentary on all facets of the back to the land life as experienced in the Ozarks. Where the *OAC* sought to maintain a regional and polished vision, *LION* was proudly homespun, wore its heart on its sleeve, and was often radical in its political overtones, at least during the tenure of Davidson as editor. (By the end of the decade, the Davidsons had embarked on new adventures in homesteading that required they give up the newsletter.) This particular voice, though, had a wide audience—by its tenth issue, *LION* reached around three thousand people an issue through subscriptions and sharing.[70] Part of this subscription base was far flung—not only were people in the Arkansas and Missouri Ozarks reading *LION*, but so were folks from eight other states.[71]

There was plenty of advice on living the BTL life in the guerilla press, but few of these offered an easily accessible and comprehensive vision of "going back to the land." There were, however, plenty of books and memoirs available that provided such an image, chief among them were the writings of Helen and Scott Nearing and Borsodi's *Flight From the City* (republished in 1972). Others also emerged, like James Bohlen's *The New Pioneer's Handbook* or *The Briarpatch Book* from the West Coast.[72] While many of the new back to the land books smacked of youthful idealism, the story of Helen and Scott Nearing seemed to hipbillies in the Ozarks as a time-tested model of how life should be lived. The Nearings' books, *Living the Good Life* and *Continuing the Good Life*, were reprinted with gusto in the early 1970s, which quickly established the aging revolutionaries as the elders of the back to the land world. These were part how-to manuals, part exhortations that provided a basic guide for many neopioneers as they headed for the hills of the Ozarks and beyond. *Continuing the Good Life*, in particular, laid out basic discussions of thriving on the land.

Focused on how the homesteading life was one of "building and maintaining a solvent family economy amid the wreckage and drift of a society that was disintegrating in accordance with the laws of its own self-destructive being," the Nearings spent the beginnings of the book discussing the necessities of gardening in an organic method and of thinking beyond simple summer gardens for producing the needed food for a household.[73] Indeed, the Nearings helped popularize "four season" gardening, to use the phrasing of one of their devotees.[74] By using certain crops and season extension materials, the Nearings showed that one could—given the work was done—successfully produce at least some produce year round, even in the harsh winters of New England.

LIVING IN THE OZARKS NEWSLETTER #2

UPPER FRILEY ORGANIZATION SCHOOL, INC.   PETTIGREW, ARK. 72752

"Homesteading has not solved the problem of living. But it has gone far
enough to convince many that no family group possessing a normal share
of vigor, energy, purpose, imagination and determination need continue
to wear the yoke of a competitive, acquisitive, predatory culture."
"The existence of intentional communities has been an expression of
dissatisfaction with an established social order and an effort to provide
a substitute that will furnish a more worthwhile life for more people
than its predecessors were able to give. Intentional communities are
practical expressions of dissatisfaction with the existing social order
and a creative effort at social improvement."
THE MAKING OF A RADICAL by Scott Nearing.

NEWSLETTER NEWS

We've moved to Spoke Plant! We
still get our mail at Pettigrew,
but now we have room to breathe,
grow and improve. Our place is
big and we welcome folks interested in sharing our work and play.
If you would like to pay us a
visit, drop us a line telling
about yourself and your interests.

OUR RESIDENT TREE EXPERT

The old-timer who lives with us has
spent over 35 years in this rough
land. On our place is one of the
widest selections of grafted trees
to be found in this region. Bob was
planting and grafting trees in No.
Carolina before he came to the Ozarks
and when he read J. Russell Smith's
book, TREE CROPS, he joined the
Northern Nut Growers Assoc. He
knows his stuff and is willing to
help others, answer questions, and
relate his experiences. If you are
interested in trees, drop him a line.

THE NEWSLETTER STARTS A SCHOOL

Last month we of the newsletter
started our own school by setting up a non-profit corporation
(very legal) by ourselves. Then
we withdrew our two 9 year old
nieces, who live with us, from
public school to teach them ourselves. If you would like to
donate something to the school
which we hope to expand, it would
really be appreciated. If you
would like to start your own
school, write to us and we will
print up a how-to manual for
Arkansas. Other states are similar, but we're really familiar
with The requirements here best.

For Young and Old Kids to do:
SPIDER WEB PRINTS

Spiders like to weave webs.
It's their thing. They make them
all the time. So if you want one
they will just make another.
Get the spider to move by
gently blowing on the web.
Spray both sides of the web
with white spray paint, while
it is still wet, carefully place a
sheet of dark colored construction paper so that it touches
all parts of the web's lower
surfaces and then cut the strands
supporting the web. The web
will make a clear print on the
paper. THANK THE SPIDER.

WHAT TO DO WITH PIECES OF THE OZARKS
LAYING ABOUT IN YOUR FIELDS - STEPS OF
OPPOSING CIRCLES. JEST PICK UM UP AND TRY IT.

1

Living in the Ozarks Newsletter (LION), edited by Joel Davidson and Sheri Davidson.
Courtesy Special Collections, University of Arkansas Libraries, Fayetteville.

SEPTEMBER 1976 Volume 3 Number 9

HARVEST 1976

Joel & Sherri's Last **LION** see page 2

1

All of this, however, was rooted in well-developed and cared for soil, something Ozark BTLs lacked. The Nearings offered a remedy: compost. Compost, a combination of decayed or mostly decayed organic materials, was essential for building up the capacity of rocky or poor soil enough to sustainably produce high-quality vegetables year after year. Healthy additions of compost, paired with sawdust and other soil amendments, maintained the Nearings, allowed their soil to transition from "tough yellow clay soil that hardened to brick-like consistency" to a soil that could "pass for a high-level sandy loam," the ideal for vegetable production.[75]

The Nearings also addressed, in detail, other issues that faced hipbillies. The couple had learned in their first homesteading experience in Vermont that homesteaders needed to understand the kinds of water usage that the farm would have. "Land without water is all but useless," Helen wrote. "In homesteading the two prime requisites are enough land and an abundance of unpolluted water."[76] There were many ways to deal with water access, but the Nearings recommended, when possible, building a pond; this would allow for natural storage of water if it was well located, a central location to pump from, and more. Structures were a different matter. Unless one bought a place with useful buildings on it, building was in order. The Nearings, due to what was readily available on *their* land, recommended working with stone; they had done so with great success in Vermont and again in Maine. Using a relatively simple slipform masonry technique, the Nearings advocated using whatever rock was on hand—no need to go out and buy stone for your walls if you have plenty already.[77] Slipformed walls were not just discussed in the Nearing's work; *Mother Earth News* would periodically have a discussion on their effectiveness and ease of use, furthering the spread of the technique throughout the back to the land community. This was not the only alternative building style discussed in *Mother Earth News*. Various articles throughout the 1970s showcased not only slipforming with rock but also with concrete or using hay bales to build homes, as well as the ever-present teepee or yurt.

A key element to the success of the Nearings was cooperation— either with locals in the community they moved into or with visitors, of which they had plenty by the 1970s. At the writing of *Continuing the Good Life*, Helen and Scott estimated they had hundreds of young people come each year who had heard of the Nearings' long home-steading experiment. They were "ready for anything that makes an idealistic appeal and that is fairly far from standard community practice . . . homeless between worlds."[78] While they could not accommodate all who came with a place to live, some were able to join the Nearings, most notably Eliot Coleman, who carried the Nearings' mantle forward into the twenty-first century.[79]

Though the Nearings made light of some of the visitors, or complained in a good-natured way about them, the sheer presence of so many hands made light work of the myriad tasks on the homestead, a reality often ignored or not grasped by some who homesteaded in other areas of the country after reading the Nearings, hipbillies in the Ozarks included. Indeed, as Eleanor Agnew noted in her memoir on the back-to-the-land movement, the Nearings had created a more "solvent and self-contained economy on their homestead" than was possible for the average back to the lander.[80] This was not openly discussed, though; the life described by the Nearings in their books of four hours of work each day set for their young readers an overly utopian tone to the business of homesteading.[81] To discuss their income would have been counter-productive; after all, going back to the land was the way for Scott and Helen to exit the economy of money. While the Nearings were not exceedingly wealthy, they had the ease of a steady income, something many of the hipbillies were often without, at least at the start of their homesteading life.[82]

Indeed, dealing with money on the homestead prompted many of the back to the landers to operate much like their native Ozark neighbors, that is, to work off the farm. Cindy Davidson remembered that she and two other women from the community in Madison County would come into the University of Arkansas in Fayetteville to work at the student dining hall.[83] Others, especially farther east into the region, became part of tree planting crews in the national forest or would join groups going around to the large cornfields and detassel. Often, many on the land would pick up part-time carpentry work, like Sam Stephens.

Bohlen's *The New Pioneer's Handbook* was part and parcel with this sort of idealized lifestyle.[84] Author James (Jim) Bohlen, a former American ICBM missile engineer had gone back to the land in Canada when he published his book.[85] The *Handbook* was typical of the times as it was environmentally focused and used examples from a diverse array of cultures to illustrate its points. The *Handbook* also contained detailed discussions of how to find land, understanding energy production and relevant technologies for the homestead, and more. As such, Bohlen's book highlighted a problem many of these new attempts to explain life on the land exhibited: little discussion on how to grow and preserve food. Though these topics were often covered, at least in a piecemeal fashion, in many of the periodicals of the day, BTLs were often in a constant state of financial crisis, preventing them from subscribing to everything they might "need" in order to become a "true" part of the back to the land era. This, however, did not mean they were adverse from buying equipment—like many in their generation, despite the generation disdain of commercialism in the youth movement, things were still bought and sold with regularity.

This was in part a symptom of the times: by the end of the 1960s, "hip" had become cool and consumable. The fashion, music, and idealism were co-opted by the marketing mandarins of Madison Avenue. The major brands and ad agencies recognized at the end of the 1960s the counterculture had formed a "powerful subeconomy" alongside a "lively print culture" that extolled an ecologically focused lifestyle.[86] This "subeconomy" functioned, by and large, as an independent world for the first years of the counterculture revolution, but by 1967's Summer of Love, countercultural imagery was in advertising campaigns by major corporations in America, institutions that saw the counterculture not as an ally, allowing for the development of a "critique of their own industries, of over-organization and creative dullness."[87] As a result of the social revolutions of the 1960s and 1970s, "hip became central to the way American capitalism understood itself and explained itself to the public."[88]

Marketing needs aside, the fact remains that these books and magazines were published and sold to prospective BTLs. While few could hold every facet of knowledge needed by a hopeful pioneer, often by piecing together a few of these how-to manuals, a young hipbilly gained useful information on a topic needed to live the revolution. Bohlen's work was one such piece thanks to its focus on alternative energy structures. Though the book was not focused on an argument as to the "pros and cons of alternative energy sources" like solar, wind, or geothermal, but in learning how to best harness contextually appropriate energy generation schemes that allowed "man to forge for himself an autonomous material life frugal in its demands on energy."[89] With a focus on learning "to live in harmony with the natural rhythm of the earth," Bohlen argued that the ideas in the book helped prospective BTLs "learn to occupy this planet without depleting the earth's material stock or its life support systems."[90]

After rather run-of-the-mill advice about buying land (which there was a whole book about by another country hippie), Bohlen launched into a numbers-heavy evaluation of energy use and needs on a homestead, often referring back to the Nearings for context. In so doing, Bohlen arrived at a series of economic figures that allowed for an avid homesteader to manipulate the environment with minimal negative impact, covering everything from income generation to waste water disposal and sanitation concerns.[91] While much of this previous discussion was difficult for someone without Bohlen's engineering background, the last portion of the book gave tutorials in physics and guerilla engineering for urbanites in the hills.[92] Though Bohlen's writing left out the issues surrounding the production of food, he provided a simple and ideal vision of how to understand and use the nascent alternative energy sources emerging in the 1970s—but this was an ideal, not reality.

Despite the problems of trying to live up to the vision of homesteading portrayed in the increasingly commercialized books and magazines, Ozark hipbillies put in the work needed to survive, and more often, thrive. Some in particular even found ways to implement the alternative energy methodologies discussed across the counterculture. Joel Davidson, for one, began a successful solar career thanks in large part to Edd Jeffords asking him to write about solar panels for the *Ozark Access Catalog*. Others created businesses or artistic careers that generated income used to pay for the homestead. And most ultimately accepted that full-time life on the farm was not be the most practical way to establish a revolutionary footing and so sought seasonal work or off-farm work on construction crews, tree-planting crews, and craft circuits.[93]

In short, living on the land was tough but made easier by the creation of community through volleyball games and letters and visits. Though some would not stay on the land for the eternity they first envisioned, those that came to the Arkansas Ozarks showed remarkable mettle in living out the deep revolution. Despite the lack of experience in homesteading, or even gardening, these intrepid neopioneers built a livelihood that satisfied their individual need for an existence of meaning rather than mindless consumerism and conformity. Along the way, they hoped to remake the Ozarks and America, one community at a time, as they pushed forward an environmental consciousness and sought to re-energize flagging rural communities.[94] Although the vision of life they offered seemingly ran in opposition to traditional Ozark communities, in truth Ozark natives and hipbillies created an alternative Ozarks, and together they quietly belied the expectations of America at large when such disparate groups meet.[95]

CHAPTER 3

Hipbillies and Hillbillies

If you're going to come, come gently.

—Crescent Dragonwagon

WASTRELS, VAGRANTS, BURNED-OUT drug addicts: these names, and more, are assumed in popular memory as a succinct description of how native Ozarkers viewed the influx of hippies seeking to rebuild their lives during the 1970s. As has been shown so far, though, this is too simple an explanation for the hipbillies in general, and their relationship to old-time Ozark natives in particular. To be sure, there were points of conflict, but these were the exception rather than the rule throughout the Arkansas uplands. Despite reality, however, a regional perception emerged that presented the back to the landers as a burned-out group intent on hedonism —a narrative that quickly dominated most discussions of the Age of Aquarius. As this chapter and the next show, the memories of the interactions between these communities was shaped not by their own voices; rather, it was shaped within the context of a "new Ozarks" dominated by other in-migrants and Ozark hamlets concerned with maintaining the fragile economic prosperity of their towns—a trend that holds true in the few deeper studies of the back to the land movement nationally as well.[1] With the story co-opted thus, conflict became the standard narrative for popular and academic discussion.[2]

Early discussions of Ozark history in the 1960s and 1970s, like Milton Rafferty's classic *The Ozarks: Land and Life*, helped establish this image of conflict, suggesting that members of the "drug culture" coming to the region knew "more about the federal assistance programs" than their neighbors.[3] Going further, Rafferty presented the in-migrants as "escapists" attempting to "reject twentieth-century life, preferring to live a back to the land communal lifestyle" and not necessarily committed to the well-being of the communities they joined.[4] Blevins's masterful work presents a similar picture by arguing that young neo-pioneers were a "less welcomed group of post-war immigrants" than Midwestern retirees and were drawn, in part, to the Ozarks by its image as a "haven of traditional, rural life and craftsmanship."[5] According to Blevins, the "vast majority" were ultimately driven back to the concrete jungle by "snakes, chiggers, heat, cold, and starvation."[6] These descriptions, accurate to a small measure, do not present a complete picture of the region and its integration of the hipbillies.[7] A more nuanced story of BTLs and their interactions with local communities shows a more positive reception by rural Ozark natives than is generally portrayed.

The question remains, though, as to how this narrative of conflict emerged. While not all facets are easily explained, a few things stand out in the Ozark region that help lay the foundation for a story of antagonism. As they were smaller in number, BTLs became easy targets as a national backlash against the counterculture evolved during the 1970s. Easily missed in media discussions of the movement were the differences between the festivalgoers, both in Mountain View's Ozark Folk Center and later in Eureka Springs, and the back to the land community. Indeed, a music festival outside Eureka Springs serves as a ready entry point in the creation of the conflict narrative.[8]

In the spring of 1973, Edd Jeffords (*OAC* publisher) organized the Ozark Mountain Folk Fair to be held at the Oak Hill Ecopark north of town.[9] The Ecopark was an outgrowth of the *Ozark Access Catalog* project as Jeffords realized that many young folk who wanted to go back to the land needed help adjusting to rural life. In a conversation with Sheila Daniels of the *Times-Echo*, Jeffords stated, "We hope that if we can build a campground that is ecologically practical, then it will set an example for others."[10] Indeed, Jeffords argued that what they were doing at the site was "undevelopment because we're trying not to change things any more than is necessary."[11] Jeffords and his partners hoped that after the Folk Fair was over that the Ecopark would be the first campground of its kind in the nation, attracting more people into the area while also providing an introduction into Ozark ecology.

Where the *Catalog* sought to connect newcomers with ways to make a life in the hard Ozark hills, the Folk Fair was billed as a way to bridge the cultural gap by introducing young, urbanized Yankees and West Coast refugees to the sounds and life of the Ozarks.[12] The three-day festival, initially projected to attract twenty-five thousand to thirty thousand people (and aimed primarily at a "general audience ranging from college students to families"), saw tens of thousands of people come from all over to hear traditional music, bluegrass, blues, and other forms of American "roots" music.[13] Though the efforts were short-lived, the Folk Fair and the *OAC* served to join the country hippies to the local communities, though often in unintended ways. Noted bluegrass pioneer Earl Scruggs played at the event, and he was joined by other regional and national acts like the Nitty Gritty Dirt Band and John Lee Hooker, to name just a few. Local artists were featured as well in the arts and crafts village, providing a boost for craftspeople from as far away as Kansas.[14]

While community integration may have been a goal, and perhaps in some measure it succeeded, the Folk Fair also brought unwanted attention to the hipbillies and the counterculture. Indeed, one noted member of the Eureka establishment alleged that the Folk Fair, though sold as an old-timey event, actually turned into a "MARIJUANA RODEO AND A COW PASTURE BROTHEL!!!"[15] Further, he noted that once the whole festival was over, the hippies that had attended and become soaked in the rainstorms that popped up over the weekend simply tossed their muddy clothes into laundromat dryers in town, ruining several.[16] Such experiences did not lend the counterculture to a widespread positive reception in the Ozarks, to be sure, and this was further compounded when the Rainbow Family of Living Light (more simply known as the Rainbow Family) came to town in 1975.

The Rainbow Family has, like much of the counterculture, been a staple of tongue-in-cheek stereotyping in American media and popular media. An outgrowth of decentralist, anti-Vietnam, and communal sentiments of the late 1960s and early 1970s, the Rainbow Family began meeting somewhat formally in 1972 to ask the universe for world peace and to "demonstrate the viability of a cooperative utopian community living in harmony with the Earth."[17] Typically, these gatherings were not permanent, lasting for a few days in a national forest somewhere. Such a gathering took place in Newton County in the summer of 1975.[18] In a letter to *LION* in October 1975, Rainbow Atma noted that, as always, "Rainbow gatherings come and go and Ark. 75 was no exception."[19] While there was the "usual paranoia," prompting the family to shift sites from Kolbs Landing, the gathering occurred along the Buffalo River in southeast Marion County with little problems. Indeed, in a "crowd that totaled about 700," only a few people ran afoul of the local sheriff and "lots of local short hairs came to visit with us who were very nice."[20] The family was quick, in the Spring of 1975, to warn Arkansas Ozarkers of their impending arrival in an open letter to the state, noting that the "gathering is not a festival or a rock concert, nor is it a big party or recreational campout. Rather it is a time for all of us to stop long enough to see what [we] have done to this planet through our carelessness and get it on the right path again."[21]

Though hipbillies often eschewed the actions of groups like the Rainbow Family, they were sympathetic enough to their cause that they were often lumped in with them. It was no surprise, then, when hipbillies and their compatriots became frequent rhetorical targets of other in-migrant groups, particularly retirees and those intent on keeping their business free of counterculture influence. As the decade wound along, country hippies increasingly rubbed shoulders with the growing power of Nixon's silent majority, the "law and order" population. These folks, coming in many cases from the same urban centers, and often for similar reasons (but with different understanding as to the cause of the problems), prompted a sea change in Arkansas politics and society based on their presuppositions about the region. Where the hippies advocated deep revolution and appropriate technologies à la Stewart Brand and *The Whole Earth Catalog*, these other in-migrants promoted something different—the development of an Ozarks that facilitated their dreams for a stable and comfortable retirement and self-imposed exile from urban centers; in short, according Blake Perkins's groundbreaking work, *Hillbilly Hellraisers*, a "new Ozarks."

Recognition of the Ozarks as a place to retreat from the excesses of urban life had been growing since the 1950s. As the state's population boomed once again, local Ozarkers searched for ways to capitalize on the in-migration. Many, especially in the older tourist areas, saw this population who flocked to the newly created lakes, retirement villages, and small towns as a way to reinvigorate the region. As scholars have shown, these crafted environments were built by and large to service the needs of newly retired families coming to the Ozarks.[22] These dammed areas and planned communities, though, supplanted older folkways, and land tenure and the promised economic benefits rarely materialized, causing frustration among rural Ozark natives.[23] In some cases, the new arrivals competed for the new jobs in the villages that serviced the retirement communities as they transitioned from full employment to semiretired, further reinforcing the divide between the groups as what little of the potential profits the local community could have realized remained, in many cases, bound within the new arrivals' community.[24] The back to the landers, by contrast, rejected this model of life in the region, and wanted to create a community that more closely resembled the Ozark world swept away by places like Horseshoe Bend. Despite this, in many cases the economic potential of middle-class, middle-aged arrivals was accepted and sought after by the economic elite in the region's towns and hamlets.

As such, it is no wonder that the arrival of both groups into the region stirred up a potent mixture of enthusiasm and consternation among the locals. At times, consternation evolved into organized antagonism, some of the most organized of which came in Carroll County's Eureka Springs and helped give birth to the prevailing narrative concerning interactions between "local" hill folks and back to the land hippies. Though now seen as a mecca for Ozarkian counterculture, in the late 1960s and early 1970s the "longhairs" newly residing around the town agitated Eureka's traditional economic leaders who had their own visions for the region (ones that did not include anything related to the Grateful Dead). Some of the strongest concern was voiced by John Fuller Cross, a bank owner, entrepreneur, and community elder. Cross, looking back on the time, characterizes the arrival of the hippies to Eureka as at first a trickle.

> And then it was a flood. And it got pretty bad. It got pretty bad. It got pretty bad drug-wise, it got pretty bad food stamp-wise, and it just got pretty bad. You know, this was the place to come. And it got so bad that I could see what was going on, in terms of drugs and fraud, with the food stamp[s] . . . So as a community leader, I picked up the phone, got the name and address and phone number

of the man who was in charge of the food stamp [program] for the entire southwestern part of the United States . . . I said "There's a lot of fraud going on up here, and we've got a lot of these unconventional young people, backlanders or back to the land people or whatever it is," saying they weren't all bad, but they've just—we've been—Every time we'd have a motorcycle wreck, or somebody would get killed, or something, they'd be wanted in Arizona, or wanted in Florida, or something like that. So we knew we had a bunch of scumbags in town, in addition to some good ones. So I really hit a nerve.[25]

Cross and his associates in Eureka's establishment, notably the weekly *Times-Echo,* alleged in the spring and summer of 1972 that the newcomers planned to take over the town during the coming fall's elections.[26] On May 25, for instance, an editorial argued that "a group, which . . . we will call a sub-culture, including hippies, and others . . . want to take over the city's government."[27] This was "not a figment of anyone's imagination. It is a well-oiled plan of a group, residing here, who plan to take over the rule of the city at the forthcoming November election."[28] The editorial went on and called for changing the city's political structure in order to defeat the hippies and urged readers to "ponder" the effect that a change in city government would have on "you as a family, and upon your children and their morals."[29]

The unhappiness of Cross and the staff at the *Times-Echo* was bolstered by Gerald L. K. Smith, a newcomer himself as well as a noted anti-Semite and a godfather of the tourism boom in Eureka. After his arrival in the hill country 1964, Smith built the Christ of the Ozarks statue, founded the Passion Play in 1968, and sought to establish other Christian-themed attractions, all to bring thousands of tourists to the area.[30] As this was happening, the transplanted Smith became interested in local politics and the impact that people like Edd Jeffords, journalist and returnee to the state and an outspoken member of the area's counterculture, would have on his interests. In general, Smith, like Cross, distrusted the influx of counterculture enthusiasts, especially after Jeffords and others began advocating for cleaning up the town's famous water supply, which had fallen on hard times.[31] The discontent Smith and Cross voiced in editorials to the *Times-Echo* grew as they feared the town would be overrun by drug-crazed "longhairs" and called on the citizens of Eureka to stand against an onslaught of moral laxity. If they did not, their right to vote would be lost to "someone else—who, for all you know, was a communist, an extremist of one sort or another, or a hippie who has added nothing to the community, but instead has through his philosophy torn down the moral fibers of the community."[32] In an effort to further describe the problems to Eurekans, the editorial explained that

> the hippies, who are parasites of the community, who bring drugs into the area, who degrade the morals of the community, who do nothing to the economy of the community, should be given a quick ticket out. These are the danger signals at any election. These are the people who will tear down the community. To rid the community of this element, there is only one answer—strong law enforcement.[33]

The editorial went on to give a scathing critique of sub- and counter-cultures across the country, arguing that such groups are un-American, meaning "any group of culture [sic] who violates the laws, the mores or the social teachings of any community."[34] The editorial staff went on to say that the only way to win against them was to remain ever vigilant: "In other words, register as a voter, and no matter how small or large the election, how significant or insignificant, get to the polls and cast your vote."[35] Only through this will "adverse social groups" fall "beneath a hail of ballots."[36] With virulent and visible reactions like this, coupled with the national perception that the counterculture movement had burned out, it should be no surprise that a mythology quickly developed that has since held sway; namely, that hippies, longhairs, and other counterculture members were often irrelevant or despised by the old-timers in Ozark communities.

This modernized, industrial vision of Ozark development was not the only game in town, however. The BTLs, and some rural Ozark residents, were skeptical of these efforts, or at least about the social and environmental cost of such plans.[37] An older generation of native Ozark hill folks and the new hipbillies instead sought an alternative form of community, placing them at odds with the economic powerhouses in the region's towns. Both groups had a vision for how to care for the region, but instead of resorts and vacation homes, the back to the land community and some native Ozarks placed a higher value on efforts to preserve and modernize traditional crafts and livelihoods. Indeed, in contrast to tourist centers like Eureka Springs or communities near the new hydroelectric dams over in Stone County, the Ozark Folk Center in Mountain View came to represent, in part, this alternative vision.[38] The Folk Center was product, in part, of the same Great Society that brought organizations to the Ozarks that later were looked on with distrust.[39] Arkansan Wilbur Mills, chair of the Ways and Means Committee in the House of Representative, ensured that a pool of money was diverted to Stone County (one of the poorest in Arkansas at the time) out of the War on Poverty. Where a type of in-migration and tourism in some places banked on leisure sports and retirement communities, the Folk Center's intention in the early days was to create a school to teach folkways to students who would return to their homes and pass the knowledge along. Due to funding issues and a change in who operated the facility, the education component took a backseat to creating a living museum of Ozark culture when it opened in 1973, though today the Center maintains a strong mixture of the two ideas.[40] While the Ozark Folk Center played up a sort of heritage-tourism (imposed to a degree from the outside), in doing so it portrayed contrasting ideas for how the Ozarks might progress in the 1970s.[41] Nevertheless, it should be remembered that both visions—the tourist meccas like Eureka or Bull Shoals and the static, heritage-tourism of the Folk Center—were rooted in misconceptions of the Ozarks.

It was into this increasingly conflicted vision of Ozark development that the back to the landers in the Ozarks arrived. Their reception by the community, then, must be seen in this light as it explains some of the rancor regarding the legacy of the hipbillies. Picking up on this tension, journalist Bill Royce, author of the regionally syndicated column In the Ozarks, attempted to evaluate various aspects of the whole migrant population and often caricatured and castigated the country hippies as antithetical to the traditional values of the Ozark hill folk. Royce proclaimed, "The trouble is, while the hippy-type refugees from the cities seek mutual admiration alongside Ozarks farmers, they are more often ridiculed because of their life-style, which permits the use of food stamps, unmarried men and women living together, and the use of dope."[42] The locals, Royce believed, were suspicious of people with "long hair and soft hands" who seemed incredibly "naïve about the Ozark hardships."[43] Royce, with no proof, gave voice to the belief that the hippies were universally disliked, based in part on their appearance.

Indeed, it seems that Royce's understanding of the BTLs was based on general assumptions that can be readily laid aside. To start with, hippies traipsing about the Ozarks did not begin with the back to the land movement or the Folk Fair in 1973. Though the region is traditionally not noted as a focal point of the counterculture, by the mid-1960s the Arkansas uplands were known to the nation's rebels as an interesting place thanks to the folk music scene near Mountain View. Some of these early interactions helped set the stage for the reception of the back-to-the-land community in the following years. In 1963 Jimmy Driftwood and others organized the first Arkansas Folk Festival in Mountain View. Only modestly linked with other regional affairs, the festival in Mountain View drew a crowd approaching ten thousand visitors who watched over the course of an April weekend as crafters and musicians displayed their talents.[44] The festival quickly grew, and by the early 1970s, crowds pushed past one hundred thousand visitors, overwhelming the area. Local Glen Orhlin remarked that "there was one year when it was almost all hippies. Of course, that's plumb outlandish right here, and . . . Anyway, one year, somehow word got out it was a rock festival, and thousands and thousands of hippies, and they camped in the forest, they blocked off the roads."[45] Soon, as developed later in Eureka Springs, the focus on folk culture marked Mountain View as a counterculture destination. Most of the incoming hippies were itinerant, moving from festival to festival, staying for a short time in any given place—not so with the hipbillies that came later. Given their highly visible nature and transience, they became a target for local police officers, who "neglected traffic control to round up dozens, even hundreds, of hippies" in the areas around Mountain View.[46] To be sure, a sudden influx of people from colleges and universities across the nation was unsettling. Some reactions were not always positive—Glen Branscum, another Ozarker, recalled, "Some of the people around here, they wasn't thrilled and joyed to see 'em, you know, some of them," but said that the hippies did not really bother him.[47] Leo Rainey, perhaps, captured the spirit of the interactions between the two groups best:

> Folk music was very big at that time, and these students came from Indiana and Illinois and different places. It was exciting . . . It was during the more-or-less hippie generation, and these people came by the thousands, and on Thursdays prior to the Festival, you'd see people hitchhiking, and vans rolling in, and I've always

said, well, the local people came to see these people, and these people came to see the local people." So it was kind of a study of each group.[48]

Indeed, stories from across the Ozarks show that while there was indeed dislike of the culture of generic "hippies," the hipbillies themselves were often received at first with caution, then with acceptance. For example, in southern Washington County, a member of the "Dome People" noted that an old-timer, Bill Huey, who lived at the front of the road, advocated for the group with the surrounding community. Huey, David Pride noted, more than once in the early days of their efforts, argued that old-timers should either leave them alone or help them out because "these kids are honest and hard working."[49] Indeed, Bill viewed the growth and use of pot by the counterculture in the hills with bemusement; he compared it to making and drinking moonshine and said, "I don't see any difference between that and this pot stuff."[50]

Brenda Moosey recalled that some local women in Newton County were concerned about the sudden arrival of lots of young women on a commune she was briefly a member of. After all, Moosey recalled, when she first arrived on the mountain, one of the men was stark naked—a shock for her as much as anybody.[51] Locals came, and leaning on the fence, watched the community figure out how to get things started, no doubt curious when the nudity would start—indeed, they treated it somewhat like a drive-in as they often brought snacks. While the men in the community were maybe not as worried about naked young hippies running around (indeed, elsewhere in Newton County, one local stopped by a hipbilly farm with the express purpose of trying to find naked folks), their wives and mothers distrusted the girls on the commune at first "because they thought it was gonna all be free love and group sex," but they quickly learned that the hippie women were interested in monogamous relationships similar to the types they had (although Moosey noted that the guys "would have fucked a post if given the chance").[52]

In truth, many in the back to the land community were concerned about the perceptions that Royce believed were dominant among native Ozarkers and worried about creating good relationships with native Ozarkers (but not always with retiree in-migrants). Early on, as a response to the naïveté of these transplanted city slickers cited by journalists and others, the publications and newsletters that emerged attempted to offer public relations advice to the neopioneers. Jeffords's *Ozark Access Catalog (OAC)*, or *Living in the Ozarks Newsletter (LION)* by Joel Davidson, aimed at filling the knowledge and experience gap for the young homesteaders. This growing knowledge base was soon paired with a growing realization that Royce had inadvertently provided; namely, "You can't trip (take dope), and function."[53] The editors at *LION* noted the influx of long-haired folk in many rural areas, and argued that instead of identifying them with the chaos often associated with 1960s, they should be acknowledged as "young folks, many with children," who "are going into isolated areas in our country to make a go of it in much the same manner as our forefathers did a hundred years ago."[54] *LION*, the *OAC*, and even national magazines like *Mother Earth News* described the life and vision of these young hipbillies, often in terms reminiscent of the great pioneer epoch in American life, and such language resonated with much of the hardscrabble life of the Ozarks that BTLs came into. [55]

Many of the articles in *LION* or the *OAC* were simple recommendations on cultural acclimatization for newcomers to the region. The *OAC*, though short-lived compared to *LION*, offered comprehensive advice on integration with the local culture.[56] This was, on the one hand, due to the *Whole Earth* style of the publication, and on the other, thanks to the solid writing and work that went into the *OAC*. That, and a little negative press. In March of 1973, after an early issue of the *OAC* was released, Jenkins Jones of the *Tulsa Tribune* wrote a piece attempting to judge the merit both of Jeffords's catalog and the back to the land movement in general. Seeing the *OAC* as a "survival manual for young and disillusioned graduates of the rock and drug scenes" who believe the "knobs and hollers" of the Ozarks hold "Shangri-la," Jones found it hard to believe that folks from Berkeley and beyond would come "gallumphing [*sic*] around the Arkansas woods" and establish a new life for themselves.[57] Stating that the hippies were in for a rude awakening when it came to the work needed to survive in the Ozarks, Jones also argued the "hill people are not entirely stupid and they've already glommed on to practically all the bottom land," meaning it would be nearly impossible for newcomers to find usable land in the area.[58] Jeffords, slightly tongue in cheek, responded with a thanks to Jones for his free national publicity (the article was syndicated), which resulted "in a great number of subscriptions."[59] With this out of the way, Jeffords went on to note that nearly half of the subscribers to the *OAC* were in fact old Ozarkers—the very Ozarkers that the back to the land community lived alongside and learned from.[60]

Thus, as a partial remedy to the problem of paradise seekers coming into the region ill-informed about how Ozark life worked, Jeffords's catalog offered advice on dealing with the local population, understanding the history, and demystifying the culture of the region, from Arkansas to Missouri. Acknowledging that most of the incoming hipbillies possessed a post-Enlightenment vision of folk culture, at least implicitly, Jeffords and his team cautioned, "Despite your philosophical orientation it is not wise to take the long-held superstitions and beliefs lightly. The mental energy poured into these concepts for centuries imbues them with a certain validity that is to be respected by even the most scientifically detached observer."[61] Quoting Vance Randolph, the pre-eminent folklorist of the Ozarks, Jeffords hammered the point home: "The Hillman is secretive and sensitive beyond anything that the average city dweller can imagine, but he isn't simple. His mind moves in a tremendously involved system of signs and omens and esoteric auguries. He has little interest in the mental procedure that the moderns call science, and his ways of arranging data and evaluating evidence are very different from those currently in the world beyond."[62] Understanding beliefs regarding folk magic, for instance, would be key to understanding the advice offered by hill folk. But it was not just folk beliefs that Jeffords attempted to educate his readers about; he also focused on how the rural Ozarks functioned. Though much had changed in the Ozarks by the 1970s, the *OAC* noted that some things stayed the same, especially things that might impact hipbillies moving in, gossip, for one. Although the telephone, newspapers, and more had broken down many barriers between the urban and rural across the nation (and the Ozarks were no different), the "community grapevine" was still holding strong as perhaps the "most effective form of local communication."[63] The system of gossip in the region could generally be seen as a "neutral force," but it could "on one hand quickly rally aid for a burned-out family, or on the other spread malicious lies about a neighbor which can leave family prejudices which last generations."[64] As mentioned earlier, this was true of the community in Weedy Rough (the Dome People), and also true up in the Missouri Ozarks, where unbeknownst at the time to a small community of hipbillies there, one local consistently went to bat for them at community meetings, arguing that the locals needed to wait and see how these folks would do. It seems they were accepted, as nothing disastrous happened to the community as it existed for many years and became part of several national studies and ecological movements.[65]

This concern about how quickly gossip can shape the community was one that Crescent Dragonwagon, a transplant to the region, noted in her comments to newcomers as well. In a short article simply titled "If You're Going to Come, Come Gently," Dragonwagon worried about people moving into the hills without giving due credit to local culture and customs: "The point remains that if you live in the country—even if you live way out and only come to town for supplies—you're living in a fishbowl. And if you want to be considered a good fish, you abide by and respect the culture of the residents in the area."[66] Like Jeffords and other commentators, Dragonwagon wanted to be sure that as the truckloads of hippies and goats came in, they did so with a soft and deft touch. This was a crucial reminder, especially as so often the hipbillies were "unaware, often, of our effect on the community—the way we looked, things we were doing, we were just oblivious to it."[67] As the efforts of things like the *OAC*, and the reality of hard work on the farm joined, it soon became apparent, then, that the message of paying attention to how you came across to native Ozarkers reached a broad audience who learned and listened from their neighbors. Publications like *OAC* and *LION* urged hippies to work hard and learn the local culture without visibly overindulging in drugs, sex, and rock 'n' roll. The back to the land population listened, and became quietly known for its desire to do all this as they strove to create a new world for themselves that blended the wisdom of the Ozarks with new ideas like solar technology. These publications and others that popped up across the Ozarks show how the in-migrant counterculture members focused on building bridges with the local community, particularly the older generation, and on gaining the knowledge needed to survive life in the hollows.

Such advice was not always successful. In southern Washington County, for example, one small group of friends (not a commune) lived the homesteading life with relative success. In return for caretaking a large farm on the middle fork of the White River in Hazel Valley, three young country hippies from Austin, Texas, received "free" rent. To supplement their income, they, like many of the BTL folks, grew their own garden, raised chickens, and had the ubiquitous herd of goats. They paid rent by watching after a medium-sized herd of cattle from time to time that their landlord would bring over to give his main pastures a break. One afternoon, the couple went out and found their friend who lived with them, a young man named Mark, lying on the ground, bloody and bruised; the extent of his wounds was such that they took him to the hospital. They found out that he had seen a group of local young men out in the pasture trying to run the cattle—that is, drive the herd into a frenzy. Mark went out and confronted the young men, who initially agreed to leave. As they were walking out of the pasture, however, they attacked him. The couple who related this story was quick, however, to point out that this action was not the result of anti-back to the lander sentiment but instead came from the fact that these young men were under the influence of a bad drug trip.[68] Other stories are present as well. In Madison County, near Pettigrew, some folks discussed a few more instances of anti-in-migrant feelings. Melinda Charles, after returning to Madison County following a brief absence, found her house had been burned down (though the culprit and reason for this is not known).[69] Another couple, Luke and Lisa Post, was threatened by a young man in a truck while sitting in front of the general store—though they were quick to point out that the relationship with the driver has progressed; in fact, he now cuts their hay.[70]

These were isolated experiences, however. Across the Arkansas Ozarks, more often than not the young counterculture members found themselves as objects of curiosity or even sources of money as opposed to being perceived as enemies. Indeed, in Madison County, the Posts and Melinda Charles, along with their friends Jack and Dana Marshall, believed that "locals around here looked on us sorta halfway as part of the new prosperity," as the newcomers bought at the local stores, helping to bolster flagging local economies. Even though it "took a while to show up as worthwhile people," the older generation was generally warm and welcoming to the young hippies.[71] As these stories and more illustrate, nearly all of the people interviewed and referenced here look back on their interactions with the local community in this way. Most of the young neopioneers, over the course of time, "gained respect from the leaders of the communities in which they lived."[72] Even those who experienced initial or fleeting negative receptions agree that within a brief passage of time (usually one winter season) the local Ozarkers accepted them as neighbors, customers, teachers, and, eventually, employers.

Indeed, even in Eureka Springs—the apparent home of the problematic perceptions of the group and home to John Fuller Cross and his worries about chaos and the breakdown of law and order—one local, Sarah (last name withheld), took time to go with her family and "check out a happening."[73] Sarah, in an article in *Down Home*, a guerilla publication out of Eureka Springs that began in 1972, was quick to note her concern about bringing her children with her—especially as she had "heard and read so much about these groups skinny dipping at the first drop of water"—but went to see what the in-migrants were all about.[74] She decided to watch the group as the gathering went along and concluded "in black and white" that, unusual attire aside, what was present was "the beauty shining from all the not less than one hundred people gathered together there on top a mountain in the Ozarks. I heard no filthy language, there were no quarrels, the children weren't spanked if they did something out of order, all I ever saw was the child swooped up into the parent's arms and soundly kissed."[75] Indeed, *Down Home* (*DH*) noted in other issues the uniqueness of Eureka and the Ozarks regarding the relationship between the BTLs and the locals. In general, despite some negative editorials that had appeared in the *Times-Echo*, the editors at *DH* noted that "hostility on either side is not generally felt on the basis of an individual's cultural belief."[76] Commenting on the *Times-Echo* pieces throughout 1972, the *DH* staff noted that the "whole controversy <u>does not exist</u> in actual fact. There is virtually <u>no conflict</u> between the different elements of this community."[77] According to the writers at *DH*, problems between the groups in Eureka were overblown by one person who disliked the counterculture and was "in a position of control over the only media, to now, that Eureka has had."[78]

Instead of rancorous reactions, the hipbillies mostly encountered locals who were bemused and helpful. In Newton County, Dan and Marylou Taylor and their two sons moved to a 160-acre farm outside of Parthenon, where they raised vegetables, varied livestock, and a small flock of chickens. They subsisted largely on what they raised themselves, and they bought very little—only things like salt, sugar, yeast, or vinegar. Their lifestyle was similar to what many BTLs in the Ozarks and across the nation achieved and aspired to: a combination of new and old technologies (the Taylors used solar ovens and a team of oxen to plow in the tough Ozark hillsides) in order to live "off the grid." They were in search of a life that attempted to achieve a relative balance with the earth and other humans.[79] It was a strenuous life, but for the Taylors the benefits were worth it. Dan stated, "We know we put a minimum load on the environment and get to live and do the things we want to do. It's being a part of the environment and not just drawing from it and consuming."[80] When asked how the local community received them, Taylor said that they had not "wildly accepted our ideas . . . Their standard response is 'we've never seen nothing [sic] like that before.' . . . We're a kind of curiosity to them."[81]

Elsewhere in Newton County, Hazel Smith and her friends purchased eighty-seven acres in 1977 and soon got to know the old-timers on their road. When asked about the local community's reaction, she said, "You know, when you go to the town, like say we'd go to Jasper, and it was Saturday, and there'd be old timers sitting on the benches whittling and that kinda stuff . . . they weren't that come over and meet ya type of people, but, the neighbors, old guys, old women . . . they seemed, first of all, they seemed sorta happy that we were visiting or stopping by . . . and second, they would ask us to help."[82] Hazel and her fellow country hippies helped hay with their elderly neighbors, an arduous task at the best of times.[83] This bought them the goodwill of the neighbors, which allowed them to stop by for a chat or to ask for help. "I wouldn't say they were warm and fuzzy, but they were certainly cordial."[84] Smith also noted, "I think because we respected them, they respected us."[85] This was the case up and down the road, based on mutual concerns such as goats and crops; in this way, these people became their closest community friends.[86]

In 1972 Cindy and Gary Davidson moved from Little Rock to eighty acres near Witter, in Madison County, intent on starting a small, self-sufficient commune in the woods. They possessed little knowledge of homesteading, knowing only that they "wanted to do something different."[87] They arrived on their land with few plans save to "build platforms in the woods and pitch tents" and "see what happens next."[88] The locals watched with bemusement until winter came to the Ozarks. Then a local named Glen Haught, their nearest neighbor, came down the hill to their place one day and told them to pack up and move in with him for the winter.[89] The people then, Cindy recalled, "just took us under their wing. They loved it that we were there. I'm sure they thought we were crazy . . . [but] they wanted to teach us their ways [because] we were interested. They embraced us. We embraced them."[90] For Cindy and her compatriots, the locals were a never-ending source of resourceful-ness, openheartedness, and insight into living in the Ozark hill country. They had help with plowing thanks to Haught's mule and learned about chickens and vegetables from his family and friends. Reflecting back on the times—though open about its hardships—Cindy fondly recounted her interactions with the locals up and down Slow Tom Road and how she kept in contact with many, especially Glen's daughter, Hazel, over the years. For Cindy and her group, the "Ozarks resonated . . . because everybody there is counterculture. Everybody that lived out in the hills were [sic] counterculture in some way. I think that's why they liked us."[91]

Down in southern Washington County's Hazel Valley, Dennis and Linda Sanders remembered their experience, save their friend's attack, with fondness as well. Linda recalled that "the whole area welcomed us," perhaps because, being from Texas, there were a lot of similari-ties in culture.[92] Dennis agreed, stating, "Well just the [Ozarks] culture was . . . similar enough to Texas culture in the way that people were generally polite and good and trusting."[93] The antihippie rhetoric and violence envisioned by the media was not present in Hazel Valley, espe-cially on the part of the local business community. The Sanders, living relatively close to Elkins, went to the Bank of Elkins to get a loan so they could build a greenhouse for tomato plants to sell at the local IGA. They easily qualified for a $300 loan and were treated well and with respect despite their—admitted—outward appearance as dirty hippies; indeed, both Dennis and Linda remarked that they actually did not look too different from other locals out in the hollers.[94] Another local, Elmer Stout, who lived just up the road from them, was the local gossip. Stout, though he did not fully approve of the back to the land lifestyle,

> was reasonable enough to see that these people were good people . . . they just didn't have the same moral values in regards to marriage and sex, drugs, stuff like that. [He saw that] they were

hard working people, they were working the land, they had a lot
of respect for the local culture . . . we felt well received.[95]

The story was the same elsewhere. Out in Searcy County, Jim
Babineaux and his wife and young son moved from New Orleans in 1976
to a farm bordering the newly created Buffalo National River. While
some were unhappy about the influx of country hippies, Babineaux
recalls that most of the ire of the large landowners was really about
the recent designation of the Buffalo as a National River.[96] But their
immediate neighbors, the people they saw regularly, treated them well.
Indeed, Harv Grinder, the old-timer who lived along the river bottom,
was about eighty years old at the time, and according to Babineaux was
"built like a brick shit house [and] could walk up and down the hills
like you've never seen." Grinder was a true local—he had only left the
county once in his life to take a load of corn to Russellville. Mr. Grinder
took the new arrivals under his wing, had them over for dinner two or
three times a week, and answered their myriad questions about life in
the Ozarks. "That's what really impressed [us], is how open they were
to us as strangers."[97] Jim told a story to help illustrate just how much
they had been incorporated into the community:

> One time, my son Seth strayed from the house off into the woods
> and we didn't know where he was . . . so I called up Harv and
> we got everybody. My nearest neighbor was about a mile away. I
> called up locals and had them keep a look out. But Harv walked
> up and down the hills all afternoon until he found my little boy in
> a field. You don't just do that for somebody you don't like.[98]

A constant thread running through the country hippies' relationships with the old-timers was hard work; indeed, many of those interviewed believed that work—and working hard over time—was what
had bound the two disparate communities together. This desire to work
the land and join with the long rhythms of Ozark life helped position
the back to the land community as a sort of surrogate generation for
those younger members of families who had left for cities and towns
in the 1950s and 1960s. This was not as simple as new hands present
to pitch in during haying or harvesting. Now, for the first time in years
it seemed, native Ozarkers had validation for their life's experiences,
someone to give their hard-earned knowledge to, and an avenue by

which the old ways could be preserved.[99] In her collection of interviews from the Ozark back to the land community, Ruth Weinstein (a hipbilly herself) found this to be true as well; long days of haying or fencing, according to one respondent, "gave them a good attitude towards us 'cause we gave an honest days work for whatever pay we were getting, and I think there was a generous respect."[100] Not only was the idea of working hard as a way into the community borne out, but also the idea that the incoming hippies were welcomed by those whose children had left the hills. "T," another interviewee in Weinstein's collection, noted, "I think (the hippies were accepted) [sic] overall very well, especially by the older locals whose—I see it sociologically—children moved to the city. And here come all these city kids say, 'Oh, I really respect the way you're living. This the way I wanna live.' So I think there was a real good energy or exchange."[101]

Though the old-time hill folk may not have understood or approved of all the aspects of the counterculture, thanks to the hard work of the BTLs across the Ozarks, a general feeling of curious affection emerged. As "J" put it, "I think everything we tried, we got so much help form the locals. We did a lot of helping locals, did a lot of fencing around here. I always thought that—and I feel it's true for almost everybody (newcomers)—we had more interaction with the local people early on. Not only did we need them economically but for their expertise on how to live in the woods."[102] And along the way, the hippies learned, thanks to constant exhortations from among themselves and a desire to live well in their new home, not to purposely offend the locals. As "D" told Ruth Weinstein, "This is their place. It's like their home, you know. . . . So we have tried to just be guests in their home."[103] Wendy out in Stone County, concurred as she discussed how many of many of the men in the back to the land community around Fox "want to distinguish themselves from the average run-of-the-mill hippy who occasionally turns up around here."[104] And like that, off came the ponytails. After all, "no one wants to appear too pretentious in front of the people around here who are so simple and god-fearing. And they are so friendly, the idea of shocking them is frightening so off with the symbol of rebellion— amazing!! [sic]"[105]

To be sure, some young in-migrants did have little concern for the locals they lived alongside—indeed, the transient Rainbow Family falls into this group—but by and large hipbillies came in and filled voids in many communities, becoming a replacement generation of sorts. This was observed by journalist Donald Katz in 1980 when he noted in an article for *GEO* that "there is a viable camaraderie of poverty that exists between the back to the lander and the unreconstructed native" that transcended their different backgrounds.[106] Katz observed:

> Hillbillies and longhairs share a strong respect for human individuality, a bullheaded sense of environmental protectionism, a mild lawlessness, a basic communitarianism, and a low opinion of the relative value and healthiness of industrialized society. It is as if the old-timers stayed poor all this time because they were waiting for a generation to come along that would see things their way and help to preserve their values."[107]

Viewing members of the back to the land movement in such a way helps scholars understand some of the rancor that other in-migrants felt toward the young hippies. The other segments of the in-migrant population, namely retirees, viewed any of the things that attracted country hippies—little urbanization, a strong folk culture, and fierce individualism—with opinions ranging from mild disdain to outright contempt.[108] By nature the retirement communities that emerged around Bella Vista, Eureka Springs, and the Norfolk River were relatively homogenous, passively hostile toward native folkways, and ultimately only marginally assimilated into traditional Ozark life.[109]

Thus, communities that espoused the maintenance of these customs were easily ignored or, if they intersected with populations retirees had fled in Chicago or elsewhere, attacked. This reaction, coupled with early stumbling by the in-migrant counterculture, resulted in the creation of a narrative of conflict that has persisted. By and large, though, this conflict was never more than rhetorical, and only flared up occasionally as former factory workers and insurance agents attempted to wrest control of the region's fate from old-timers, imposing an imported vision of modernity onto the region with their newly asserted economic might. Indeed, their efforts spelled doom for the BTLs most formal effort at community development and preservation, the Ozark Institute.

CHAPTER 4

―――

Hipbillies and the New Ozarks

More people mean more needs to be met, and that's where the problems begin.

—Anonymous

IN THE SUMMER of 1976, Mrs. Margaret McGrade of Eureka Springs wrote a letter filled with firm opinions about the Ozark In-Migration Conference that had occurred that spring. Mrs. McGrade, it seemed, was not at all in favor of the arrival of the counterculture in her town, nor of their self-appointed leader, Edd Jeffords. The whole affair was just "a project that was pointless, unnecessary, unproductive, and it was spearheaded by recent migrants whose major achievement, both here and elsewhere . . . seemed to be obtaining government grants that make what for them is an easy life appear purposeful."[1] Despite Mrs. McGrade's criticisms, the back to the land community sought to use their grant-writing ability not to make an easy life for themselves but to better the life of the region they called home. In so doing, however, they encountered the growing power of the "new Ozarks:" a place where folks in the towns and hollers no longer viewed government funded programs with the acceptance they once did, sparking a conflict that helped bring down Bill Clinton in his bid for reelection in 1980 and that signaled the beginning of the end for Democratic dominance in the Ozarks and Arkansas.[2]

There is perhaps no more interesting illustration of this than the man Mrs. McGrade denounced, Edd Jeffords. Jeffords had made himself known to Eureka's citizens not just as an organizer of the In-migration Conference in May 1976, but also through his organization of the Folk Fair in 1973, the *Ozark Access Catalog*, and the Ozark Access Center.[3] In part because of these projects, Jeffords was uniquely positioned to emerge as a visible leader in Arkansas's counterculture. It helped as well that Jeffords was an Arkansas native, though he had moved away to Tacoma, Washington, where he finished school and established a career as a journalist, writing for the *Auburn Globe-News* and *Rolling Stone*.[4] Jeffords returned to Arkansas in 1971, first to Mansfield (near Fort Smith), and then to Eureka Springs, where he worked for area newspapers and began attempts at integrating hipbillies, locals, and other in-migrants throughout the Ozarks.

Jeffords, through his efforts at community organization with the Ozark Access Center, edited the *Ozark Access Catalog* and its sister publication, *The Ozark Digest*. Both aimed to help young hipbillies gain a better understanding of the region. Though these met with limited success, Jeffords sought to expand his reach and put together the Ozark Mountain Folk Fair for 1973's Memorial Day weekend. Jeffords attempted to use the *Catalog*, the Folk Fair, and later the Ozark In-Migration Conference and Ozark Institute to bridge the gap between local Ozarkers and the in-migrants.[5] While these endeavors were part of the reenergized tourist economy of the region, Jeffords often ran afoul of established figures like John Cross or Gerald Smith. Nevertheless, Jeffords forged ahead and made use of Eureka's unique infrastructure to further his own goals, though not without incurring the wrath of the traditional power structure.

While Mrs. McGrade worried that Jeffords was just drumming support for his lifestyle, Jeffords had identified a potential problem in the region. To address it, in 1976, he and others hosted a conference in Eureka Springs that sought to understand the larger movement of people into North Arkansas as well as the particular issues associated with subgroups of newcomers. The purpose of the conference, as set out by Jeffords and his staff, was "to assess through public dialogue the impact of continued migration into the Ozarks region, to consider potential future implications of regional population growth, and to develop a list of concerns to which scholars, planners and public policy makers can address themselves."[6] Weighing heavily on the minds of Jeffords and other conference goers were the recent statistics from the Census Bureau: the combined population of the Ozark and Ouachita regions of Arkansas was projected to double by 1984. The Bureau also noted that as of 1976, the state's population growth rate was 7.2 percent, double the national average, with the Ozark-Ouachita region at the even higher rate of 9.4 percent.[7] The massive influx of people had the potential to wreak havoc on the beauty of the Ozarks, overrun the remnants of traditional folk culture, and alter the state's economy—perhaps in ways not in line with the values of the area.[8] An editorial in the *Springdale News* from that April noted the rapid growth the area was experiencing brought both "benefits and headaches . . . more people mean more needs to be met, and that's where the problems begin."[9] While the back to the landers were at times blamed for these issues, Gale Baldwin, writing for the *Springfield News-Leader* in 1977 noted that such complications came from retirees and other in-migrants whose presence necessitated increased spending on infrastructure of all kinds.[10]

Population statistics provide context for the changes and challenges in the New Ozarks and the in-migrants that, in many ways, directed its course. Between 1970 and 1980, Ozark counties saw an average of 42 percent growth in population (97,252 people). Of this, only a little over 11 percent resulted from natural increase—the other approximately 89 percent was due to in-migration. While we do not have exact numbers on those from out of state during the decade, we know that at least 19 percent of the region's expansion was due to people who lived out of state in 1975.[11] Statistical evidence also provides some context for these increases: all of the Ozark counties experienced increases in their rural population, at an average rate of 35 percent over the course of the decade. Despite this increase in population, the number of farms declined from 16,006 in 1969 to 13,472 in 1974, and finished the decade with a slight bump to 15,555. Farm sizes by 1970 had also increased, from an average of 134.5 acres in 1950 to 233.63 acres in 1974, reflecting the contraction of agriculture as a primary profession in the area.[12] Indeed, by 1980, the rural nonfarming population of the Ozarks totaled 178,781 people, or 85.9 percent of the rural population, compared to 29,322 farmers, native or hipbilly.[13] Urban areas experienced similar levels of increase as well. Though the data is incomplete, there was nearly

58 percent growth in urban centers in the region over the decade, bringing the urban population up to 32 percent of the region by 1980.[14] Such
data allows one to make an educated guess about the nature of the
rural increase; namely, that it was one that did not reflect the traditional
Ozark systems of small-scale agriculture and community networks.[15]

Indeed, it seems that this population played a large role in many
areas of Ozark life over the course of the decade, the least of which was
politics. At the start of the 1970s, Ozark counties, save Newton, Searcy,
and Madison counties, were brittle Democratic bastions, largely as a
result of Civil War legacies.[16] By 1980, however, the Arkansas uplands
were largely Republican when it came to presidential politics. The trend
toward Republican dominance had begun with the presidential contest
of 1960, when all but two Arkansas Ozark counties voted for Nixon over
John Kennedy.[17] While Benton and Baxter counties may have held out
and led the charge in the 1964 cycle for Johnson's sweep of the region, in
truth they were a dying breed. The 1968 election saw nine Ozark counties go overwhelmingly for Nixon, while four were split between Nixon
and the Alabama reactionary George Wallace. It seemed a sure thing
for Republicans, at least in national races, from this point on as Nixon
swept the hill country in 1972 by strong margins. Perhaps because a
Southerner was running, or because of the national perception that
Democrat Jimmy Carter was more conservative than he turned out to
be, the former peanut farmer won the majority of the region in 1976,
losing only Benton and Baxter County. By 1980 the Reagan Revolution
flipped the country, and where Carter had won nearly 100 percent of
Ozark counties only four years before, Reagan held strong majorities
in 80 percent of the mountains, with close calls in the remaining area.[18]
Indeed, by the end of the decade, Ozark counties were voting solidly
for Republican candidates at the national level (though at the local
level, conservative Democrats retained power until the twenty-first
century) and the margin for Democrats with long ties like David Pryor
and young ones like Bill Clinton became slimmer and slimmer (though
Clinton claimed victory in the Ozarks).

Thanks to such data presented at the conference, columnist Ernie
Deane and others were aware of these momentous changes in the
region. Deane, however, noted that while many worthy questions
were asked at the conference, little was immediately achieved other

than building hope that those at the conference "will generate discussion in their home communities."[19] Perhaps fearing this, as the hubbub from the In-migration Conference died down, Jeffords and his associates worked to ensure Dean's concerns did not come to fruition. Initially, they sought to better understand the plight facing rural Ozark communities in the face of such rapid population expansion. With the help of an Arkansas Humanities Council grant, Jeffords and Ozark Institute staff initiated the "Ozark Futures Forum," (OFF) a series of county-level meetings held across the Arkansas uplands.[20] The meetings, organized to "consider the effects of projected population growth in the context of local counties and communities," were held in the seats of seven counties and had varying degrees of community engagement.[21] In Berryville (Carroll County), for example, only twenty-five residents showed up. In Newton County, though, some 150 participants offered their opinions to the panel, giving voice to concerns ranging from chemical usage to federal interference in agriculture.[22]

Across the region the influx of migrants, be they longhairs or long in the tooth, was dealt with in a typically decentralized Ozark fashion. In Madison County, for example, the Fayetteville paper the *Grapevine* reported that there was a unanimous "disapproval" for any sort of federal control, yet one hipbilly, Joel Davidson of *LION* fame, was noted for calling for the increase of industrialization across the region, a scheme that would have benefited from—if not required—some level of federal intervention for infrastructure upgrades.[23] Over in Newton County, community members voiced concerns about increased usage of the herbicide 2,4-D, clear cutting in the National Forest, and were interested in how to best organize and push the US Forest Service to create better policy.[24] In the seat of Baxter County, Mountain Home, the discussion was intensely local. It focused on the need for a stronger sewer system, in part to service the needs of those who attended the meeting who were "overwhelmingly persons of retirement age" and in many cases did not "even live [t]here yet, but . . . [were] property owners" and wanted the area to be in good shape when they settled.[25] One reporter at the Mountain Home meeting noted that only three Ozark natives were there and that the newcomers argued that social safety nets for the elderly "weren't needed" as "most of those retired in-migrants have sufficient means."[26] The journalist went on to note with disbelief that

BAXTER COUNTY
FUTURES FORUM

POPULATION & ECONOMIC GROWTH • LAND USE PLANNING • WATER & NATURAL RESOURCES • ENERGY NEEDS • TAXES & REVENUE

- What will life in Baxter County be like in 1996?
- Will we control growth, or will it control us?

A CITIZENS MEETING ON REGIONAL GROWTH AND ITS FUTURE EFFECTS ON BAXTER COUNTY.

WEDNESDAY, NOV. 3

7:30 P.M. - BAXTER COUNTY COURTHOUSE

SPONSORED BY

THE ARKANSAS HUMANITIES PROGRAM, EUREKA SPRINGS CULTURAL AFFAIRS COMMITTEE AND THE BAXTER BULLETIN

Flyer promoting an Ozark Futures Forum in Baxter County, 1976.
Ozark Institute Files (MC 252), series 1, subseries 1, box 1.
Courtesy Special Collections, University of Arkansas Libraries, Fayetteville.

"one man accused the county's 'Meals for the Aged Program' of being an 'elite dinner club.'"[27]

Indeed, as Perkins has shown, such a varied set of responses reflected the changing nature of the Ozarks as the age of Reagan dawned. Where once Ozark communities wanted government assistance in dealing with economic and structural injustices, they now had a "new ethic of defiance" toward federal programs.[28] Responses Jeffords and his associates received from some at the OFF highlighted this changing attitude. When asked about government aid to small farms, some respondents noted that what programs existed failed; after all, if such efforts had been around since Teddy Roosevelt with no success, that proved their uselessness.[29] In Carroll County, one member of the crowd noted that if the government really wanted to help small farmers, new programming was not the way to go. Instead, it should stop raising agricultural import quotas when American farmers were close to making money; in short, "stop making us political pawns in the interests of manipulating world policy."[30] Such standoffishness meant groups like the Institute, especially given their relationship with the counterculture, needed to find ways they could speak to the real and felt needs of Ozark communities— and do so in ways that differed from projects that brought in "Yankee" VISTAs (Volunteers in Service to America) with low opinions of Ozark culture.[31]

Indeed, the forums were part of the Ozark Institute's (OI) early efforts to develop an effective working strategy for the hill country.[32] As the fall of 1976 progressed, OI staff focus coalesced on rural poverty for their first round of grant proposals. All of their ideas would be implemented via "work in support of regional Community Action Agencies in areas of community nutrition and energy conservation."[33] The OI was seen by its creators as "a public interest organization which will provide research and informational resources to individuals and organizations in North Arkansas and the Ozark Mountains."[34] Wallace Smith, executive director of the Office of Human Concern, stated that the OI was also sought "to mobilize academic and community resources in the field of appropriate technology, and to coordinate with the National Center for Appropriate Technology" (NCAT) when appropriate.[35] As such, the Ozark Institute had a particular focus on working within the Ozark bioregion and within low-income populations, regardless of age or ethnicity. Joel Davidson, an occasional program manager for the OI, articulated their working vision of bioregionalism as a "wholistic [sic] approach that takes into consideration all ecological realities, recognizing no state lines."[36] One of the first grants the OI submitted was to NCAT to create such a system, based primarily in community networking via a regional newsletter, *Ozarka*, similar in distribution and content to the more informal creations like *LION* or the *Digest*. The newsletter "address[ed] the problem of rural poverty through advocacy of appropriate technology and systems, and to create an exchange of information leading to greater public awareness of the a.t. [appropriate technology] concept."[37]

Another of the OI's early projects was the creation of small canneries in Madison, Carroll, and Benton Counties. The Board of Directors, which included Wallace Smith of the Office of Human Concern in Benton County and rising Arkansas political activist Stephen Smith, began discussing the creation of these canneries in May as part of a "bioregional Community Food and Nutrition workshop" for groups in the Ozarks.[38] It was hoped that the canneries would improve the nutrition of rural areas and also increase economic opportunity for the patrons of the facilities as well. The community canneries were in full swing that October, just as the OI applied for its first Comprehensive Employment and Training Act (CETA) grant for "developing and implementing a comprehensive program of consumer education, training and technical assistance with the goal of alleviating nutritional deficiencies among rural low-income families in North Arkansas." [39]

By January 1978, the canneries received regional and national attention, as commentators noted that while they were "initially unsuccessful with regard to their prime purpose—production of canned goods at costs lower than prices of canned items at neighborhood stores—the canneries have provided a successful tool for community organization," something that Bill Brown, Deputy Director of the Office of Human Concern was proud of, as "food provides the strongest single base upon which to build coalitions."[40] The cannery project gained stronger structure via the charter of the Ozark Producer-Consumers Alliance (OPCA), a unique partnership as rural producer cooperatives in Madison and Carroll County merged with consumer cooperatives in Benton County to establish a market for excess foodstuffs, an arrangement that "proved profitable for small farms and owners of large vegetable gardens who had previously given excess produce away or simply left it to rot."[41]

The canneries also proved a good way for the OI and its affiliates to gain recognition from other community action groups and identify potential partners.[42] In October of 1978, Jerry McMahon of the National Catholic Rural Life Conference wrote to Jeffords and asked for more

The Canning Centers were made available to the citizens of Benton, Carroll and Madison counties in 1975 through a grant provided by the Office of Human Concern. In conjunction with OHC, the Ozark Institute provides assistance to the Canning Centers through management support and training. Special support in staffing the facilities is provided by the County Judges of the three counties.

WHY A CANNING CENTER?

The object of the Ozark Producer-Consumer Alliance's self-help canneries is to bring locally grown fruits and vegetables to the tables of local consumers. By encouraging local consumption of local production, eating what we grow or what our local farmers produce, we will eat better, more nutritious foods, at lower costs. We can eliminate transportation costs and any excess profits, and individually benefit from the savings, as well as provide for the existence of small farmers in our Ozark bio-region.

**"EAT WHAT YOU CAN -
CAN WHAT YOU CAN'T"**

INFORMATION AND APPOINTMENTS

In Benton County:

Ozark Producer-Consumer Alliance Community Cannery, on New Hope Road, just one block east of Highway 71, in *ROGERS*.

Telephone: 636-9189

In Carroll County:

OPCA Food Preservation Center, at Springfield and Ada Streets, in *BERRYVILLE*.

Telephone: 423-6300

In Madison County:

OPCA Community Canning Center, on Governor's Road near the Fairgrounds, in *HUNTSVILLE*.

Telephone: 738-2610

APPOINTMENTS

All the Community Canning Centers are open for appointments from 9 to 5, Monday through Saturday. Evening canning is available at the Madison County Community Canning Center, by appointment only.

***

OZARK PRODUCER-CONSUMER ALLIANCE
Main Office
(501)253-7384

OZARK PRODUCER-CONSUMER ALLIANCE

COMMUNITY CANNING CENTERS

**in
BENTON, CARROLL,
MADISON COUNTIES**

Pamphlet promoting the Ozark Institute's community canneries.
Ozark Institute Files (MC 252), series 4, subseries 1.
Courtesy Special Collections, University of Arkansas Libraries, Fayetteville.

details about the program. Jeffords was quick to respond and noted that the program had been beneficial to area residents via the integration of "canneries with food co-ops, farmers markets, community gardens and educational and technical assistance programs."[43] Part of the success stemmed from the location and operation of the canneries: in Madison County, for example, it was the near the county fairgrounds and offered cheap prices to use specialized equipment, like large steam kettles.[44] Apparent success also stemmed from efforts by the Ozark Institute and the Office of Human Concern to streamline the management and integration of the canneries with the other elements that Jeffords noted in his letter to McMahon.[45]

The canneries were not permanent, however. In July 1978 Craig

Fuller, manager of the OPCA, recommended to the board that they dismantle parts of the program. The promotion of natural foods had "never proven to be profitable and their benefit to our members and our Producer-Consumer Alliance is questionable."[46] Prices were going up on the other goods the OPCA was trying to provide also, and this was compounded by problems of "spoilage, waste, local competition, and the small amount of working capital" left in the OPCA coffers.[47] Despite this, Fuller was in favor of continuing other elements of the OPCA, including community education efforts on a host of issues, central of which were the canning operations—though this was subject to change if CETA grant funding did not remain at sufficient levels to continue paying staff.[48] Jeffords echoed these concerns in his October letter to McMahon, as he noted that the combined operations of the OPCA were financially "marginal" and relied on CETA and Community Action grants to stay in operation.[49] Jeffords noted at the end of the letter that because the OPCA required a continual subsidy to operate, there were doubts as to the ability of the group to achieve self-sufficiency in any "reasonable period of time."[50] Indeed, though an internal review of the OPCA in 1979 noted that the canneries served over fifty local families in some fashion, of which thirty-five families canned "a total of 1,378 quarts of garden produce" and twenty-one families dried twenty-six bushels of fruit, "participation [was] still less than desired," perhaps due to lack of community knowledge about the canneries—and, most likely, because locals, old or young, had their own equipment and had little need for a newcomer to teach them what they already knew.[51]

While the cannery operations ultimately closed their doors with little impact on popular memory, the publication of *Uncertain Harvest* in 1980 and the creation of the Family Farm Development Service (FFDS) in July of 1978 proved to have lasting importance in the region and the state, though not, perhaps, in the way the Jeffords and the staff at the Ozark Institute intended. During 1978 and 1979, the OI identified ways to make a positive impact in rural Ozark communities. In 1978 Institute staff focused on the problems facing small-scale farms and farm families in the region, especially after research showed these communities were buffeted by an increasingly large array of forces outside their control. Rising energy costs at the end of the 1970s, disintegrating sales opportunities, and USDA policies that prioritized large-scale agricultural operations created an environment that was forcing "70 per cent of the state's agricultural sector" into dire straits.[52] By creating a "unique para-professional rural assistance program for Arkansas," Jeffords hoped to build a system that delivered "employment and training to small farmers and rural residents;" increased access to technical assistance, education, and management principles for community organizations; and worked to distribute information on new growing practices, appropriate technology, and more to farmers and rural folk.[53]

What was supposed to be a one-year program soon turned into a multi-year employment training and empowerment project, complete with the support of the young state governor, Bill Clinton, who was, according to Jeffords, "very receptive to our FFDS project. He envisioned the Institute's FFDS as a possible vehicle for program efforts of the state administration's progressive farm policies." [54] Support came not just from the Governor's office, but also from the Community Services Administration (CSA), the Arkansas Department of Local Services, and private donations, all of which built on preliminary funding from the Arkansas Endowment for the Humanities and CETA.[55] Such wide-ranging support allowed the initial actions of the FFDS to quickly encompass twenty-six Arkansas counties, from the Ozarks to the Delta, all primarily focused on "providing employment training and career development opportunities," a task facilitated by forty-three newly hired staff members.[56] For Jeffords, reflecting on the first year of the FFDS, this meant that "two important objectives" were accomplished: staff was hired, trained, and sent into the rural communities to help empower rural residents of the Ozarks and elsewhere; and small farmers now had a chance at greater self-sufficiency due to the FFDS's emphasis on self-reliance.[57]

Indeed, early evaluations of the FFDS showed the OI had one of the higher success rates in implementing employment objectives in the region, with a 69 percent placement rate.[58] This level of success was reflected elsewhere in audits of the FFDS program. As a jobs training program that was often the "first good working environment ever experienced," the Institute was commended for its work culture filled with "motivated and competent personnel," as it left those who transitioned out of its programs with an increased "likelihood of finding employment" and was an asset in those places.[59] In short, the training systems, research processes, and community engagement of the Institute were held up as a model by CETA reviewers.

Part of the FFDS worked to include traditional Ozark folkways into poverty alleviation and nutrition enhancement programming. Seed banks, seed saving, and the associated hope for gains in food security became a focus of OI staff and the Governor's office. By June 1980, the FFDS personnel had distributed 2,400 packets of garden seeds to community members in its service areas, paid for by a series of grants from the Ozarks Regional Commission.[60] In the June press release about the program, Jeffords noted that the seed-distribution project encompassed the whole idea of the FFDS, namely, that it was about building individual and community self-sufficiency and not giving a "handout."[61] Jeffords noted that "if handled properly, each seed pack gives a family the ability to grow its own garden vegetables for years on end, multiplying the economic effect."[62] Indeed, the crux of the program was "to provide low-income rural residents and limited resource farm families with non-hybrid garden seeds suitable for home vegetable production at minimal costs, and the establishment of permanent Community Seed Banks."[63] The FFDS estimated that within a short time this would provide vegetables valued at approximately $456.70 per family per $3.20 invested.[64] The OI staff, led by Craig Fuller, went above the goal of 2,000 families and served nearly 2,500 across the region, all while coming in under budget. Jeffords noted in a letter to Harold Daricek at the Ozarks Regional Commission in September of 1980 that the OI was returning $1,339.29 of the ORC's initial grant of $9,780 because "I can state at this point that all objectives of the project were met and exceeded at cost below our original projections."[65] Indeed, Jeffords and the OI staff were hoping that they would be able to return funds as early as the previous May, when Jeffords noted to the ORC director in Little Rock, Frank Iuen, that "the Institute was able through bulk purchasing" to maximize the impact of the grant money and reach the extra families.[66]

In the midst of this programmatic success, the OI experienced the beginning of the end. Edd Jeffords had been the target of local ire since he had put together the Folk Festival in 1973. It seemed his new success and visibility with the OI, and the large grants it applied for (and often won), drew increased negative attention.[67] By the summer of 1980, Jeffords sent the OI's board of directors a collection of press clippings that represented what he viewed to be "local political opposition to our new CETA contract" of some $960,000.[68] In particular, Jeffords warily watched as Clinton's challenger in the gubernatorial race, Frank White, picked up the OI as a political bat to hit his opponent with in July and August.

While White was quick to use the OI against Clinton, the first-term Democrat was not lacking in scandals. To be fair, not all the problems Clinton was blamed for during the 1980 campaign were of his making, at least in their entirety. When Clinton took office in 1978, over eight thousand miles of the state's roads were deemed in need of repairs and the state's economy was stuck between the old industrial order and the new economics of Walmart, Tyson, and others. The young politician also had to balance pet projects, like reorienting Arkansas's energy use patterns, with these harsh realities. In short, Brother Bill was caught between a rock and a hard place. When it came to the state's roads, Clinton enacted a controversial weight-based fee schedule in which car owners paid a registration fee based on the weight of their car to raise money for infrastructure improvement. This prompted a quick back-lash throughout the state, especially as most Arkansans owned older, heavier cars—especially in the poorer counties of the Ozarks. The car tag fiasco was compounded by Clinton's stance on other issues, like changing the economic development emphasis from large industries to small businesses and holding hearings on clear cutting forest areas that angered timber companies. These issues were made worse when it came out that his administration handled money poorly. A favorite target of the growing anti-Clinton press, led by op-ed writers like Meredith Oakley, was a program to cut firewood for the needy.[69] At first glance, the Sawyer Program—which also aimed to create jobs—was a good idea; but public opinion shifted as the program cost some $62,000, created only six jobs, and produced a mere three cords of wood.[70]

Clinton also poorly navigated the Carter administration's policy on Cuban refugees. In May 1980 the White House informed Clinton that Fort Chaffee, outside Fort Smith in Sebastian County, would become transitional housing for some twenty thousand Cubans who sought asylum. Though Clinton supported Carter, he was left to address the new arrivals alone, stretching an already taxed state budget. By the end of May 1980, the population of Cubans at Chaffee surged and relations between them and locals reached a boiling point. By June 1, it was too much and the Cubans jumped the barricades and rushed out of Fort Chaffee while federal soldiers stood by. Chaos reigned in the streets around Fort Chaffee and the neighboring town of Barling. By August, the Carter administration asked Arkansas to take in more Cubans, which Clinton refused—after all, tensions were still high and he faced accusations of capitulating to Washington. This accusation gained power as the White House ignored him and sent the new round of migrants, infuriating the state's growing antifederal population.

In this environment, then, opposition to a large federal grant like CETA should have come as no surprise to Jeffords and the Institute staff, no matter how successful previous work was. The grant would expand the Family Farm Development Service with a budget of nearly one million dollars, quickly sparking outrage by some locals and antifederal in-migrants who viewed it as continuing a pattern of government waste. Opposition to CETA was somewhat ironic. The Comprehensive Employment and Training Act of 1973 was established by President Nixon to help train workers and empower the nation's workforce to face the new American economy of the 1970s and beyond.[71] The program, while lauded by Nixon as "one of the finest pieces of legislation to come to my desk this year," was not universally loved, particularly by those opposed to the types of projects the OI embarked upon.[72]

Despite the conservative credentials of program's origins, by the start of the 1980s, old-style New Deal liberalism was out of favor in Washington and in Arkansas. The emergence of neoconservative forces in domestic politics ensured that social welfare programs became pariahs.[73] Astute local candidates like Frank White capitalized on the shifting regional mood and used issues like the Institute's grant as an effective bludgeon against the struggling incumbent. White's rhetoric resonated with voters throughout the northern part of the state, at least according to op-ed writers in places like Carroll County. Jim Lair, a staff writer for the *Carroll County Tribune*, wrote a series of stinging commentaries about the OI in his column, "Reflections of an Outlander." Lair was unimpressed with the OI's efforts "to help . . . poor rural residents of the Ozarks," and were, in his opinion, "another classic example of much that is wrong with our nation today." Further, he said, "We have gone too far now in the creation of a welfare state. As a taxpayer

Political cartoon, newspaper unknown, ca. 1980.
Ozark Institute Files (MC 252), series 3, subseries 1, box 5.
Courtesy Special Collections, University of Arkansas Libraries, Fayetteville.

this writer [*sic*] is definitely opposed to programs of this nature."[74] The Ozark Institute and its kind were simply a "cancer on society" whose unchecked growth was paid for by the taxpayers.[75] Lair, however, was no native of the Ozarks. Self-described as an "outlander" and "adopted son," Lair, like many in-migrants who arrived in the region during the 1960s and 1970s, passed himself off as speaking for "true" Ozarkers.[76] In so doing, his diatribes against Jeffords and the Ozark Institute perhaps spoke less for rural hill folk and more for the residents of the "new Ozarks" detailed by Perkins.

While White used the Institute as a whipping boy in his campaign against the extravagancies of the Clinton government, he nearly overplayed his hand, and in so doing provoked Jeffords and the OI board to file a libel lawsuit against him that fall. The suit stemmed from comments White made during the summer's state Republican convention regarding the nature of the OI and Jeffords personally; namely that Jeffords had recently been convicted of assault with a weapon, which was not true. White, Jeffords believed, was simply using the story of a recent altercation to discredit the OI and Clinton during the campaign season and to score quick points in Carroll County and elsewhere.[77] White was correct in noting that Jeffords had been arrested, but the story was not as salacious as he wished. In reality, Jeffords had a charge of aggravated assault filed against him on July 26, 1980, thanks to a fight the day before.[78]

The incident took place on the evening of July 25 as Jeffords left his home for dinner. As he backed out into the road, his son yelled something to him, prompting Jeffords to stop just as David Vanderboom came along at a "rapid speed."[79] Vanderboom began honking and yelling at Jeffords and yelled, "I'm going to teach you a lesson, you son of a bitch." He got out of his truck and struck Jeffords several times in the face and ripped his shirt.[80] He then tried to pull Jeffords from the truck, twisting his leg and telling Jeffords he was going to break it. In the chaos, Jeffords hollered for his son to call the police while the assailant's wife tried to get her husband to calm down. Instead of ceasing his attack, the assailant slammed Jeffords's leg in the door several times, requiring Jeffords to go to the hospital later. Ultimately, the assailant gave up, telling Jeffords he was going to take his family home and saying to Jeffords, I'll "come back for you, motherfucker."[81] Michael Mager, an eyewitness to the event, noted that at "no time did I see either man brandish a weapon," and that "it was quite apparent that the man driving the blue pickup [Vanderboom] was the aggressor."[82] In the end, Jeffords settled for possession of an unlicensed firearm in his truck—not assault with a weapon—and Vanderboom was charged with assault and battery but convicted only of disorderly conduct and fined.[83]

The event fed into White's narrative about the Ozark Institute, as well the general narrative about the recipients of federal grants, being unfit to continue receiving funding for the FFDS. White started in on the OI after reading articles by newspaper columnist Jim Lair, an immigrant himself, prepared by his campaign staff. When the Republican candidate read a piece about Jeffords's altercation, White quickly weaponized the story as leverage against Clinton. Before he did so, Frank White tried, in some minor measure, to verify parts of the story. White first called John Fuller Cross, his campaign manager in Carroll County and an old friend "to ask him what he knew about the Ozark Institute and Edd Jeffords," and Cross replied that there had been opposition to

Jeffords in the past.[84] Indeed, in September 1980, Cross was noted in a report by the *Arkansas Democrat* as having "compiled a thick dossier on Jeffords' activities, both here and on the West Coast."[85] The reporter went on to note that "Cross'[s] opposition to the Ozark Institute and Jeffords seems to be of the oldtimers-versus-newcomers variety" and that he "'wouldn't mind' if the Ozark Institute were closed forever."[86] It is no surprise, then, that Cross elaborated further by stating that "Jeffords'[s] enterprises are 'growing like a cancer' in the area and do nothing but add to inflation and hurt the people they purport to help."[87] White also tried to get information from John Tyson, police chief in Eureka at the time. Tyson noted that he only gave over the information required of him by law, but by this time the press had constructed the story that White ran with; namely, that Jeffords was charged with "allegedly brandish[ing] a handgun during an altercation with another Eureka Springs man."[88]

As White's attacks increased and Jim Lair's columns became more strident, the OI's board of directors felt the need to push back on behalf of their director. Wallace Smith, then Executive Director of the Office of Human Concern (OHC), wrote in to Jim Lair and the ownership at the *Tribune*, wryly noting that he had read their assessments of the OI with "amusement," and wondered who would write up the story of the most recent OHC meeting, as he had seen no representative of their paper at the meeting. That was, no doubt, because he had a "slight vision problem."[89] Smith concluded the letter by asking the paper, Lair in particular, to revisit the definition of words like "subjectivity" and "objectivity" as this might help them in future endeavors.[90]

As Jeffords and the OI board attempted to correct the record with the *Tribune* and began the lawsuit against White, more trouble emerged. A former contract employee of the Institute, Billy Rojas, sent a long tirade against the *Tribune* to Lair and others early in October. Rojas was hired by the OI for a brief time during the summer to create general educational materials on the Ozarks and the work of the OI.[91] It seemed that when Rojas left the OI, he took some of the group's stationary with him, unbeknownst to Jeffords, and used it to inform the *Carroll County Tribune* that "frankly, I think you stink."[92] In between screeds against homosexuality, Rojas went on to castigate Ted Larimer, the editor, and the whole of the *Tribune*, stating, "Your newspaper, and your political fellow-travelers, have poisoned many minds in this part of Arkansas," and that the arguments made by the paper were "small-minded to the extreme" and were "irresponsible."[93] The ensuing hullabaloo forced Jeffords to write an open apology to the *Tribune*, explaining that Rojas was not affiliated with the Institute and that they did not agree with his depictions of the paper or its employees, at least in that language.[94]

The grant application, already politicized as a part of Frank White's efforts to smear Bill Clinton and take the governor's mansion in November of 1980, was further endangered by the investigation of State Senator Kim Hendren, who jumped into the fray thanks to his concerns about the money the OI used in its suit against White and with the FBI inquiries. Hendren, as the summer of 1980 wound to a close, asked Clinton to deny the grant, at least until a proper investigation into the allegations from White, Carroll County Judge Wayne Farwell, and others could be dealt with.[95] Hendren was given greater voice by the *Arkansas Gazette*'s Meredith Oakley, who ran a series of articles that attempted to lay out the issues surrounding the Institute. Oakley noted that "Hendren left no doubt in my mind that he believes White's criticism of the Institute, not [that] any 'misstatement' White might have made in public, provoked the lawsuit."[96]

The campaign theatre surrounding the CETA grant only heightened when Hendren; Clinton staff member BJ McCoy; Anthony Marty, the state CETA administrator; and others made the trip up to Eureka Springs—at Hendren's request—to meet with the Institute's beleaguered director. The meeting was a fact-finding session, wherein Hendren asked Jeffords several questions about issues "bothering him in connection with the Ozark Institute."[97] Despite Jeffords's answers, Hendren was not satisfied and maintained his belief that the CETA grant should be denied.[98] Hendren, as Lair reported, also noted his displeasure with the Institute's recent *Uncertain Harvest*, and in particular what he felt were negative statements about private citizens in Arkansas paid for by public money.[99]

Uncertain Harvest: The Family Farm in Arkansas was the ultimate presentation of research and policy advocacy the OI created. *Uncertain Harvest* was put together by Jeffords and Ralph Desmarais, an expert on food and agriculture, and it was billed as "a first step" to address and solve the problems that rural Arkansas faced.[100] Throughout the book, the OI described a complicated portrait of the state's agriculture system in the aftermath of large-scale agricultural mechanization and consolidation, and argued, in part, that with "70 per cent of Arkansas farmers" deemed "small farmers," only solutions for their context would reinvigorate rural communities across the "Land of Opportunity."[101] Jeffords and the Ozark Institute were not the only ones seeking answers for these problems. Thomas McRae, head of the Winthrop Rockefeller Foundation (now Winrock International) in Little Rock, noted during the Family Farm Symposium in June 1979, that small farmers in Arkansas were "on the verge of extinction."[102] Jeffords, McRae, and others argued that despite the relatively minor economic impact of small farms in Arkansas, "new social problems" will emerge if these communities were not supported and given similar access to institutional support as large-scale agribusiness.[103]

In order to craft a solution, Jeffords and his contributors attempted to give a holistic picture of how the shifting tides of farm policy and practice impacted Ozarkers and others. With special attention paid to minorities and portions of the state often neglected, the book allowed the Institute to illustrate the impacts of agricultural aggregation—a force that between 1940 and 1976 pushed some 72 percent of the state's farmers out of the fields (a process that impacted black farmers disproportionately).[104] While no silver bullet was given, Jeffords and his staff published a list of policy solutions that prioritized the preservation of farmland, small farm practices, and the creation of tax incentives and other financial enticements, including the job training programs put forward by initiatives like the FFDS.[105] Nevertheless, state legislators like Hendren found the book troubling in its efforts to check the growing power of companies like Riceland.

Despite growing agreement on the OI's findings by groups like the Rockefeller Foundation, the blows kept coming. In August Institute staff learned that the FBI had launched an investigation into their use of grant money at the request of an unknown party. That October Douglas Wilson, then president of the OI board, sent an inquiry to Larry McCord, the US Attorney in Fort Smith, to try and get to the bottom of the issue. Through "leaks to the press from someone outside the Institute," Wilson noted they had learned in August of FBI efforts to investigate alleged misuse of federal funds at the Institute.[106] The OI was concerned as "the

UNCERTAIN HARVEST
The Family Farm in Arkansas

EDITED BY RALPH DESMARAIS AND EDD JEFFORDS

Edd Jeffords and Ralph Desmarai, *Uncertain Harvest*, 1980.
Ozark Institute Files (MC 252), series 4, box 8.
Courtesy Special Collections, University of Arkansas Libraries, Fayetteville.

leaks occurred about the time local political opposition to a certain grant proposal of the Institute's materialized."[107] That was not the only problem. FBI agents, in the course of their inquiries, set up shop in the OI headquarters and dogged FFDS trainees around the region, which created morale problems as "employees see a vicious circle of allegations, investigations, and adverse action" while also hampering their ability to get on with the job at hand.[108] The FBI investigation into the accounting of the OI, though quite thorough, was ultimately fruitless for those who hoped to hear that Jeffords and his staff inappropriately used funds. In a news report on October 23, 1980, the agent in charge of the inquiries, William Kell, noted that since the Bureau had been notified of the allegations on August 11, teams had combed through the Institute's files and interviewed former and current employees.[109] By early November, the investigation was over and the OI had been cleared. Jeffords noted in a press release that the whole thing had "clearly reinforced the integrity and accountability of the Ozark Institute, but we cannot help but feel victimized by unseen accusers and false witnesses."[110] Indeed, at no time had the Institute staff or board been notified about the "specific accusations which stimulated the inquiry into our operations, although we became aware of numerous allegations which were investigated."[111]

Ultimately, the combined impact of the FBI investigation and negative press that the OI received during the 1980 governor's race proved too much for the Ozark Institute to endure. The death knell for the OI began on October 6, 1980, when it was notified it would not receive the CETA grant to continue and expand the FFDS, though it received a six-month extension to wrap up its CETA programs. The FFDS limped along until the spring of 1981, when the OI shut it down, despite the FFDS having "been cited as one of the most successful in the state in terms of training and placement rate."[112] Before the end came, though, Jeffords and OI did win a hollow victory against the newly elected Governor White thanks to a $7,000 settlement that they donated to campaigns. Jeffords noted in a donation letter to State Senator John Lisle from Springdale, "This contribution, by the way, came out of Frank White's pocket as a result of that affair and we are enjoying spreading it around to good Democrats this year."[113] Despite the bright spot of being able to give to Democrats in 1982, Jeffords was unrealistically optimistic throughout 1981, noting that the sales of *Uncertain Harvest* and fees from training sessions were bringing in enough money to keep the lights on.[114] This ultimately slowed down, however, as the Institute began shrinking its office size and ultimately faded away. By mid-October 1982, Jeffords noted that he had enclosed the "final forms filed during the calendar year 1982 as this organization anticipates having no employees beyond the current reporting period."[115]

Despite the troubles the Institute faced, the issues championed by Jeffords and his compatriots remained relevant to the Ozarks. Indeed, as the OI fought for its survival, hipbillies across the mountains organized to build economic and environmental security for Ozarkers and rural communities across the state. Thus, while attempts at large-scale organization fueled by the grants decried by Mrs. McGrade in 1976 proved futile, smaller efforts more in tune with traditional Ozark concerns prospered, often in unlikely ways. Intervention that appeared to be a handout or wasteful had never been well received in the hills, but BTLs had learned action that spoke from lived experience on the land could prevail.

CHAPTER 5

The Ozark Mystic Vision

The revolution in our own lives has us . . . becoming much closer to the land and its seasonal rhythms and requirements.

—Jerry Friedberg

THE WORK OF the Ozark Institute was not the only way in which hipbillies sought to become an asset to their new home. As they established themselves and learned from native Ozarkers, hipbillies became deeply involved in their local communities, often in ways meant to bridge the gap between ideals of the deep revolution and lived experience in the Ozarks. While the Institute might have been a flashier vision of this, it is best understood within a larger network of community-based activism that emerged alongside of, and perhaps despite, its efforts. These grassroots efforts are, in many cases, what has served as the lasting influence of the hipbillies on the Ozarks.

As the back to the landers settled into the rhythms of Ozark life, they faced certain realities. Hipbillies arriving in the region had envisioned the Ozarks as pristine, a place where the impurities of America were erased. However, instead of a bucolic paradise, they encountered the growing use of chemical herbicides by the US Forest Service (USFS), larger farms, power companies, and others—something that, given Rachel Carson's then-recent *Silent Spring*, should have come as no surprise to the hipbillies.[1] One hipbilly noted years later, "It was one of those things that you kind of think *that happens someplace else, that doesn't happen here.*"[2] But it was happening in the Ozarks. Faced with such a reality, the neopioneers did what they had done elsewhere: organized with gusto.

In what became an ongoing act of back to the land engagement in local politics and economy in the Ozarks, the hipbillies protested the USFS's attempts to escalate the use of 2,4 D and 2,4,5 T throughout the Ozark and St. Francis National Forests. The USFS had previously used the herbicide in ground applications in clear-cut areas, but in the fall of 1974 and in early 1975, it announced it would begin an aerial spraying program. Opposition within the back to the land community began almost immediately, as groups throughout the larger Ozarks raised concerns. In November 1974, Fayetteville resident Sidney Bell wrote to *LION* about the efforts of the Women's Center Committee on the Environment in Fayetteville to have the chemical banned in Arkansas.[3] Just what made 2,4 D so controversial? According to Gary Turner, 2,4,5 T was a hormone-based herbicide, "which kills many plants by causing them to grow themselves to death."[4] It was often used to clear weeds in rice or soybean fields, as well as to make space in timber stands for fast-growing pine trees. Indeed, as Kathryn Newfont has shown in her work on forest commons in Appalachia, USFS was engaged in a broad strategy throughout the south to create single-aged forests for easy harvesting and replanting. While in some areas—like the Blue Ridge Mountains—clear-cutting was the USFS's first choice to manufacture forests for harvest, in others, surplus chemicals from Vietnam, like 2,4 D in the Ozarks, were the weapon of choice.[5] Opposition to the use of the herbicides, like clear-cutting or coal mining in Appalachia, and water planning elsewhere in the South, was often most powerful in the local context as farmers, timber professionals, or impacted residents protested to local and state officials, and such efforts often prompted change to occur throughout the regulatory structures.[6]

To put the use of the chemical into perspective, *LION* reminded its readers that the herbicide was surplus from Vietnam where it had been used to defoliate Vietcong forest cover with lasting impact on the beleaguered nation.[7] Sidney Bell alleged that the chemical, despite being incredibly effective at killing plants, had negative effects on humans: illness after spraying (abdominal pain, nausea, dizziness and more), birth defects, miscarriages, and damage to a person's genetic material.[8]

It was not just spraying that was a problem, however. When plants sprayed by the chemical were burned, Bell argued, the result was the creation of dioxin, a deadly chemical. According to a biochemist consulted by *LION*, "One drop of dioxin is estimated to be able to kill 12000 men."[9] These were not problems located far away; *LION* detailed how in Missouri, after an area was sprayed, "dozens of domestic animals" died mysteriously, and allegedly, some young girls developed "a strange kidney disease" while their mother and others had constant migraines.[10]

Members of the back to the land community and their local partners used *LION* and other guerilla publications as an outlet for distributing information about the fight against use of the chemical. Indeed, many groups pushed to ban the herbicide throughout the Arkansas Ozarks, notably the Newton County Wildlife Association (NCWA) and Care Enough About Saving the Earth (CEASE) in Madison County, as well as a strong, decentralized group in Stone County. The informal social network of *LION* and other newsletters was crucial for mobilizing the resistance.[11] The back to the land community, though, did not focus only on protests. *LION*, the *Ozark Digest*, and more distributed information about protecting oneself from the negative impacts of 2,4 D. The advice was simple: stay away from sprayed areas, test your water and urine, avoid foods with lots of fat (where it was alleged they stored herbicides), and use alternative weed controls.[12]

Farmers and ranchers throughout the region were using increased amounts of herbicides as well. The surge in herbicide use resulted from a combination of things by the 1970s. To begin with, the ready availability of the chemicals in combination with their promotion by groups like the University of Arkansas's Extension Service and the Arkansas State Plant Board (ASPB) increased the visibility of the herbicides. While the ASPB numbers do not include all private application of chemicals like 2,4 D, they do illustrate this increase. In 1968 the Plant Board devoted 1,721 man-hours to dealing with issues related to 2,4 D and 2,4,5 T (permitting, inspection, education, and complaints).[13] That same year, the state-wide acreage with some form of these herbicides used was just under 148,000 acres.[14] By 1979 these numbers had increased sharply. ASPB man-hours jumped to 7,387 (down slightly from the peak of 7,821.5 hours in 1976), and acreage sprayed with 2,4 D now sat at 366,244.[15] In 1979, the ASPB experienced a 329 percent increase in man-hours devoted to the issue, while the acreage sprayed grew by nearly 150 percent. One back to the land publication attributed the increased use of 2,4 D to greed: "The growing controversy over the use of aerial poisons boils down to the old disease of people versus profits."[16] The ASPB reports over the decade show only a modest increase in the number of those with permits to sell the substance (from 298 in 1969 to 363 in 1978), which certainly lends credibility to the idea that some of the expansion, at least, was beneficial for a few.[17] One back to the lander stated that "the county extension agent was pushing that [2,4 D] like there was no tomorrow, and there were people out here who thought it was the greatest thing."[18]

Another reason for the increase in chemical usage was the rapid growth of larger farm acreages throughout the nation and the state. Since the 1950s, officials like Earl Butz, once Eisenhower's undersecretary of agriculture and later secretary of agriculture for Nixon and Ford, advised farmers to "get big or get out."[19] While Ozark farmers did not go big in the same way that farmers did in the wheat fields of the Midwest, they were at least indirectly influenced by Butz's advice. Between 1950 and 1982, agriculture in the region experienced a sea change along multiple fronts. To begin with, as Brooks Blevins has shown, the nature of farming in the region changed dramatically. Throughout the late nineteenth and early twentieth centuries, much of the Ozarks' agricultural economy was dominated by the small-scale production of row crops like cotton or corn. After World War II, this pattern shifted, as it did elsewhere in the upland South. In the Ozarks, this was seen in the proliferation of beef cattle operations and poultry houses. Corn acreages by 1963, for example, had dropped some 90 percent since 1939 as farm after farm traded row crops for livestock.[20] By the end of the 1970s, the number of cattle in the Ozarks had jumped from 220,000 in 1940 to 640,000.[21]

These changes were coupled with a significant shift in population and land use in the region. During this period, the number of farms in the Arkansas uplands dropped by more than 55 percent, from 37,691 to 16,751. Many farms consolidated (or went under) and the average farm size grew by 66 percent, from 136 acres in 1950 to 226 acres in 1982.[22] In the face of this change, farmers left the hills for factories and towns across the Midwest and West, resulting in the "largest outmigration in

Ozark history," a combination of farm closure and greater availability of stable jobs in town.[23] Herbicides like 2,4 D, Silvex, and 2,4,5 T made managing the larger pastures and fields with fewer hands feasible— indeed, even marginally profitable. Dealing with weeds in a crop field or toxic weeds in a stock pasture with herbicides allowed farmers across the region to keep the family farm going as the younger generation left the farm for bright lights and the big city.

Despite these potential gains, the herbicides caused their fair share of problems. During the summer of 1975, the *Ozark Digest* ran a series of articles that detailed complications associated with 2,4 D.[24] Beginning with the experiences of several women in the community, the *Digest* noted that the USFS was preparing to start a new round of spraying, continuing a pattern begun in 1966. The editorial staff argued "there is no longer any doubt that the Dioxins contain in 2-4-5-T and 2-4-D are deadly to humans."[25] To help underscore the seriousness of the issue, that June the *Ozark Digest* published a letter by Anida Frans from Van Buren County.[26] Described by *Digest* staff as "a good expression of the concern [by] rural Ozark families threatened by the unknown effects of aerial poisons," Frans's letter described the experiences of three families affected by the use of 2,4,5 T near the source of their drinking water.[27] Frans detailed how after a neighbor sprayed the headwaters of the spring with herbicides, "six out of eight babies conceived on that farm died."[28] If that was not stunning enough, she also noted how near Clarksville, some folks had goats die after an area was sprayed.[29]

Hipbillies were not the only people voicing their concerns. In Little Rock, David Glenn, a long-time staff reporter for the *Arkansas Democrat*, allegedly resigned his job in protest in 1975 before he published the conclusion of a three-part series on 2,4,5 T, thanks to a representative of Dow Chemical who called the newspaper and pressured his editors to cut off the stories.[30] His article was picked up by the *Ozark Digest* in the summer of 1975, and while it covered some of the same ground that *LION* and others had discussed for the past year, it added to the conversation a new level of documentation. Glenn detailed how the Plant Board had established that the safe level for the herbicide should not exceed 0.1 parts per million (ppm) in the mix used for spraying. This was a bit of a problem, though, as the episode detailed by Frans in the *Ozark Digest* was the result of a solution containing 60 ppm of 2,4,5 T.[31]

Efforts to end the practice of using 2,4,5 T in the Ozarks did not stop at the region's borders. Throughout 1975 residents across the region wrote to newly elected Senator Dale Bumpers detailing their concerns about the use of the chemical in their area. Brooke Ligon, a Fayetteville resident, wrote in with concerns that the herbicide had not been properly studied, and that she felt the "EPA should prohibit the spraying of phenoxy herbicides until we can know scientifically and assuredly the positive and negative consequences which might occur immediately and in the future."[32] Aside from the potential health concerns, Mary Tuttle from Mountain View wrote to Bumpers about her interest in "preserving the environment and ecology of our wonderful State of Arkansas" and asked that the Senator "please do something about outlawing this aerial spraying [of] timber from helicopters with tree poison that kills the trees, as well as polluting our pure water supply."[33] Concerns were also voiced to Bumpers about the lack of legal options for people opposed to the broad use of herbicides. M. L. Pardue, a back to the lander, noted in August that he and his neighbors had no way to "protect our families from these dangerous chemicals" and that, despite his wife's efforts to talk with the regional EPA office and Arkansas State Plant Board, there was "no legal way to protect" themselves or, he said, to even "guarantee that the chemicals used are what they say they are."[34] Pardue then detailed his concern more directly:

> Last year thousands of gallons of something labeled 2,4,5[-]T was dumped on Stone County. It was later discovered that the spraying company switched labels because they were out of 2,4,5 T and didn't want to lose their contract! We have many here who will testify about losing gardens, bees, and fruit trees because of drift of the spray. One lady even lost her unborn baby![35]

Bumpers was quick to respond to growing constituent concerns. Groups from NCWA, the Women's Center Committee on the Environment, and others sent letters and called his offices in an attempt to push him to take action. Throughout the summer and fall of 1975, he continually assured Ozarkers of his efforts to look into the matter and offered his own "rather serious misgivings about the use of this herbicide, particularly on the forests of Arkansas."[36] The new senator, though, was also quick to note he was concerned about the economic impact of banning something as powerful as 2,4,5T, something that BTLs interviewed for this project made sure to note—often with a healthy dose of skepticism as to whether or not Bumpers was a true ally in the fight against 2,4,5T.[37]

As Bumpers responded to his constituents, area news agencies reported on the developing fight between the Forest Service and anti-herbicide groups in federal court. Buried in the classified pages of the *Northwest Arkansas Times* in June 1975, a brief article noted that Federal Judge G. Thomas Eisele issued an injunction against the USFS which prohibited them spraying on public land until they produced the required environmental impact study. In so doing, Judge Eisele sided with the NWCA's claim from June that the Forest Service had violated National Environmental Policy Act (NEPA) regulations.[38] Government lawyers objected to the NCWA's characterization of NEPA regulations, arguing that they did not apply as the herbicide program was "not a major federal action substantially effecting the human environment."[39] Judge Eisele dismissed this argument, noting that the USFS had believed differently at some point, as they had submitted a preliminary impact study and indicated their intention to produce a final version. Faced with this, the Forest Service was forced to agree with the NCWA and Sierra Club that the use of 2,4,5T and its companion chemicals did indeed pose a threat to the environment, if for no other reason than the fact that the use of these herbicides resulted in the shift of the "natural stand in the forest from hardwoods to conifers."[40]

In the wake of the injunction the outcry against the herbicides grew. Aubrey Shepherd, an outdoor sports columnist for the *Northwest Arkansas Times*, argued in October that "regardless of the truth of the charges made against the chemical," it only seemed logical to wait until thorough studies were completed.[41] For Shepherd it was a simple matter:

> Anyone who enjoys the beauties of the Ozarks should of course be dead set against spraying the hardwoods. Sprayed hardwoods not only are dead and ugly but also represent a terrific waste of natural resources . . . Let us not allow the very agency which is supposed to preserve it—the National Forest Service—to destroy it [sic] in some misguided attempt to turn parts of it into the relatively sterile pinelands so common to the South.[42]

The ban, however, was not permanent and had no impact on private citizens.[43] The hipbillies, led in part by the NCWA and CEASE, continued to fight federal use of the herbicide, not content with the limited ban on using 2,4,5T in the National Forest.[44] The August 1975 issue of *LION* noted the difficulty of the fight, as the "burden of proof [as to harm] rests on the public, not on the manufacturers or users of the hormone herbicide 2,4,5 T."[45] Joel Davidson, detailing his long attempts to communicate with the Forest Service, noted that their responses argued the "chemical was safe to use"—despite having no completed studies to offer as proof, and that they planned on spraying more public land that year.[46] The Forest Service was bolstered, no doubt, by the fledgling Environmental Protection Agency's (EPA) sluggishness to address herbicide use anywhere, much less the National Forest.[47] Confronted with this, and with David Glenn's ouster from *Arkansas Democrat*, Davidson was less than optimistic about the chances of true success, arguing this meant "the ordinary citizen is helpless to stop the government which he is supposed to control. It means that the Ozarks are not immune to the exploitative rape resulting from shortsided [*sic*] so-called 'economics.'"[48]

Faced with such a problem, the readers of *LION* wrote in and offered camaraderie through stories of illness, land spoilage, and advice related to the continued use of 2,4,5T. Robbie Pardue, author of a book on homebirth popular in the back to the land community, provided advice on approaching neighbors who used the herbicide. Pardue recommended requesting those spraying chemicals near vegetable fields and gardens to stop but admitted this was at best wishful thinking as neighborly notifications required nothing of the herbicide user. Indeed, Pardue noted that despite the growing anecdotal evidence of the negative impacts that 2,4-D had on the Ozarks, EPA researchers charged with understanding the problem took few samples from the region to inform their recommendations for the chemical's continued use.[49] Pardue's letters, then, had a defeated air about them.[50]

As the back to the land community continued the struggle against herbicides, they dealt with the fallout of other forest management battles occurring throughout the upland South.[51] While the USFS in the Ozarks was challenged on herbicide use in its forest management, in Appalachia they utilized clear-cutting—something that residents were upset about. Just as in the Arkansas uplands, legal challenges in the Carolinas forced the Forest Service to reevaluate its processes.[52] No matter the technique to achieve it, across the South as the USFS argued for the development of single-aged forest tracts, local communities banded together against the mass application of herbicides and clear-cutting and advocated for a return to an older style of forestry that prioritized multi-aged timber stands and more community input. The ensuing legal battles spilled into forestry debates across the region, with the clear-cutting debate reaching Arkansas in 1976 as the herbicide battle was ramping up. That March, the *Northwest Arkansas Times* ran a short piece discussing how the state's timber industry was concerned about the impact of new clear-cutting legislation. William F. Chestnut, executive director of the Arkansas Forestry Association, worried that if the standards discussed in the 1897 Organic Act were applied across the region, Arkansas timber companies would lose over $700,000 in revenue.[53] Chestnut's concerns, though, were met with a large amount of skepticism from area critics who doubted that he and the state's timber industry were candid about the impact of these regulations, much like other groups who predicted dire consequences with little real impact.[54]

Court battles were not the only way the hipbillies and locals worked to ban the use of 2,4D. At the start of 1976, Jerry Ashworth wrote to *LION* about the NCWA efforts to "get this whole environmental mess straightened" by tackling the 2,4,5T fight.[55] Ashworth and the NCWA were not alone; in Madison County, CEASE was up and running, and it advocated a county-wide ban on the use of 2,4D and similar substances in the air, on land, and in water.[56] CEASE was born a few years earlier in 1974 after a letter-writing campaign was organized by the Sierra Club and the Women's Center Committee on the Environment in Fayetteville for the cessation of aerial spraying of 2,4D. The first CEASE meeting in June 1974 drew twenty to twenty-five people, remembered Gary Turner, one of the chief organizers of the group.[57] As a result of their efforts, 882 Madison County residents signed a petition to challenge the use of 2,4,5T, though there was clear opposition to the idea of a ban on herbicides.[58] In Turner's opinion, those who argued for the continued use of 2,4D did so from an economic standpoint. Farmers—especially those with larger and growing farms—sent letters to the editor that "pointed out that using the herbicides to clear land (for cattle pasture, for instance) is several times more economical than brushhogging the acreage."[59]

The effort to ban the chemicals at the ballot box was ultimately unsuccessful, though it continued mobilizing back to the landers against the rapid growth increase in chemical use throughout the Ozarks. Not long after this, hipbillies in Newton and Stone Counties engaged in a strong door-to-door campaign aimed at convincing locals and in-migrants alike to refrain from using the herbicides. "T" noted that "Many people in Madison County/Newton County stopped using agen orange [sic] because they were educated—or told some facts—by the hippie community, who went around and said, 'This stuff is really nasty shit, and it's very harmful.'" Although an effort to ban the use of 2,4,5T throughout Madison County failed, "T" recalled, "A lot of people stopped using it. So I'd call that a social change that had a lot to do with the hippie folks."[60] In Stone County, a resolution was proposed to gauge public opinion and potentially pave the way for county regu-lations decrying 2,4,D.[61] In 1976, though, the anti-2,4D group lost the opinion ballot by a scant sixty votes out of 3,174 cast.[62]

By 1978, while legislative victories were in short supply, things were looking up for the NCWA and its allies, at least at the community level. After the initial fight in 1975, the group held fundraiser after fundraiser and continued attempting to convince Ozarkers, native and imported, of the dangers of the USFS herbicide program. During that same time, the Environmental Protection Agency declared 2,4D "to be a potential haz-ard that may cause cancer and birth defects," a declaration that proved to be indicative of a victory of sorts.[63] The Associated Press reported on November 21, 1978, that the USFS in the Ozarks announced "it had no plans to resume using 2,4,5T and Silvex," as it had developed a new forest management plan that did not rely on these chemicals.[64] William Haring, a lawyer with the Sierra Club, noted that this was a major victory for environmentalists, seeing as the government had never before "conceded an intention to be bound by law" and not use such substances.[65] This victory was made even sweeter, Haring argued, by the fact that this was the first time a challenge to federal herbicide use had been settled by the Forest Service in favor of environmentalists.[66]

This was no doubt a blow to the corporations who produced the herbicides, as was the waning support for the use of 2,4D by state legis-lators. In 1976 and 1977, Grant County State Senator Harold King and Representative Bill Clark of Sheridan pushed for and won approval to have the usage and impact of 2,4D in the state studied by politicians in Little Rock. Where before the struggle had been cast as something "inspired by 'outsiders' and 'hippies,'" such sponsorship lent the efforts to ban the herbicides greater legitimacy.[67] Tom Foti with the Arkansas Ecology Center wryly commented that the "legislature could ignore some hippies up in the hills, but they can't ignore good citizens down in Grant County. They have credibility. They are *real* Arkansans."[68] King and Clark argued that given the US military's decision to stop the herbicide application in Vietnam, as well as their restricted use throughout America, that it only made sense to ask some deeper questions.[69] Though they acknowledged that the substances in question were widely used by farmers and foresters across the nation, many of whom argued they were "a vital tool," King in particular felt he needed to respond to concerns his constituency was voicing.[70]

The inquiry highlighted that there had not been any definitive proof from scientists that usage of the herbicides was harmful to human health when "used with reasonable caution," something that Dr. C. A. Goring, a Dow Chemical scientist, noted. Goring was part of a "parade of experts who say the herbicide is entirely safe" that focused on "nip[ping] in the bud the Arkansas legislature's threatening concern."[71] Goring's testimony, during which he "scoffed" at allegations of health problems related to 2,4D usage, was buttressed by economic arguments from farmers and forestry officials across the state, in particular Andrew Whisenhunt, a rice grower who argued that banning the chemical would result in a personal loss close to $100,000 a year. Forestry Association official Bill Harbour claimed that outlawing the chemicals in the national forest would cost the national timber industry $1 billion annually ($404 million for weed control and $606 million in lost yield).[72]

Despite the legislature's study and the testimonies in favor of the continued use of herbicides, the Forest Service opted to cease using them in the new forest management plans of 1979. At the same time, Judge Eisele put in place a consent decree to "ban the use of the herbicides 2,4,5T and Silvex in the Ozark-St. Francis National Forests for the next ten years," reflecting the settlement reached between environmentalists and the USFS.[73] This was not permanent—in the future, after a "long environmental review," the judge noted that usage of the herbicides might resume if they had negligible impact on human well-being.[74] It seemed, then, the use of 2,4D and its companion products was over in the Ozark and St. Francis National Forest.[75]

The fight surrounding 2,4D in the Ozarks, as well as hipbilly efforts to sustain organic agriculture practices in the region add to the nuanced story of environmental activism in the South during the 1960s and 1970s. Indeed, both organic agriculture and the antiherbicide campaigns illustrate how the efforts of the back to the land community in the Ozarks, and nationally, had a vision of environmental stewardship that offered an alternative to the accepted way of doing things. While much has been made of the impact of the 1960's socio-cultural rebellion on the development of a "modern" American wilderness policy, it should be noted that although the hipbillies agreed with much of this, they also advocated a land-use structure closely aligned with agrarian movements in US history. In so doing, they advocated the preservation of working landscapes, an idea at times at odds with the prevailing understanding of the wilderness ethic espoused in legislation like the 1964 Wilderness Act.[76] Such a stance provides nuance to what William Cronon has described as the American wilderness ethos; namely, the idea that wilderness is a "cultural invention" that takes "flight from history."[77]

Cronon and other scholars are correct to point out that the creation of a wilderness spirituality in American life from the mid-nineteenth century onwards laid the foundation for twentieth-century debates about wilderness and the environment. That being said, a more thorough integration of the back to the land movement into the narrative of environmentalism in the nation provides a corrective to the views described (and critiqued) by Cronon. Though the counterculture did indeed see wild places, even the Ozarks, as "the original garden . . . a place outside of time, from which human beings had to be ejected," the deep revolution offered a revision to this idea. As self-proclaimed heirs to the agrarian ideal, the back to the land community saw the need for portions of the land to remain in use as working farms.[78] Thus, the idea of wilderness—parks, forests, rivers—could only exist in juxtaposition to working land; indeed, increasingly the Ozarks back-to-the-land movement advocated a land ethic rooted in the notion that only those who *worked* the land understood the deepest ascetic and cultural value of wild places. On one hand, the counterculture writ large held fast to the idea that rural and wild places represented some measure of escape from the responsibilities of the modern world; on the other hand, however, hipbillies, inspired in part by authors like Aldo Leopold and Wendell Berry, argued that the appreciation of wild spaces only made sense in the context of working land no longer in disrepair.[79]

Undeniably, this approach helped Ozark hipbillies define themselves. The back to the land community quietly prided itself on being, as the group outside Pettigrew noted, "real" hippies as opposed to "down low" hippies.[80] The distinction made between the two was not merely related to competing philosophies of work and play, but also in understanding the varying ways the land impacted one's life. One BTL in Washington County noted, "very quickly I discovered there was a huge difference between city hippies and country hippies. The ones in the country were almost always on a whole other level, actively living in a positive way, whereas the ones in town were fringe dwellers, very cynical and big dopers."[81] That "whole other level" perhaps was the impact of the deep revolution taking root and shifting the BTLs toward creating the new community they hoped to see emerge from the wasteland of modern life.

Here the role of certain drugs is useful in understanding their perspective. Back to the landers who engaged in limited use of LSD noted that, as their perceptions of the world shifted, they felt they had no choice but to engage in working *on* and *with* the land.[82] Those in the counterculture who opted to use higher amounts of LSD and at greater frequencies became associated with the "down low" hippies, as they were unable or unwilling to engage in the hard work required of living out the deep revolution. Though the back to the land community came to the agrarian lifestyle via a far different route than that of native Ozark farmers, they arrived at the same basic assumptions about how to incorporate wild and working spaces into the creation of their own "new" Ozarks at the end of the 1970s. The hard beauty of the Ozarks and its sparse soil, experienced via the combination of psychedelics and work, mandated an approach toward the natural world that aligned with an older agrarian model.

For the back to the land community, then, agricultural work—however grand or modest—provided an intimacy of knowledge and emotion that inspired action against environmental degradation, such as the protests against herbicides.[83] Therein lies the crux of the back-to-the-land contribution to the environmental movement, in the Ozarks at least: while they believed with a Muir-like awe in the church of nature, they also argued through a living agrarianism that wild spaces needed to be put into a particular interpretive context, one defined by agrarian ideals. That is to say, for the hipbillies, agricultural work provided the context by which wilderness could be known at an intimate level. Indeed, the back to the landers built friendships with the land akin to those seen in old-order Amish communities and traditional Ozark communities. Only such a nuanced familiarity brought about the work of the deep revolution as it applied to the natural world. To a degree, the same sort of impetus can be seen in Newfont's discussion of how residents of the Blue Ridge Mountains dealt with the forest commons. The act of working in and near the forest gave rise to some of the strongest efforts to preserve and use the resource with stewardship in mind.[84] In an agrarian context, humanity, instead of being outside nature and dropping in for quick experiences, was very much in membership with it thanks to cyclical acts such as birth, plowing, and harvesting.[85] This perspective provided a corrective to the problem of bourgeois environmentalism— namely, that accessing the "wilderness" was no longer bound to a social class that possessed little practice in understanding the natural world. Despite the fact that the back to the land community was undoubtedly a product of the stagnating American middle class, it opted to approach environmentalism from the perspective of agrarian people by incorporating agriculture into the conversation. If midcentury environmentalism entailed caring about a natural place far from where you lived, setting up farms provided a stronger incentive for environmental stewardship. The work of a homesteader doubly recentered one's focus on nature thanks to the hard—and at times defeating—work in and with the land. Where critics of the wilderness ethos worried about the creation of a "dismissive" or "contemptuous" attitude about local and "humble" places, the hipbillies showed that the intimacy of agrarian life provided a corrective, and indeed, might be the only way forward.[86] Only by inhabiting a working landscape could the preservation of wild spaces make sense; the pairing of the two provided incentives for land preservation as well as for good farming, thereby creating multiple shades of natural space that ranged from wild to urban.[87]

In such a spirit, it is no surprise that the back to the land community played an outsized role in the evolution of the bioregionalism movement in the Ozarks. The idea of bioregionalism had emerged in the early 1970s as "both a philosophy of life and a social movement" based on the idea that human community exists in a "unique region definable by natural (rather than political) boundaries with a geographic, climatic, hydrological, and ecological character capable of supporting unique human and nonhuman living communities."[88] The national bioregional movement, led in part by Peter Berg, a cofounder of the Diggers, began as an outgrowth of the counterculture's evolving conceptions of nature and human action in a place. Berg began refining the idea of bioregionalism after he met Raymond Dasmann, an ecologist, at the 1972 United Nations Conference on the Human Environment.[89] By 1973 Berg and his partner Judy Goldhaft founded Planet Drum, an organization dedicated to spreading the ideas of bioregionalism, inspiring groups across the country to organize.

Such an idea was pivotal in the foundation of the "official" bioregional group for the Arkansas and Missouri Ozarks, the Ozarks Area Community Congress (OACC). Though it did not form until 1980, various groups throughout the region, like the Newton County Wildlife Association, operated in a manner that matched Berg's vision for a bioregional movement for several years. The idea of bioregionalism coalesced more formally in the region in 1979, thanks in large part to the work of "G" and others.[90] "G," alongside a crew of back to the landers that hailed from Michigan, arrived in the Missouri Ozarks in the spring of 1971 after having scouted the area the previous year.[91] Thanks to the enduring popular imagery of the Ozarks—Li'l Abner in particular—they had been introduced to the region before they visited, and their scouting trip in 1970 only served to convince them of the beauty and potential bounty of the area. After all, like many hipbillies noted, the Ozarks had a respectable growing season and land was cheap; the group purchased forty acres of land in Howell County, Missouri, for $4,000.[92]

By 1974 "G" had begun incorporating a bioregional perspective into his life in the Ozarks. This came about because he, like other hipbillies, faced the difficulties of farming in a place with scant topsoil, and in part because his understanding of ecosystems had evolved, "G" began developing a sustained criticism of the "normal economy" and advocated for the creation of an "authentic life" that followed the "natural cycles of the world."[93] From this emerged what he termed a "counter analysis of society" that employed an "ecocentric" system apart from the broad tenets of environmentalism.[94] Citing authors Gary Snyder (who provided what he termed the "most significant evolution of human thought" yet encountered) and EF Schumacher, "G" formulated what he called a "unified field theory for the planet."[95]

This theory began with a simple premise: the Ozarks was its own unique biological and cultural nation. As such, it should be dealt with according to *ecological* laws and norms, as opposed to political or economic laws.[96] "G" was not alone in thinking this. In late 1975 and early 1976, he was joined by ten or twelve folks at an early meeting of what would become OACC outside of Cabool, Missouri. There, the group tossed around ideas for what kind of imagery might capture the public's attention and convince them to reconceive how they approached ecological issues in the Ozarks. They arrived at the image of an oak—a ubiquitous tree throughout the region that signified strength and resiliency in difficult ecological conditions.[97] By 1977 the group had organized in earnest, and in 1979 preparations were made for the inaugural OACC meeting the following year. In the interim, the women involved with the nascent Ozarks bioregional movement formed "Mother OACC" which, as Barbara Harmony of Eureka Springs noted, was an effort to ensure that OACC did not go the way of so many other counterculture groups—namely, that it did not inadvertently maintain mainstream cultural dynamics.[98]

The 1980 meeting convened of all the "eco holo-fractals," as "G" termed them, that is, the various human components that made up the Ozark bioregion: midwives, farmers, energy experts, land-trust representatives, and more.[99] Central to OACC was the idea of an "Ozark Free State," an "Ozark ecological nation" that brought "all good and ethical things together, and run [*sic*] on solar energy, appropriate technology, and co-operative economics, while defending the Ozarks' ecological integrity."[100] As Brian Campbell has noted, these ideals were exemplified by the site of the OACC gathering at New Life Farm in Drury, just west of West Plains.[101] The 240-acre New Life Farm was established in 1972 by one of the members of the Ozark bioregional movement.[102] The founder had degrees in engineering and business and tried to apply alternative energy and appropriate technological solutions to common farm problems.[103] The next four years saw OACC engaged in the tough and "ambitious" work of creating resolutions and guiding principles for interacting with the natural world. Such efforts provided the model for the first North American bioregional congress in 1984, attended by some two hundred people in Excelsior Springs, Missouri.[104] All of this served to establish the Ozarks as a crucial hub in the bioregional movement, which remains true today.[105]

Bioregional efforts via OACC were not the only way hipbillies worked to foster this combination of working and wild spaces. Building in part on the foundation left behind by the Ozark Institute as well as OACC and New Life Farm, many small-scale organic growers in the mid 1980s searched for a new way to work together and promote their efforts—especially as farmers markets and Community Supported Agriculture movements had yet to coalesce in the area. Formally established in 1980, the Ozark Organic Growers Association (OOGA) was a collection of friends and farmers who had partnered as early as 1979 to market local produce to area grocers and individual consumers. Initially focused on getting bulk prices for organic nursery stock and fertilizers, it grew in size and scope, ultimately reaching across three states with over 250 members involved. The association's goal, in part, was to define growing standards for fruits and vegetables in the Ozarks, setting quality benchmarks that allowed producers to use when marketing their products, making them competitive when selling goods to the first two Whole Foods stores in Austin and Dallas.[106] In fact, in the late 1980s, OOGA spoke out against the use of chicken litter as an "organic" fertilizer for fields, though they were overruled by the Arkansas State Plant Board.[107] These efforts by groups like OOGA helped, as one paper put it, hipbillies shed the "hippie image" in parts of the Ozarks. Organic growing standards, as defined by OOGA over the course of its existence, required a complex agrarian practice of its members that included detailed crop records outlining every system input, annual soil samples, crop rotation schemes, and more.[108] OOGA was also realistic in its goals, aware that this style of agriculture "might not be feasible for everybody," bound as it was to the cycles of land and community.[109]

Though the group did not last beyond the mid-1990s, they were successful in attracting enough national attention to win development grants, bring in nationally recognized speakers on organic agriculture, and help lay some of the foundation for groups like the Northwest Arkansas Farmers' Market Alliance.[110] For example, today in the Ozarks several initiatives exist to help with continuing education for organic and organic-preferred farmers in the area. Such efforts build, in part, on the legacy of OOGA's "New Directions in Agriculture for the Ozarks" conference in Harrison in the fall of 1986.[111] The conference featured several nationally respected organic growers who spoke about various ways "sustainable, ecologically sound techniques of farming" might continue or evolve in the Arkansas and Missouri uplands, all in keeping with the hipbillies' dreams of deep revolution.[112]

While none of these individual efforts were as successful as the BTLs hoped, combined, they created a lasting impact on the Arkansas uplands. Indeed, such piecemeal success was the hallmark of the deep revolution put in motion by people disillusioned with fast, simplistic political change. The hipbillies may not have conquered the ASPB and forced the region's farmers and lawn enthusiasts—or even the USFS—to abandon the use of herbicides, but they succeeded in causing enough of a stir that they won modest changes in how the Forest Service, at least, approached their management of the nation's timber. In the same vein, groups like OACC and OOGA pushed for greater citizen awareness about the impact of chemical-based agriculture on the region, a battle OACC and others, like the NCWA, still wage today. After all, a revolution so intimately bound to the land could only progress at nature's pace. Building a membership, for the hipbillies, worked like planting trees: the full measure of the work can only be measured years later.

CHAPTER 6

——

Hipbillies Triumphant

For lack of better terms, we came and we invaded and sought to alter (it).

—"H"

THE BACK TO THE LAND movement made large claims for itself—indeed, it sought nothing less than the restructuring of American life. With claims so large, evaluating the impact of the back to the land-movement has often veered into a simplistic dismissal of youthful exuberance and hedonism. While such interpretations are understandable, they avoid any detailed discussion of the group's and the counterculture's impact on Ozark and American life. The deep revolution's goals, though, should be measured in decades and not immediate impact, as it argued from the start. The flashy, fast-paced political revolutions had not gained all they promised. This prompted the resurgence of self-sufficiency ideologies and prompted this generation of revolutionaries to move toward the slower, deep revolution. It was an effort that required rediscovering everything that was once common knowledge: how to grow food, build homes, give birth. What was sought, then, was a rehabilitation of American culture—one that began in the dirt and grew over time like the forest that slowly reclaims and heals a ruined field. Judging a revolution by its parts is tricky, but a few components of the back to the land movement allow for a partial assessment of the group on its own terms. Birth, gender, and child-rearing, taken together with the deep revolution's discussion of an agrarian environmentalism, provide a lens through which the success—and failure—of the revolution might be evaluated. For the time being, though, a final judgement on the hipbillies and their revolution is impossible: it is history still in the making.

Understanding this might be best started by thinking about gender and birth. Wendy Neidhardt in Stone County highlighted the difficulties faced by a generation who advocated both equality and homesteading. While "second wave" feminism had gained a great deal of ground during the 1960s, thanks to the success of figures like Betty Freidan (*The Feminine Mystique*, 1963) and the inclusion of the word *sex* in the 1964 Civil Rights Act, much work was still needed to ensure equality for women. This was no less true in the counterculture than in suburbia. In 1974 Wendy wrote to a friend about some of these issues, asking for relationship advice. Wondering about how to balance the new definition of womanhood with the pleasure of being "a woman (children, house, etc.)," Wendy noted that it was "difficult to accept a secondary role, which nevertheless occurs quite naturally, especially when you have children" and that Richard, her husband, was a bit of a chauvinist pig, "not intentionally, but unconsciously," something that was hard to deal with.[1] She then quickly added that in the Ozarks it was normal "that a man and a woman stuck off in the woods alone together naturally will share all burdens, especially when all labor is hand done + time consuming . . . The modern day [sic] equivalent is women working at the shirt factory in order to keep the men at home working on the farm."[2] She noted that there were exceptions to this, even her own life. Richard, her husband, was often gone six days a week on a construction crew while trying to keep up with the daily chores of milking and splitting wood as well as the weekend work of building the homestead. "Meanwhile, however, I am equally overloaded" with children, gardening, laundry, and more.[3] Although there is a "separate, but equal" status between male and female in country life, this was difficult to stomach "when for years in school and at home, we women nowadays are trained to think of ourselves as men—have careers, etc. But no one says *how* it can be possible to raise a happy family + work, too . . ."[4]

This Ozark realization reflected the larger counterculture's effort to work out this problem. Peter Coyote, author of *Sleeping Where I Fall* and a founding member of the San Francisco Diggers, was part of a relatively short-lived back to the land effort, the Turkey Ridge Commune.[5] Describing the hard work of the self-sufficient group, Coyote quoted Joanna, a long-time member of the Digger tribe, on gender balance at the time:

> "Even though the women may have embraced and enjoyed their tasks, they were not tasks that were coveted." She is right, of course. All of our "appreciation" of the women and their work did not extend to valuing the work as dearly as our own. With hindsight, our division of labor seems archaic, particularly for a visionary community. The Digger scene was quite conventional in terms of men's and women's roles . . . Sam [Coyote's partner at the time] remembers very clearly the creak of my inner wheels adjusting the first time I had to cover the house while the others went to the fields: "So Coyote finally gets his day in the kitchen, and as we're pulling out, he comes running out of the house going 'Hey, look, you can't leave all the *kids* here. I've gotta *cook*!' The women all looked at each other and said, 'Right!'"[6]

This "chastening experience," as Coyote termed it, was ultimately still a problem.[7] In many ways, despite the gains of the 1960s and 1970s, it seemed citizenship for women in the counterculture and beyond was, at least indirectly, predicated upon motherhood and all that came with it. The back to the land movement perpetuated the national gender binary, often unintentionally, while at the same time stating all should be equal in the deep revolution. Indeed, this was what Lucy in Stone County and others addressed in their comments, namely that 1970s America—hipbilly or square—was still "a culture where motherhood [was] a prerequisite for women to seek full citizenship or a measure of power" and as such "[was] not a culture that regard[ed] women as fully human."[8]

Limiting life to traditionally defined modes of gender production on homesteads and communes was not taken lightly by back to the land women. While some women were perhaps less bothered by the contradictions, or less inclined to push back against them, others readily stood in the gap. Brenda Mooscy moved to the Ozarks from Austin, Texas, in 1971, and joined a commune near Red Star, Madison County. In some respects, her experience on the land was fairly typical—though she, and others in the group, had been exposed to the literature surrounding the movement, such as Alicia Bay Laurel's *Living on the Earth*, Moosey described that nevertheless they "brought city consciousness with them:" the commune owned some 260 acres but they had set up a makeshift camp on the top of the mountain, crammed together and far away from the nearest spring.[9]

The camp, especially the location away from the spring, became a point of contention for Brenda and the other women. Though both genders were there to go back to the land, it quickly became apparent that the hard work of community building was done by the women; the men on the commune hung out, drank beer, smoked weed, and planned. The women washed the clothes and dishes, hauled water—"'cause of course we set the cook tent far away from the spring"—cooked, gardened, watched the kids, "and we fucked the guys in the evening, and they sat out there and smoked pot and drank green beer and planned. Not a damned thing got built."[10]

The planning by the commune's menfolk, according to Brenda, centered on sourcing more beer—often at the expense of the women's well-being. To illustrate this, Moosey described how after a few weeks of living on red beans and rice, a big grocery run was planned to take advantage of a recent paycheck one of the men had received. He and the other guys went into Huntsville, where it was assumed they would purchase the supplies Brenda and the other women expected. In particular, they hoped the men would bring back fruit, vegetables, and other staples needed for the well-being of three pregnant women on the mountain. Instead, when the men returned from the store, they had brought back "twenty-seven dollars-worth of booze."[11] Recurring actions like this prompted Brenda, despite the general rules of the commune, to keep her money rather than give it to the men. Indeed, her refusal to hand over her money and to not accept the general order of things on the commune was not the only challenge to male governance in the camp. She recounted that another woman, Shirley, was also less than pleased with the status quo. Shirley's boyfriend, Reggie, returned from fishing one day and handed his catch to Shirley. He then commanded, "Here, cook these fish!" Shirley looked at Reggie with a surprised expression and mentioned something about how she might cook them. Reggie cut her off and yelled about how he wanted it done, at which point Shirley beat him about the head while the rest of the women cheered.[12]

Actions like Brenda's and Shirley's were not unique to the Ozarks, nor were they isolated to communes and homesteads. Women throughout the back to the land movement actively attempted to shift the conversation toward building the world they wished to see. *Communities*, a journal founded in 1972, was devoted to life on communes and gave considerable space to gender equality.[13] Contributor Kate MeWhinney's article, "Women and Communal Societies," jumped straight into the deep end: "We've noticed that in many contemporary communes the worst sex roles of society are often perpetuated. To provide a meaningful alternative to society's dominant institutions and to be successful in human terms, intentional communities must step out of the sexist framework."[14] Other commentators, following on MeWhinney's observations, offered advice on how to break the age-old gender structures. Dianna MacLeod and Rachel Bedard, noting that most women who moved back to the land wanted to "leave sex roles and other cultural conditioning behind," offered advice on how to recognize and deal with these structures and see "feminism as a priority life-style and political issue."[15]

In recognition of the quest to see feminism implemented on the farm, publications emerged that addressed the needs of women, both lesbian and straight, going back to the land. Chief among them was *Country Women* (*CW*), a California publication that began as a magazine and became a book (both of which made it to the Ozarks thanks to subscribers and to articles published in them). The journal began in 1973 as an extension of the "vision and the voice of a group of country women who had come together to explore 'consciousness raising.'"[16] Like the other guerilla presses established by the back to the land movement, *CW* and its companion publications focused on connecting groups—specifically women—across California and the country partaking in the back to the land movement. The magazine and the book were, in the spirit of the *Whole Earth Catalog*, to be an "encouragement and a tool," and this desire colored the language of the publication.[17] As they compiled story after story from across the nation, the editors of the magazine decided to utilize a collective "I" to represent the "single country woman, and all women" as their "experiences in consciousness raising validated this, for much of what [they] learned was personal/collective, unique/universal."[18] As such, Jeanne Tetrault and Sherry Thomas, the driving team behind *CW*, argued in the book's introduction something that women like Brenda Moosey and others in the Ozarks noted time and again; namely, that:

> In the country, there is room for a women's renaissance. The space and time is there for a total redefinition of ourselves, our relation to the earth, our relation to each other. This has become very clear . . . We have the skills, the enthusiasm, the resources to build our dwellings, raise our food, take care of our most basic needs and real needs. This self-reliance fosters an incredible strength.[19]

Country Women did not simply serve the coastal counterculture; it allowed for voices from periphery areas like the Ozarks to be heard. Very simply, the magazine offered a classified system for groups to participate in if they wanted property or people to join them on the land. Lynne Smith, outside Pea Ridge, and Diana Rivers from the Sassafras group near Ponca, both wrote in looking for women to come and join their respective homesteads—and the two reflect the different scales of the back to the land movement in the Ozarks. Smith had a small, five-acre homestead and sold produce and crafts at weekend markets. Rivers and the group at Sassafras, by contrast, had embarked on dividing 520 acres in Newton County into private, wild, and community land in an effort to create a more holistic life.[20]

Women in the hipbilly community, as they built the feminist revolution on the land, also worked to reassert control over their own bodies—particularly their reproductive rights. While much has been made of the sexual revolution, created in many ways thanks to the pill, women in the counterculture revolted against the medical establishment's practices for pregnancy and childbirth. Birthing at home, once the norm throughout America, had been largely abandoned as the medical establishment professionalized its technocratic method during the early decades of the twentieth century. By the 1960s, the use of midwives and home birthing was seen as a practice only poor and remote communities maintained.[21]

The Arkansas Ozarks, despite the region's rurality and economic woes, were no exception to this trend. Though less so in the Ozarks, as trained doctors across the country became common, midwives were cast as poorly prepared competition for a steady business.[22] The counterculture, though, rejected the medical establishment as cold and part of the war machine that spawned Vietnam and 2,4-D. As a result, it attempted to re-appropriate traditional birthing practices to allow a greater expression of women's rights. American women, thanks to the ready availability of birth control, could manage not just when they became pregnant, but also the manner in which they gave birth— revolutionary in an era when women gave birth in a hospital with little knowledge as to what was going on around them during this seminal moment in their lives.[23] Thus, while chemistry was increasingly used to allow women to control their bodies, there was also a resurgence of natural methods as well. In February of 1976, *LION* offered a brief discussion of several books on the topic. For instance, *The Natural Birth Control Book* by Art Rosenblum and Leah Jackson, published by the Aquarian Research Foundation, gave "complete information on combining the astrological and ovulation methods of contraception for maximum protection. You can figure your own astrological status with the charts included which can save the astrologer's fee." There were also selections from more mainstream presses, like Bantam Books' *Natural Birth Control* by Shelia Ostrander and Lynn Schroeder, which professed to give scientific backing to the astrological method, noting most significantly that it should be paired with something else.[24]

Indeed, for Steve and Ina May Gaskin, the main leaders of The Farm in Tennessee, reclaiming womanhood (and humanity) was the point.[25] At The Farm, birth was (and is) a spiritual and revolutionary act, and the Gaskins even argued it was a sacrament akin to the Eucharist. And, in true hipbilly fashion, if it was spiritual, it was revolutionary because "it is our basic belief that the sacrament of birth belongs to the people and that it should not be usurped by a profit-oriented hospital system."[26] Instead of a commodity, birth was about "life force. It's the same thing you deal with at death. It's there for everybody to feel and see," said "L."[27] Not only was birth something that capitalism should be removed from, but for the Gaskins and other members of The Farm (and the counterculture writ large), birth symbolized the beginning of the enumerated rights of the constitution.[28] Indeed, it went beyond the constitution in some cases, as young people giving birth used the act as a way to question the right of the government to certify or make a legal entity out of sex or the product of a sexual act.[29] In the Ozarks, at least, homebirth and midwifery were often practiced by families who wanted few records given over to a government bent on warfare. Indeed, many people "didn't want to have a social security number; they didn't want to have a birth certificate or anything like that . . . There is a whole counterculture of people that don't want to pay taxes, don't want to the support the system."[30] Rejecting the certification of marriage and of birth meant that the back to the land movement rejected a society that required the registration of everything—in their minds, for war and consumption.[31]

Aside from its political nature, natural birth was a rite of passage, a way to reassert traditional community-building norms as the back-to-the-land movement lived out the revolution. Barbara Katz Rothman, perhaps the leading scholar of midwifery practice and culture in the United States, notes, "Home birth resonated with 'traditional' values too, not just feminists and hippies. Amish communities have been big supporters of midwifery, and there's a whole collection of homes-school, Christian traditionalists."[32] This helps to underscore yet another way the land communities integrated with the cultural norms of the Arkansas uplands. Birth was also freeing, as "sharing the experience of creating life is viewed as an essential part of life itself. It becomes a liberating ritual. A natural birth in the home is the antithesis of production-line maternity wards where the mother is unconscious and the infant is separated immediately."[33] For Rothman and the back to the landers, birth at home became part of the rejection of a mindless, con-sumerist world and about the empowerment of a thoughtful, careful existence.[34] Women, through the act of natural birth, went through a "rite of passage—something for which you could gather up your cour-age with the help of your friends and contemporaries" and move into a new phase of life naturally and organically, as opposed to the mechanis-tic and sterile vision of the beginning of life offered by a hospital.[35] This would, hopefully, help the newly emerged child begin life in a way that allowed for greater connection to humanity and the natural world.[36]

Though many who opted for homebirth did so with the help of a midwife or nurse, the back to the land community sought to compile a sufficient amount of information to help those who wanted to go for it on their own. Chief among this effort was the visit in 1976 by mid-wives from The Farm. "K," an Ozark BTL, remembered the visit as the moment when "a lot of us learned about home birthing and that whole lifestyle, the language, the food, the ways of caring for each other [and] that kind of community from those Farm midwives."[37] While many were already giving birth at home, "K" believed that The Farm women helped establish a safe and efficient system for giving birth, even sharing the early versions of what became *Spiritual Midwifery*, now the go-to book for home birth.[38]

The Farm midwives were not the only aid pregnant hipbillies received, though. *LION*, throughout its run under the Davidsons, advertised various sources of information on birth, including self-published guides like the one put together by Robbie and Michael Pardue of Mountain View entitled *Home Childbirth: The Miracle of Sharing*, a "work of love which is full of information, ideas, thoughts and feelings."[39] Placing such an ad—the book was for sale for three dollars—in *LION* was wise, as there was a general stream of letters coming in looking for information like this or connections to midwives in the area. Indeed, in the same issue, Pat Lurowski wrote in from Moody, Missouri, seeking a midwife to assist with the birth of her baby, as well as information about birth in general.[40]

Such information was quick in coming. In the next issue, Donna Hudson, an expectant mother in Orlando, Florida, wrote to *LION* about basic concerns in homebirth, beginning with notes as to good schools for midwives as well as information on a *Mother Earth News* reprint about preparing for childbirth.[41] After briefly discussing planning for a natural birth in the hospital, Hudson outlined how readers could prepare for a home birth. Proper prenatal care was essential, as were clear medical test results. When seeing a doctor for prenatal visits, Hudson encouraged parents to ask lots of questions—and even float the idea of having the baby at home past the doctor, even though "999 doctors out of 1,000 will tell you it's a terrible idea. Do not, under any circumstances, press the matter or try to defend the idea."[42] One should also be stealthy when preparing the home, she cautioned, lest neighbors become suspicious. She then went on to outline the basic concerns that might arise as well as advice on how to deal with them. In the end, Hudson simply stated, "Be sure that if you really are serious about having your baby at home that you have your proper prenatal care and learn the breathing exercises for labor. If you cannot find a midwife and still want to go thru with it, study the obstetric nursing book till you know every move, every detail, and every possible complication by heart. If you are going to do it, by all means do it right."[43]

Midwives in the traditional sense, that is, women, were not the only game in town. The back to the land community in the Ozarks also boasted one male midwife. In the mid-1970s, Joe Baldwin and his girlfriend lived in Newton County. Brandt's girlfriend had trained as a midwife and visited The Farm in Tennessee, and along the way Brandt picked up training as well. For him, it was less about delivering babies—though he was qualified to do so; rather, it was about being there to support the fathers during the birth process.[44] The systems that surrounded childbirth during the 1940s and 1950s had, alongside removing control from women, removed men from the system as well, divorcing them from their particular rite of passage. Just as giving birth was one of the ultimate rites of passage for mothers, the same was true for fathers, and there were only remnants of a cultural support system remaining. Brandt wanted to help alleviate this, making it easier for men to take part in the process. This aside, it was also helpful to have more hands in the region—Joe recalled that at the time, 1976, Newton County had no birth facilities to speak of, and given changes in how the state dealt with rural communities, he and his girlfriend, like others in the back-to-the-land community, served to fill a gap in the community—native and hipbilly alike.[45]

For those who planned to birth on the land, the right techniques or midwives were not always the issue. In the 1970s, homebirth and midwifery existed in a nebulous legal terrain in Arkansas. To help alleviate those concerns, "AD" wrote in to *LION* in March 1975, stating that "midwifery is legal in Arkansas in those counties with medical support."[46] "AD" went on to detail where medical and prenatal services were located in Newton County and offered to help put together a class with a local doctor in Jasper to prepare hipbillies for birthing in the back country.[47] "AD" was only partly correct. Indeed, despite a long-documented history of midwifery in Arkansas up through the 1950s (with a particularly powerful impact in the African-American community), times had changed for the state's midwives.[48] In 1926 some four thousand midwives were registered in Arkansas, and by 1940 Arkansas had the third-highest rate of midwife-attended births. By 1952, however, midwives practicing without a license were prosecuted as part of the state's ongoing efforts to improve infant mortality rates. Midwifery in Arkansas, then, had followed the rest of the nation during the 1960s and early 1970s and became increasingly marginalized. In 1983 the state legislature passed Act 838, which allowed for the return of registered midwives in Arkansas, but only in counties with at least 32.5 percent of their population below the poverty line. No counties in the Ozarks qualified under this stipulation; indeed, only six counties in the state would, according to the poverty statistics from the 1979 US Census. The closest Ozark county was Newton, with a poverty rate of 31.73 percent, followed by Searcy and Stone counties, with 30.60 percent and 30.23 percent, respectively.[49] This act was later amended in 1987 by Act 481, which allowed for midwives to be licensed and practice across the state.[50] It should be noted, however, that until 1983 homebirths occurred and midwives practiced throughout the state, and in the Ozarks in particular, despite the law.

This desire to empower women and facilitate a gentler entry into the world for children was often discussed by the Ozark BTLs. Writing in to *LION* in 1974, Suzanne McCarthy noted that a woman preparing for childbirth "must have her body and mind in a healthy educated state with positive thoughts that she knows she will be able to help her baby be born [for] the baby's experience during birth will affect it for life."[51] For hipbillies, midwifery embraced just such a vision of birth. The discussion regarding the health and development of children born at home or in the "hippie" style was not isolated to the Ozarks or the Gaskins' Farm. In 1970 the *American Journal of Orthopsychiatry* (a journal focused on issues pertaining to mental health and social justice, particularly as these issues are dealt with in early childhood development) published a study conducted by David Smith and James Sternfield out of the Haight-Ashbury Medical Clinic in San Francisco. Noting that, while the communal and back-to-nature aspects of the counterculture in 1970 were not new in American life, there was a certain commonality between new groups in California and Oregon that perhaps past iterations of the back to the land impulse lacked. Most of these young people, it seemed to Smith and Sternfield, had a "belief system of mysticism and nonviolence derived primarily from the use of psychedelic drugs, with LSD and marijuana maintaining premier positions."[52] The authors were prompted to write their study by the realization that not only were the parents focused on living a life highly influenced by "psychedelic information environments" but that they intended to raise their children in such a way as well.[53]

This environment had little to do with LSD or other mind-altering substances; rather, it was focused on creating a world in which children developed along natural lines. Beginning instantly, with birth, a child would be with the mother nearly always, in a setting that was often built to allow the utmost freedom for all people, not just adults. Breastfeeding occurred as long as possible; David and Sternfielder found that mothers in communes often breastfed until a child was two years old.[54] This was based on the same logic as the rest of their childcare and childbirth practices: it was a naturalistic system that had psychological and nutritional benefits.[55] Smith and Sternfield also noted child-rearing approaches were an indicator of a successful commune; if there was a parent education group that facilitated learning, centered around music, arts, and practical skills, this often signified that the commune was organized enough to be stable.[56] The communes discussed in the study rejected public education and mass media as mediums by which children were indoctrinated into the desires and aims of society writ large.

Such an approach was not found only on communes. Back-to-the-land parents noted that the lifestyle was "really good for kids, almost under any circumstances, with or without good parents."[57] Growing up on the land helped to ensure children knew "how to survive," a skill bolstered by the fact that the Ozarks offered "no terrible alternative for them. There's no going to the streets and dealing drugs or hanging out or going ripping off a store. There's no real crime to get involved in."[58] Some back to the landers in the Ozarks argued their children turned out well because "we held our babies, we nursed our babies, we talked to our babies. We were so *into* being with them as people, and I think in society as a whole that's lost 'cause the mother goes to work. So when ours [our children] go out, they have that interpersonal thing that makes them actually influence the people they're around."[59] Such an outcome was crucial to further the revolution, create better children, and break the power structures. While not a coordinated strategy, BTLs on communes and homesteads across the nation attempted to build alternative lives for their children, beginning at birth and continuing through childhood.

The effort to raise children apart from the mainstream did not just exist in the home. In some cases, hipbillies in the Ozarks created alternative education models. Key in this effort was the Headwaters School, a free school formally incorporated in 1976 outside of Red Star in Madison County. Originally established to supplement homeschool efforts by young back to the land families, the building itself reflected the ethos of the deep revolution: it was built on donated land out of recycled materials (with lumber also donated by local loggers). Initially, reflecting the population, it served younger children and also became a hub of community action.[60]

For a revolution to truly deepen, working to create a new world could not stop at exiting society or reclaiming birth practices. The revolution had to be transmitted to the next generation. That begs the question, then, as to how the "children of the land" viewed their parents' attempts to rebuild the world. If part of the success of the revolution could be measured in terms of how well children retained their parents' ideology in the face of the Reagan era and the dot-com boom, then, like with gender concerns, the success of the back to the land generation is somewhat mixed. What often characterized the outlook of the back to the land children, according to *Spectrum*, was "their attitude. They seem to share a relaxed, receptive side," said an article from 1990, "a reflection of the parents' open-ended beliefs."[61]

Jennifer Billig, daughter of Bob and Eileen (discussed earlier), noted in 1990 that growing up as a back to the land child did a few things for her outlook on life; namely, it gave her a "distaste for 'normal' life" while also instilling in her the desire to "check everything out [and not] take everything at face value . . . a very, very valuable lesson."[62] Her sentiments were echoed by "S," who noted that growing up in the woods provided a home for her heart, so much so that, she said, "Moving to a town away from the community that was pretty much all I knew was hard."[63] Her transition, in part, was made difficult by having to reconcile the free-form educational style of the back to the land community, as evidenced by schools and groups like Headwaters, with a system that was "competitive." It "really upset me when I had to do that," "S" recalled.[64]

The passing on of these values—noncompetiveness, at home in nature, and other hallmarks of the 1960s and 1970s counterculture— did not always translate into the children of the land staying on the homestead. Indeed, Lee McCoy, a homesteader in the Pettigrew area, noted that he and other parents watched the children in the area decide that "though their parents chose a homesteading life, the offspring have higher expectations and aren't interested in settling in."[65] Despite the fact that few of the children of the BTLs remaining on the land, the deep revolution proved to be successful in creating a broad shift in the mindset of a generation. This was true not just in Madison County, but also out in Stone County, with Sunshine Broder and her friends in and around Mountain View.[66] Most no longer live on the land, but they all still have strong roots to the area and, like Sunshine, continue to be influenced in many quiet ways by the decisions their parents made in moving to the land.

Indeed, when asked to describe her family's life on the land, Sunshine's home was typical of many others in the back to the land community. Her family moved to forty acres outside of Mountain View in 1973, and her parents, like many hipbillies in the area, were attached to the Folk Center in various ways over the years. They had a big garden, raised rabbits for meat, and built the house out of recycled materials from nearby lumber mills.[67] This ethos of eco-consciousness, whole foods, and self-reliance is still underscored in her life today. While she may not have a huge garden, raise livestock, and have solar power, Broder noted that much of her response around things like energy use or composting is unconscious, so much so that throwing away food of any kind takes "everything I have."[68]

While composting and energy conservation are commonplace for Broder, perhaps the most complicated influence of the back to the land community for her revolved around gender and community. For several years, she was one of the children in her parents' friend group; as such, she went everywhere and saw everything. From an early age, then, the mysteries of life were normal: skinny dipping, parties, gardening in the nude, marijuana use, and the evolving conversation about women's rights were part and parcel in her childhood. At the same time that the back to the land community provided a safe outlet and support network in a community that could be harsh on newcomers, Sunshine argued that the growing power of gender equality and the strong circle of women around her and her mother were double-edged swords. On one side, she grew up hearing and thinking, "I can be anything, anything I wanted," which was not the norm in Stone County.[69] The flip side of this was, she said, "The women of that generation sat around a lot and talked a lot of shit about how you don't need a man and he's nothing . . . we can, we can, we can."[70] She argued that this built into her and her girlfriends a sense of "low expectations" for the men around them, while also complicating relationships with men. She said, "[It became] so ingrained that I was so capable and to never let on that I wasn't."[71]

Such a perspective helps illustrate the difficulties in understanding gender balances on the homestead. The breakdown of traditional gender norms on the land, while it did move to be more in line with the rise of the feminist movement, did so slowly. Despite this, in some areas the back to the land generation amended prevailing Ozark male-female relationships, in particular in Fayetteville and Eureka Springs where women's rights were more often directly discussed and acted upon. This is particularly the case with the broadening of gender norms in the 1970s and 1980s as the LGBT community made itself more openly known in the wake of the Stonewall riots and the actions of local groups.[72]

Like so many other issues in the 1960s and 1970s, the gender revolution served to redefine much in American life. Indeed, as historians have increasingly detailed, the midcentury gender revolt centered around the twin ideas that "citizens have *a* sex and they *have* sex."[73] While understanding how the various aspects of the gender revolutions played nationally was (and is) still underway, in Arkansas at least, the Ozarks provided a testing ground for some of these communities. In Fayetteville, home to the state's flagship university, there was a nascent feminist- and gay-rights presence, centered around the Fayetteville Women's Center and the "Razodykes," a student organization at the University of Arkansas. While the relationship between the two groups has been portrayed as conflicted, perhaps mirroring the perceived national divide between second-wave feminists and the newly ascendant lesbian rights efforts, in part the split contributed to a thriving back to the land consciousness amidst the lesbian community.[74] The Ozarks came to be seen, at least by parts of the lesbian community, as a safe haven for those interested in creating a separate life apart from the mainstream. Isolated hilltop farms, though not without their own particular risks, were ideal locations in which to live out their lives in relative seclusion.[75]

Creating the deep revolution, beyond building houses and growing gardens, required organization of the kind many in the back to the land world had left behind. Despite this, throughout the 1970s country hippies across the Ozarks enacted their vision of the world. As one BTL, "N" said, "[We created a venue for] social change, to create that society, because we weren't happy with the one that was out there."[76] In short, getting Nixon—or even Carter—was not good enough for the back to the landers. Through reorienting birth and childhood and fighting for preservation and prosperity of the region they had adopted, the hipbillies proudly ignored Crescent Dragonwagon's early warning to come gently, and in so doing served as a catalyst to a region on the cusp of economic and cultural expansion.

CONCLUSION

——

The Affection for Place

WENDELL BERRY, IN his 2012 Jefferson Lecture for the National Endowment for the Humanities, told a story that would have resonated with the hipbillies of the 1960s and 1970s. Describing the flawed industrial economy that plagued tobacco farmers dominated by tycoons like James B. Duke, Berry noted that in 1906 his grandfather—a tobacco farmer—had nothing to show for the year's work thanks to prices set by industrialists. Some years later, when Berry came face to face with Duke's statue in front of a Methodist chapel at Duke University, he suddenly juxtaposed the tycoon with his grandfather:

> After my encounter with the statue, the story of my grandfather's 1906 tobacco crop slowly took on a new dimension and clarity in my mind. I still remembered my grandfather as himself, of course, but I began to think of him also as a kind of man standing in thematic opposition to a man of an entirely different kind. And I could see finally that between these two kinds there was a failure of *imagination* that was ruinous, that belongs indelibly to our history, and that has continued, growing worse, into our own time.[1]

Imagination was, and is, the key for Berry. Imagination, in its truest sense, is the ability to see the world with clarity, familiarity, with a "force of vision and even with a visionary force." Thus, imagination is not passive; rather, it is intimately connected with "truth and knowledge" and "grasps securely the qualities of things seen or envisioned."[2] Imagination must have a real connection to the world, humans must imagine themselves in the world, for only this can "enable sympathy" which in turn brings about affection, and "it is in affection that we find the possibility of a neighborly, kind, and conserving economy."[3] Such a call is, in the twenty-first century, what the deep revolution in the Ozarks during the 1970s was about.

This idea of an affection for place, though, is not often associated with these hills. Indeed, when the Ozarks, or Ozarkers, come up in conversation around the country, the idea of revolution or imagination is not often associated with this landscape. Indeed, in popular conception today, the Ozarks are quintessential "fly-over" country, a region so set in its ways, so stodgy and traditionalist, that it would be unthinkable to imagine a rebellion here, much less that thousands of middle-class youth during the 1960s and 1970s flocked to the region, plowed the rocky hillsides with mules, and built geodesic domes. So then, what should be said about the back to the land movement in the Ozarks? It is easy, and simple, to say that all the stories and popular memories about the counterculture were right—the political system was not overturned, the economics of the country stayed firmly capitalistic, drugs were consumed, and people ran around in their birthday suits. But as this study has tried to illustrate, a more honest exploration of the movement shows a complicated story. The hipbillies were indeed idealists filled full of utopian dreams, and like all idealists they did not succeed as well as they had hoped. But that should not remove them from serious study by scholars of the Ozarks or of American life. Indeed, as I believe I have shown, the back to the land community had a clear vision for itself, and it believed that it was revolutionary. To be sure, it needed to occur on a private scale at first and then move to the larger, community—something that makes evaluations of the back to the land movement difficult. But if scholars and pundits make the effort to use their own ideals as the measure of their successes or failures, then it is safe to say that the back to the landers were more successful than popular memory has allowed.

Hipbillies came to the Ozarks seeking refuge and a place in which they might build a new world for themselves, and hopefully, all of humanity. They learned how to live in a place, became a part of its rhythms, and from there worked both to preserve and advance it. By helping hold small farm communities together, slow the spraying of toxic chemicals across the region, start businesses, and advocate for social justice across many fronts, hipbillies wove themselves into the fabric of Ozark life. While in some places they may still be called "hippies" or "longhairs," these days the terms have lost their sting and become, often, terms of bemused endearment. And while the hippies' and long-hairs' children may not stay on the land, and while the world has not totally transformed into that which the deep revolution envisioned, the back to the land generation, as the long-standing gentle warriors of the counterculture, ensured that the revolution happened.

Day to day existence, though, was far more mundane than the lofty revolutionary rhetoric might imply. After all, as one BTL said, "What we were doing at that time was trying to demonstrate that attitude, to accept a more cooperative way of living, to realize that we would do with less, be happy with less. That more wasn't always better."[4] By initially withdrawing from society at large and accepting less, the deep revolution was teased into existence and ultimately provided the foundation for future political action on the part of hipbillies—and, on occasion, locals. The Ozarks, like so many places throughout the nation became a "stronghold" for a "grand experiment," a place where the myriad changes being asked of the nation were sorted out as best as they could be.[5] Often, the difficulties arose not around protesting 2,4,5T or childbirth but around questions about educating children, what the future might hold, or how a group organized. Despite the problems, the hipbillies thrived in the Ozarks, learning the answers these questions and countless others gave them.

These lessons are of particular importance today and not just to this population. With the rise in power of a popular slow food movement and a surge in young, college-educated people once again heading back to the land, turning back to ask what can be learned from the hipbillies only seems prudent. Aside from this practical application, understanding the back to the land movement within a distinct American tradition not just of casual self-reliance, but as an extension of the founding agrarian mythology serves to highlight, in part, why the back-to-the-land story still resonates with so many across the nation and why the hipbillies were successful in the Ozarks. In truth, there is no simple explanation for these two phenomena.

As a native of the Arkansas hill country, I believe that some of the explanation must lie in Cindy Arsaga's observation that the Ozarks have always been countercultural, though not always in the tie-dyed and weed sense. After all, to stick it out here—especially in the hardscrabble hollers in the central portion of the region—means you most likely are going against the grain of modern America anyhow, no matter who you vote for or how you live. As scholars and commentators have shown for a century, this region defies simple explanations and attracts a diverse array of people, from Holy Rollers to the Rainbow Family. The hipbillies were another wave of people at once both enamored with, and empowered by, the mythology of the Ozarks; so much so that they found the wherewithal to root themselves deep in the hills and build the world they envisioned. While they did not always succeed, the story is not over—they are still alive and are still powerful cultural, political, and economic forces in the Arkansas highlands. In the Democratic primaries in 2016, Newton County, a hub of hipbilly activity, was the only county in Arkansas to vote for Bernie Sanders over Hillary Clinton (though Sanders came close—within 0.3 percent—to beating Clinton in Madison County, another mecca of back to the landers).[6] Their voices are present in the ongoing fight against herbicide application in the national forest and along power lines, for the continued protection of the Buffalo River, advocacy for small farms, and the furtherance of civil rights for all. Like all Ozarkers, then, at first glance the hipbillies appear to be silenced stereotypes, but instead of going quietly into the night, they are going out with a roar. Behind them is left an indelible imprint on the land of ridge runners and yarb doctors.

NOTES

PREFACE

1. Indeed, in the process of writing this book I was misquoted by the *Arkansas Democrat-Gazette* about communal life in the region.

INTRODUCTION

1. Jack Kerouac, *The Dharma Bums* (New York: Penguin Books, 2006), 9.

2. Allen Ginsberg, "Howl for Carl Solomon," in *Collected Poems, 1947–1980* (New York: Harper Perennial, 1988), 126.

3. Even in the 2014 CNN documentary on the decade this is the image portrayed of the truly countercultural aspects of the age. Tom Hanks and Gary Goetzman, *The Sixties* (CNN, 2014). See also Jeremi Suri, *Power and Protest: Global Revolution and the Rise of Détente* (Cambridge, MA: Harvard University Press, 2005) for placing the end of the social revolt in America in a global context. Suri presents the culmination of the decade as one focused on maintaining, rather than upending, the status quo.

4. Indeed, new work is appearing weekly, it seems, to highlight the impact of the revolution. For example, see Jonathan Kauffman, *Hippie Food: How Back-to-the-Landers, Longhairs, and Revolutionaries Changed the Way We Eat* (New York: William Morrow, 2018).

5. Indeed, the historiography is beginning to show this as well, illustrating how the 1960s, instead of dying, continued and gained strength well into the 1970s. See, among many, Thomas Borstelmann, *The 1970s: A New Global History from Civil Rights to Economic Inequality* (Princeton: Princeton University Press, 2013); Stephanie A. Slocum-Schaffer, *America in the Seventies* (Syracuse, NY: Syracuse University Press, 2003); Jefferson R. Cowie, *Stayin' Alive: The 1970s and the Last Days of the Working Class* (New York: The New Press 2010); Beth Bailey and David Farber, eds., *America in the Seventies* (Lawrence: University of Kansas Press, 2004); Bruce J. Schulman, *The Seventies: The Great Shift in American Culture, Society, and Politics* (Boston: De Capo Press, 2002); and Robert O. Self's impeccable *All in the Family: The Realignment of American Democracy Since the 1960s* (New York: Hill and Wang, 2013).

6. The period of the 1950s and 1960s saw various forms of soul searching throughout the country as "alternative" religions associated with the counterculture surged alongside mainstream Christianity. See Randall Bennett Woods, *A Quest for*

Identity: America Since 1945 (Cambridge: Cambridge University Press, 2005), chap.
5, 6, 8, and 11; Rebecca Kneale Gould, *At Home in Nature: Modern Homesteading and
Spiritual Practice in America* (Berkeley: University of California Press, 2005); Darren
Dochuk, *From Bible Belt to Sunbelt: Plain-Folk Religion, Grassroots Politics, and the Rise
of Evangelical Conservatism* (New York: W. W. Norton, 2012); David R. Swartz, *Moral
Minority: The Evangelical Left in an Age of Conservatism* (Philadelphia: University of
Pennsylvania Press, 2014); Sherri Smith, *Hippies, Indians, and the Fight for Red Power*
(Oxford: Oxford University Press, 2012).

7. For an excellent discussion of the spirituality of back to the land movements
in American life, see Gould, *At Home in Nature*. Particularly useful is her discussion of
the "ambivalence" of the homesteading life, especially regarding its efforts to both
remake culture and respond to culture. Gould highlights how homesteading, for
many back to the landers "expresses itself in terms of inherited understandings of
what nature, the self, spirituality, and the Good Life *have* meant and in terms of what
these concepts might mean in the future" (103, emphasis in original). Questions such
as these are not necessarily supposed to be answered; rather, those practicing the deep
revolution attempt, to borrow Gould's phrase, to put "themselves in a particularly
intense relationship with nature" that forces them to address these questions daily,
"in part to gain access to experiences that will fuel their intellectual and spiritual
development" (104). It should be noted, though, that the back to the land population
in the Ozarks, at least, did in fact seek to transfer such sentiments into practical social
action.

8. Henry David Thoreau, *Walden and Civil Disobedience* (New York: Barnes
and Noble, 2003), 33. This is especially true with those involved in the bioregional
movement.

9. It might be argued that this is evidence not of a lasting revolution but rather a
consumer choice revolution. While there are aspects of this in the lasting success of
the deep revolution—for example, the ability to buy organic products at stores like
Walmart. Such a distinction, though understandable, is a problematic way to evaluate
the impact of the back to the land movement. By placing this community within a
consumer choice framework (something they eschewed), the revolutionary goals
and intentions of back to the landers are overshadowed. Indeed, the BTL movement
saw itself as separate from the broader counterculture in part because of this (this
distinction is dealt with later in the book). This is not to say that there is no aspect of
commercialism that appears in the movement but that to overly emphasize it is to
abandon our ability to evaluate the group on its own terms.

10. See, for example, Grace Elizabeth Hale, *A Nation of Outsiders: How the White
Middle Class Fell in Love with Rebellion in Postwar America* (Oxford: Oxford University
Press, 2011); Marianne DeKoven, *Utopia Limited: The Sixties and the Emergence of the
Postmodern* (Durham, NC: Duke University Press, 2004).

11. Terry Anderson, *The Movement and the Sixties: Protest in America From
Greensboro to Wounded Knee* (New York: Oxford University Press, 1995), xvi.

12. See Theodore Roszak, *The Making of a Counter Culture: Reflections on the
Technocratic Society and Its Youthful Opposition* (Berkeley: University of California Press,
1995 reprint).

13. See Anderson, *The Movement*; Hale, *A Nation of Outsiders*; DeKoven, *Utopia
Limited*; David Maranis, *They Marched Into Sunlight: War and Peace, Vietnam and
America, October 1967* (New York: Simon & Schuster, 2004) for examples of this.

14. The literature on these ideas is vast and growing. For brief discussions of the American Dream, consumption, and similar issues, see Thomas Borstelmann, *The 1970s: A New Global History from Civil Rights to Economic Inequality* (Princeton: Princeton University Press, 2012); Roland Marchand, *Advertising the American Dream: Making Way for Modernity, 1920–1940* (Berkeley: University of California Press, 1986); Cowie, *Stayin' Alive*; Louis Hyman, *Debtor Nation: The History of America in Red Ink* (Princeton: Princeton University Press, 2012); Lizabeth Cohen, *A Consumer's Republic: The Politics of Mass Consumption in Postwar America* (New York: Vintage Books, 2003); Karal Ann Marling, *As Seen on TV: The Visual Culture of Everyday Life in the 1950s* (Cambridge, MA: Harvard University Press, 1998). For discussions about American foreign policy during the Cold War, the Cold War in general, and American cultural intersections with the Cold War, see John Lewis Gaddis, *The Cold War: A New History* (New York: Penguin Books, 2006); Borstelmann, *The Cold War and the Color Line: American Race Relations in the Global Arena* (Cambridge, MA: Harvard University Press, 2003); Elaine Tyler May, *Homeward Bound: American Families in the Cold War Era* (New York: Basic Books, 2008). For discussions about the national counterculture and its shifting nature, see Anderson, *The Movement*; Roszak, *Counter Culture*; Todd Gitlin, *Sixties: Years of Hope, Days of Rage* (New York: Bantam Books, 1993); Peter Braunstein and Michael William Doyle, eds., *Imagine Nation: The American Counterculture of the 1960s and '70s* (New York: Routledge, 2002).

15. It is hard to nail down the exact ethnic composition of the group. Anecdotally, there were some Latino, Native American, and African American members of this portion of the counterculture, but far fewer than can be found in other segments of the counterculture. This is perhaps a reflection of the material ability and social freedom of this group to leave the safe spaces of suburban life for the hills, especially as they went to one of the whitest portions of the country at the time.

16. One member of the back to the land community in Newton County remarked that "we didn't know shit" about farming or gardening. Guy King Ames, conversation with the author, April 20, 2015.

17. The notable exception to this is Jeffery Jacob, *New Pioneers: The Back-to-the-Land Movement and the Search for a Sustainable Future* (University Park: Pennsylvania State University Press, 1997) but his work deals with back to the landers in the 1980s and beyond and makes little linkage to the counterculture of the 1960s.

18. This is true save two useful studies, Dona Brown's *Back to the Land: The Enduring Dream of Self-Sufficiency in Modern America* (Madison: University of Wisconsin Press, 2011) and Gould's *At Home in Nature*. Gould, however, is more focused on spiritual and philosophical aspects of the homesteading life as they relate to the American Northeast, whereas Brown attempts to provide a brief overview of the back to the land impulse in America. This goal, however, falls short when Brown arrives at the time period discussed here, the 1960s and 1970s, as she falls into some of the same tropes and casual dismissal found elsewhere.

19. Guy Ames, conversation with author, March 18, 2015.

20. Ames, conversation.

21. Ames, conversation.

22. Not long before this, Arkansas senator J. William Fulbright had put such a question before the American people in his critique of American empire, *The Arrogance of Power* (New York: Random House, 1967).

23. Guy Ames, conversation with author, March 18, 2015.

24. See Joel Selvin, *Altamont: The Rolling Stones, the Hells Angels, and the Inside Story of Rock's Darkest Day* (New York: Dey Street Books, 2016) for an insightful recent look at the Altamont concert and the attending chaos.

25. Guy Ames, conversation with author, March 18, 2015. This sentiment is true across most of the back to the landers interviewed by the author. See also Cowie, *Stayin' Alive*, for an excellent discussion of this.

26. Woods, *Quest for Identity*, chap. 11. See also Randall Bennett Woods, *Prisoners of Hope: Lyndon B. Johnson, the Great Society, and the Limits of Liberalism* (New York: Basic Books, 2016) for a recent discussion of Johnson and the limits of the Great Society.

27. Herbert Marcuse, *One-Dimensional Man: Studies in the Ideology of Advanced Industrial Society*, 2nd ed., (London: Routledge, 1991), xl. For discussions of this conflict, see Suri, *Power and Protest*; Self, *All in the Family*; Cowie, *Stayin' Alive*; Anderson, *The Movement*; Darren Dochuk, *From Bible Belt to Sunbelt: Plain-Folk Religion, Grassroots Politics, and the Rise of Evangelical Conservatism* (New York: W. W., 2012); Lisa McGirr, *Suburban Warriors: The Origins of the New American Right*, updated ed. (Princeton: Princeton University Press, 2015).

28. For the phrase "silent majority," see Richard Nixon's speech, "Address to the Nation on the War in Vietnam, November 3, 1969," The American Presidency Project (website), accessed February 23, 2016, http://www.presidency.ucsb.edu/ws/?pid=2303.

29. President Nixon quoted in Jefferson Cowie, "Nixon's Class Struggle: Romancing the New Right Worker, 1960–1973," *Labor History* 43, no. 3 (2002): 258–59.

30. Nigel Bowles, *Nixon's Business: Authority and Power in Presidential Politics* (College Station: Texas A&M University Press, 2005), 236.

31. See Cowie, *Stayin' Alive*, for an excellent discussion of this from a labor point of view, as well as Self, *All in the Family*, for an erudite discussion of social issues occurring at the same time. This national fracturing is also represented in microcosm in the Ozarks. See J. Blake Perkins, *Hillbilly Hellraisers: Federal Power and Populist Defiance in the Ozarks* (Urbana: University of Illinois Press, 2017) chap. 6, 7.

32. Vision of the "country life" will be examined later in this work, but it is worth noting that only two major studies are readily accessible of Midwestern or Southern counterculture: Jeffery Turner's *Sitting In and Speaking Out: Student Movements in the American South* (Athens: University of Georgia Press, 2010) and Beth Bailey's *Sex in the Heartland* (Cambridge, MA: Harvard University Press, 1999).

33. Turner, *Sitting In*, 5. This is not to say that the efforts of the Civil Rights Movement were not countercultural; rather, the ideas and aims of the "counterculture" were often less defined and poorly executed in contrast to the efforts of SNCC (Student Nonviolent Coordinating Committee) or CORE (Congress of Racial Equality).

34. Bailey, *Sex in the Heartland*, 4.

35. See R. Douglas Hurt, *American Agriculture: A Brief History* (West Lafayette, IN: Purdue University Press, 2002) chap. 7, 8. See also Willard W. Cochrane, *The Development of American Agriculture: A Historical Analysis* (Minneapolis: University of Minnesota Press, 1979); Pete Daniel, *Dispossession: Discrimination Against African American Farmers in the Age of Civil Rights* (Chapel Hill: University of North Carolina Press, 2013).

36. Secretary of Agriculture Earl Butz, quoted in Daniel, *Dispossession*, 153–54. See also Wendell Berry, *The Unsettling of America: Culture and Agriculture* (San Francisco: Sierra Club Books, 1977) for contemporary commentary on this process.

37. Hurt, *American Agriculture*, 327–28, 358. See also Brooks Blevins, *Hill Folks: A History of Arkansas Ozarkers and Their Image* (Chapel Hill: University of North Carolina Press, 2002), for a discussion of this.

38. Blevins, *Hill Folks*, 199–200.

39. See Blevins, *Hill Folks*, 195–98.

40. Reprinted in Donald Katz, *The Valley of the Fallen and Other Stories* (New York: AtRandom Books, 2001) pp. 152–73.

41. See Michael Liensech, *In the Beginning: Fundamentalism, the Scopes Trial, and the Making of the Antievolution Movement* (Charlotte: The University of North Carolina Press, 2009).

42. For interesting discussions of these seemingly competing ideas, see, for example, T. J. Jackson Lears, *No Place of Grace: Antimodernism and the Transformation of American Culture, 1880–1920* (Chicago: University of Chicago Press, 1981); Dona Brown, *Back to the Land: The Enduring Dream of Self-Sufficiency in Modern America* (Madison: University of Wisconsin Press, 2011); Gould, *At Home in Nature*. The newer historiography on the American populist movement is also noted for its discussion of such dualities, in particular, see Charles Postel, *The Populist Vision* (Oxford: Oxford University Press, 2009).

43. Guy Ames, conversation with author, March 18, 2015.

44. Ames, conversation.

45. This movement is similar to many other back to the landers that move into the Ozarks. Most do not initially come to the region first, though many will have heard of it through travelling with family, reading about it, or other means.

46. Edwin Way Teale, *Wandering Through Winter* (New York: Dodd, Mead, 1965).

47. Teale, *Wandering Through Winter*, 187.

48. Blevins, *Hill Folks*, 2.

49. Blevins, *Hill Folks*, 149, 150.

50. Blevins, *Hill Folks*, 150. Blevins points out that in 1945, some 95 percent of Ozark farmers relied on animal power on the farm, a statistic that would not change substantially until the mid-1960s. Blevins, *Hill Folks*, 150.

51. Blevins, *Hill Folks*, 161, 180. Between 1960 and 1975, the Northwest Arkansas and White River development districts of the Ozark Regional Commission absorbed some 63,274 and 18,309 in-migrants respectively. Of the total in-migrants, 48.02 percent moved into non-metro areas. George H. Dailey Jr. et al, *A Quarter Century of Population Change in the Ozarks, 1950–1975* (University of Missouri Department of Rural Sociology, 1978), 66–69.

52. Blevins, *Hill Folks*, 161, 180.

53. Blevins, *Hill Folks*, 187–89. See also the long history of the Ozarks referenced in popular culture thanks to comic strips like *Lil Abner*, novels like *Shepherd of the Hills* by Harold Bell Wright, and regional booster efforts. For a longer discussion of these sorts of impacts on the national perception of the region, see Blevins, *Arkansaw/Arkansas: How Bear Hunters, Hillbillies, and Good Ol' Boys Defined a State* (Fayetteville: University of Arkansas Press, 2009).

54. Blevins, *Hill Folks*, 212. See also Perkins, *Hillbilly Hellraisers*.

55. Blevins., *Hill Folks*, 220–22. For discussions of packaging and selling the South and its cultures, see Jane S. Becker, *Selling Tradition: Appalachia and the Construction of an American Folk, 1930–1940* (Chapel Hill: University of North Carolina Press, 1998); Rebecca Cawood McIntyre, *Souvenirs of the Old South: Northern Tourism and Southern Mythology* (Gainesville: University Press of Florida, 2011); Richard D. Starnes, "Tourism, Landscape, and History in the Great Smoky Mountains National Park," in *Destination Dixie: Tourism and Southern History* ed. Karen L. Cox (Gainesville: University of Florida Press, 2012).

56. Otto Earnst Rayburn, *Ozark Country* (New York: Duell, Sloan & Pearce, 1941). See also Wayman Hogue, *Back Yonder: An Ozark Chronicle* ed. Brooks Blevins. (Fayetteville: University of Arkansas Press, 2016). I am greatly indebted to Brooks Blevins for this insight. See Blevins's presentation, "When an Ozark Boyhood Really Isn't: Reconsidering Wayman Hogue's Back Yonder," at the 9th Annual Ozarks Studies Symposium, Missouri State University-West Plains, September 18–19, 2015. This comparison between the two regions—the Ozarks and Appalachia—by the counterculture is summarized best by Bob Billig, a back to the lander who moved with his family to the Ozarks over Appalachia partly because the poverty and lifestyle of Ozark hill folk was not as "desperate." Bob Billig, conversation with the author, June 3, 2014.

It should also be noted that to date, with one exception, detailed examinations of the folk culture of the Ozarks have rarely been separated from assumptions based on the Appalachian experience. Though they indeed offer useful insights into rural, the upland culture (and even the relatively recent creation of "culture") of Appalachia is different. Thus, excellent studies such as David Whisnant's *All That Is Native and Fine: The Politics of Culture in an American Region* (Chapel Hill: University of North Carolina Press, 1983) are useful for context, but scholars of the Ozarks would be better served at following the path blazed by Brooks Blevins in *Arkansas/Arkansaw* (2009) and *Hill Folks* (2002) and by J. Blake Perkins in *Hillbilly Hellraisers* (2017).

57. Joe Neal, "A Historical Note on the Arkansas Mountains In-migration," *The Grapevine*, March 16, 1977.

58. Neal, "A Historical Note on the Arkansas Mountains In-migration"

59. Neal, "A Historical Note on the Arkansas Mountains In-migration."

60. Nan Lawler, "William R. Lighton," *The Encyclopedia of Arkansas History and Culture* (website), accessed February 20, 2016, http://www.encyclopediaofarkansas .net/encyclopedia/entry-detail.aspx?entryID=1046.

61. William R. Lighton, "The Story of an Arkansas Farm," *Saturday Evening Post*, January 22, 1910, 14.

62. Lighton, "The Story of an Arkansas Farm," 14.

63. Lighton, "The Story of an Arkansas Farm," 14. For the complete collection of stories from Happy Hollow, see William R. Lighton, *Happy Hollow Farm* (New York: George H. Doran, 1915).

64. Charlie May Simon was the daughter of Wayman Hogue, the author of *Back Yonder: An Ozark Chronicle*, who also offered a somewhat nebulous definition of Ozark geography.

65. While today Perry County would not likely make the normal list of "Ozark" counties in Arkansas, at the time the Ouachitas and other areas south of the current understanding of the Ozarks were viewed as one region. This shift in geograph-

ical boundaries has come through the continual refinement of the idea of the Ozarks, seen in things like Milton Rafferty's work, *The Ozarks: Land and Life,* 2nd ed. (Fayetteville: University of Arkansas Press, 2001).

66. Charlie May Simon, "Retreat to the Land: An Experience in Poverty" *Scribner's,* May 1933, 309–12. It must be said that while Charlie May Simon was an Arkansan, both she and Howard had been circulating in rather rarified circles in Paris and New York at the time they decided to move to Arkansas.

67. See in particular Eleanor Agnew's discussion of this in *Back from the Land: How Young Americans Went to Nature in the 1970s, and Why They Came Back* (Chicago: Ivan R. Dee, 2004), as well as Gould, *At Home in Nature.*

68. Don West, *Broadside to the Sun* (New York: W. W. Norton, 1946). The Don West discussed here should not be confused with the Highland School Don West, author of *Between the Plowhandles* (1932) and *Clods of Southern Earth* (1946).

69. The impact of *Broadside to the Sun* is hard to gauge: W. W. Norton, the publisher, has not retained distribution records for the book. (Doris Dorough, sales representative for W. W. Norton, email correspondence with author, July 10, 2015).

70. West, *Broadside to the Sun,* 193. While the West family had their experience eloquently chronicled, hundreds of others also moved into the Ozarks during the Depression years. According to Sue Webb, between 1929 and 1932, Arkansas gained nearly two hundred thousand farmers and thirty-nine thousand new farms, roughly an 11 percent increase over the previous three-year period. Such an increase even prompted the University of Arkansas in Fayetteville's College of Agriculture to tell its students that "the depression was an opportune time to begin a career in agriculture." See Sue Webb, "By the Sweat of the Brow: The Back-to-the-Land Movement in Depression Arkansas," *Arkansas Historical Quarterly* 42, no. 4 (Winter 1983): 334–35. The economic pressures and interest in returning to the land even prompted, in 1931, a farm plan campaign by the state Agriculture Extension Office that offered a "ten commandments" (that are remarkably similar to what counterculture publications like *Mother Earth News* would publish in the 1970s). The list included such advice as "let every farm have at least one milk cow" and "keep at least thirty laying hens on every farm." "Farm to Make a Living, 1931 Farm Plan," *Extension Cooperator* 12 (February 1931).

71. Blevins, *Arkansas/Arkansaw,* 4–9.

72. Blevins, *Arkansas/Arkansaw,* 79–80.

73. Paul Durand, "Advice on Ozarks Homesteading," *Mother Earth News* May/June 1975, accessed September 30, 2016, http://www.motherearthnews.com/nature-and-environment/ozarks-homesteading-zmaz75mjzgoe. Durand's full discussion of the Ozarks will be revisited later in this work.

74. See Neil Compton's *The Battle for the Buffalo River: The Story of America's First National River* (Fayetteville: University of Arkansas Press, 2010). Suzie Rogers, "Buffalo National River," *The Encyclopedia of Arkansas History and Culture* (website), accessed February 23, 2016, http://www.encyclopediaofarkansas.net/encyclopedia/entry-detail.aspx?entryID=7. See also, Neil Compton, *The Battle for the Buffalo River: A Twentieth Century Conservation Crisis in the Ozarks* (Fayetteville: University of Arkansas Press, 1992); and Dwight Pitcaithley, *Let the River Be: A History of the Ozark's Buffalo River* (Santa Fe: Southwest Cultural Resources Center, 1997). A definitive history of the Buffalo River has yet to be written. Perkins's *Hillbilly Hellraisers* discusses the

ongoing competition and, at times, bad blood between those in the hills and smaller communities and those in the wealthier towns and cities across the region. See Perkins, *Hillbilly Hellraisers,* chap. 1, 4, 5, and 6 for different variations of this issue.

75. Blevins, *Hill Folks*, 221.

76. Blevins, *Hill Folks*, 221–31.

CHAPTER 1

1. James Andrews, "The New Settlers: Hipbillies," *Ozark Access Catalog (OAC)* 4 (November 1973): 1.

2. Andrews, "The New Settlers: Hipbillies," 1.

3. Andrews, "The New Settlers: Hipbillies," 1.

4. A few notable exceptions to this gap exist; namely, Jeffery Jacob, *New Pioneers: The Back to the land Movement and the Search for a Sustainable Future* (University Park: Pennsylvania State University Press, 2006); Brown, *Back to the Land*; and Timothy Miller, *The 60s Communes: Hippies and Beyond* (Syracuse: Syracuse University Press, 1999). See Ryan Edgington's excellent article "'Be Receptive to the Good Earth:' Health, Nature, and Labor in Countercultural Back to the Land Settlements," *Agricultural History* 82, no. 3 (Summer, 2008: 279–308; and Jinny A. Turman's "Appalachian Alter-Natives: The Back-to-the-Land Migration and Community Change in Appalachia, 1970–2000" (PhD diss., West Virginia University, 2013).

5. Blevins, *Hill Folks*, 200.

6. See, for example, Jacob, *New Pioneers* for a discussion of the "ecological con- sciousness" of the back to the landers in the 1980s; Eleanor Agnew *Back from the Land: How Young Americans Went to Nature in the 1970s, and Why They Came Back* (Chicago: Ivan R. Dee, 2004), for what she terms the failed idealism of the back to the land movement; Gould's refreshing *At Home In Nature* for a more nuanced discussion of the philosophy of northeastern BTLs; Brown, *Back to the Land*, for a brief discussion of the troubled political dreams that fueled back to the landers; and, finally, Turman's recent dissertation on the country hippies in West Virginia, "Appalachian Alter- Natives," which seeks to bring together all these disparate arguments to create a more cohesive vision of the group in the Appalachians.

7. Not referenced in this statistic are the stories found in Weinstein, *Force for Social Change* (funded by the Arkansas Humanities Council), Denele Campbell, *Aquarian Revolution: Back to the land, Thirty-Two Interviews* (Self-published through CreateSpace Independent Publishing Platform, 2013), or stories from the Missouri Ozarks. The interviews conducted by Campbell and Weinstein are presented anon- ymously, and I have chosen to not pursue them beyond this based on conversations with the authors, save where I was able to match the stories with interviews I con- ducted. Thus, in all likelihood, the averages I discuss in table 1 would be slightly dif- ferent. For instance, if these stories were able to be included, average time on the land would most likely adjust down from 14.6 years to near 12.0 years. It should be noted this is still far higher than the presumed average nationally.

8. Brown, *Back to the Land*, 206.

9. This assumption might hold true for the counterculture writ large (though this seems suspect), but the back to the land community, in the Arkansas and Missouri Ozarks at least, was certainly not lackadaisical.

10. Indeed, one member of the counterculture in Eureka Springs never meant to stay in Arkansas—he meant to spend one night and never left. Anonymous, conversation with author, July 25, 2014.

11. A note on source identification is in order. In some cases, as in the case of Bob Billig, per the wishes of some in the back to the land community, I have not preserved the anonymity of people interviewed. In other cases, which will be noted, I have operated in accordance with the wishes of each respective person. In the rare cases where interviewees expressed no opinion on the issue, I have preserved their anonymity.

12. Bob Billig, interview with author, June 3, 2014; Bob Billig, author's questionnaire, June 2014.

13. Billig, questionnaire.

14. Billig, questionnaire. It should be noted that this imagery is not to essentialize the counterculture's experiences. Rather, it is meant to highlight this sudden exposure to a community or membership that the Billigs had been seeking. As Billig noted to me, and as was echoed by countless others in the back to the land community, far too much has been made of nudity in relation to the BTL, in effect creating a trope that has obscured serious inquiry into the group. While nudity does play a role in some early interactions with Ozark natives, most often—at least in the memories of conversations between hipbillies and locals—it was treated with a healthy dose of bemusement, especially as the young pioneers were quick to learn that working with hay, dealing with fences, and operating tractors meant wearing clothes if you were serious about building a farm and not getting hurt.

15. Joel Davidson, interview with author, August 15, 2014.

16. Henry David Thoreau, *Walden and Civil Disobedience* (New York: Barnes and Noble Books, 2003), 11.

17. Thoreau, *Walden*, 19.

18. Davidson, interview.

19. An additional complexity in the makeup of Ozarks back to the land groups was growth of intentional communities, for example, general commune groups like Lothlorien outside of Eureka Springs in Carroll County or women's communal-living groups like Yellowhammer in Madison County. While this study does not go into great detail on the issue of communal living, the little historiographical discussion of these groups supports the conclusions drawn here.

20. Weinstein, *Force for Social Change*, 21.

21. Weinstein, *Force for Social Change*, 22–23.

22. Weinstein, in an effort to provide anonymity for the majority of her respondents assigned code names—a single letter, sometimes corresponding with a letter in the person's name—to each of her interviewees. As such, it is difficult to go back and check many of the stories, though in some cases (as with Crescent Dragonwagon), this was possible.

23. Weinstein, *Force for Social Change*, 24.

24. Weinstein, *Force for Social Change*, 27.

25. "T," Weinstein, *Force for Social Change*, 26.

26. Jacob, *New Pioneers* discusses this desire to leave a consumption economy behind as well, arguing that BTLs are a piece of a larger critique of the material consumption prevalent in American life by the end of the 1970s.

27. David Shi, *The Simple Life: Plain Living and High Thinking in American Culture*

(Athens: University of Georgia Press, 2007), 248–50. Shi is highlighting here what other authors have noted as well, in particular Roland Marchand, *Advertising the American Dream: Making Way for Modernity, 1920–1940* (Berkeley: University of California Press, 1986).

28. Shi, *Simple Life*, 252.

29. Shi, *Simple Life*, 252.

30. This is not to say that only these figures were known or key to the back-to-the-land movement. Others were present and noted, but the selection here reflects the conversations and stories from the Arkansas Ozarks.

31. This list of authors is partially based on survey's and conversations conducted by the author with back to the landers from April 2014 through August 2015.

32. Nearly all BTLs interviewed for this project noted familiarity with Borsodi's work either prior to leaving for the land or soon after arriving.

33. Ralph Borsodi Interview, *The Plowboy* no. 26 (March/April 1974). Available at "Dr. Ralph Borsodi," Soil and Health Library (website), accessed January 14, 2016, http://goo.gl/w1FZ8M, January 14, 2016. See also, Bolton Hall, *A Little Land and a Living* (New York: Arcadia Press, 1908).

34. Allan Carson, The New Agrarian Mind: The Movement Toward Decentralist Thought in Twentieth Century America (New Brunswick: Transaction Publishers, 2000), 55–56.

35. Carson, *Agrarian Mind*, 62–63.

36. Carson, *Agrarian Mind*, 64.

37. Ralph Borsodi, *This Ugly Civilization* (Philadelphia: Porcupine Press, 1975 reprint), 1.

38. Borsodi, *Ugly Civilization*, 6.

39. Borsodi, *Ugly Civilization*, 284–85.

40. Borsodi's views on the issue of technology, quoted in Brown, *Back to the land*, 168.

41. All interviewees for this project had a great familiarity with the Nearings prior to moving to the land and continued to reference their work throughout their time homesteading. For a full biographical account of Nearing, see both Stephen J. Whitfield *Scott Nearing: Apostle of American Radicalism* (New York: Columbia University Press, 1974) and John A. Saltmarsh, *Scott Nearing: An Intellectual Biography* (Philadelphia: Temple University Press, 1991) as well as Nearing's own autobiographical works, including *The Making of a Radical: A Political Autobiography* (New York: Harper and Row, 1972) and the collected *The Good Life: Helen and Scott Nearing's Sixty Years of Self-Sufficient Living* ((New York: Schocken Books, 1989); Gould, *At Home in Nature*, 139; Nearing, *Making of a Radical*, 40–41.

42. Gould, *At Home in Nature*, 157.

43. Nearing and Nearing, *Good Life*, 5.

44. Nearing and Nearing, *Good Life*, 5.

45. Nearing and Nearing, *Good Life*, 6.

46. Nearing and Nearing, *Good Life*, 7.

47. To see the development of Leopold's land ethic and ecological consciousness, see Susan L. Flader and J. Baird Callicott, eds., *The River of the Mother God and Other Essays*, (Madison: University of Wisconsin Press, 1991). In many ways Leopold serves as a more accurate model of the back to the land lifestyle achieved by many in the counterculture—Leopold and his family lived part time on a derelict farm outside of

Madison, Wisconsin, that they worked on for years to restore to fertility before his tragic death in 1948.

48. Max Oelschlaeger, *The Idea of Wilderness: From Prehistory to the Age of Ecology* (New Haven: Yale University Press, 1991), 206. To a large degree, Leopold was redis-covering the natural philosophy of Alexander von Humbolt. See Andrea Wulf, *The Invention of Nature: Alexander von Humbolt's New World* (New York: Knopf, 2015).

49. Aldo Leopold, "The Land Ethic," in *A Sand County Almanac: With Essays on Conservation from Round River* (New York: Random House, 1970), 239.

50. Leopold, "Land Ethic," 240.

51. Leopold, "Land Ethic," 240.

52. Leopold, "Land Ethic," 263.

53. Oelschlaeger, *Idea of Wilderness*, 206.

54. Oelschlaeger, *Idea of Wilderness*, 220.

55. Oelschlaeger, *Idea of Wilderness*, 235–237.

56. Snyder is cited by all Ozark hipbillies as key in the formation of their ideas. Those affiliated with the bioregional movement saw him as particularly inspiring.

57. Gary Snyder, "Energy is Eternal Delight," in *Turtle Island* (New York: New Directions Books, 1974), 105.

58. Gary Snyder, "The Call of the Wild" and "The Wilderness," in *Turtle Island* (New York: New Directions, 1974), 23; 107.

59. Oelschlaeger, *Idea of Wilderness*, 261–262.

60. Wendell Berry also held, and holds, the same saintlike status among the back to the land community in the Ozarks. While only 70 percent of the hipbillies were familiar with his work before they came to the region, they quickly became enam-ored of his vision for rebuilding rural communities across the country, but in particu-lar the upland South.

61. Stegner, a noted author and teacher who would win the Pulitzer in 1972 for *Angle of Repose* and the National Book Award for *The Spectator Bird* in 1977, had estab-lished a writing workshop at Stanford. In 1958, when Berry was a part of the group, other noted American authors were there, including Larry McMurtry, Ken Kesey, and Robert Stone.

62. Much of this friendship is chronicled in Chad Wrigglesworth, ed., *Distant Neighbors: The Selected Letters of Wendell Berry and Gary Snyder* (Berkeley: Counterpoint Press, 2014). This collection picks up their correspondence in the early 1970s up through the present, charting the joint intellectual development of these giants of American countercultural and literary life.

63. Wendell Berry, *Nathan Coulter*, rev. ed. (New York: North Point Press, 1985), 85.

64. Berry, *Unsettling of America*, 30.

65. Berry, *Unsettling of America*, 31.

66. Southern Agrarians are deserving of their own new history. Two interest-ing, though dated, examinations of key figures, works, and lasting influences of the Southern Agrarians are Paul Keith Conkin, *The Southern Agrarians* (Knoxville: University of Tennessee Press, 1988) and Paul Murphy, *The Rebuke of History: The Southern Agrarian and American Conservative Thought* (Chapel Hill: University of North Carolina Press, 2001). The key collection of Southern Agrarian writing is Virginia Rock's *I'll Take My Stand: The South and the Agrarian Tradition, by Twelve Southerners* (New York: Harper and Brothers, 1930).

67. Brown, *Back to the Land*, 174. Brown provides a nice summary of the main

currents and influences in decentralist back to the land thought in the 1920s and 1930s.

68. E. F. Schumacher, *Small Is Beautiful: Economics as if People Mattered* (New York: Schocken Books, 1975), 13.

69. Schumacher, *Small is Beautiful*, 13 and chap. 4, esp. 58.

70. See Roszak, *Counter Culture*. Roszak published this first in 1968 in an attempt to both understand and explain the youth of the 1960s to mainstream America. The "invasion of the centaurs" is a reference to chap. 2, where Roszak uses the story from Ancient Greece in which the centaurs, drunk and angry, invade a festival taking place. Apollo, interpreted by Roszak as the protector of civilized culture, strides forth into the fray and forces the barbaric centaurs back into the wilderness. Roszak argues that though mainstream America might see the counterculture as similar to the centaurs, perhaps they were not a destructive force but rather a force ushering in a new era for humanity.

71. David Pride, conversations with Author, April–May 2015. Name withheld for privacy.

72. Martin A. Lee and Bruce Shlain, *Acid Dreams: The Complete History of LSD: The CIA, the Sixties, and Beyond* (New York: Grove Press, 1992), xxv.

73. Lee and Shlain, *Acid Dreams*, 60.

74. Lee and Shlain, *Acid Dreams*, 72. See Robert Gordon Wasser, "Seeking the Magic Mushroom," *Life*, May 13, 1957, 100–120, https://books.google.com/books?id=Jj8EAAAAMBAJ&lpg=PA100&ots=biwwlEN8c4&pg=PA100&hl=en#v=onepage&q&f=false October 11, 2016.

75. Timothy Leary, quoted in Lee and Shlain, *Acid Dreams*, 73–74.

76. Lee and Shlain, *Acid Dreams*, 76. For a more recent discussion on the history of hallucinogenic drugs, see Andy Lecther, *Shroom: A Cultural History of the Magic Mushroom* (New York: Ecco, 2007), esp. chap. 12.

77. Anonymous, conversation with author, December 23, 2015.

78. See Berry, *Unsettling of America*; Wendell Berry, *The Way of Ignorance and Other Essays* (Berkeley: Counterpoint Press, 2006); Leopold, *Sand County Almanac*.

CHAPTER 2

1. This agrees with Bruce Schulman's assessment of the 1970s back to the landers in his *The Seventies: The Great Shift in American Culture, Society, and Politics* (New York: Free Press, 2001).

2. Grace to Wendy Neidhardt, February 4, 1973 and Wendy Neidhardt to Nana, February 11, 1973, in *The Fox Letters, 1973–1980*, ed. Sarah Neidhardt (self-published, no date), 5–8. The acreage is noted in a letter from Lucy to Nana, August 26, 1973, in Neidhardt, *Fox Letters*, 34.

3. Wendy Neidhardt to Nana, February 11, 1973, in Neidhardt, *Fox Letters*, 7.

4. Wendy Neidhardt to Mom, February 15, 1973, in Neidhardt, *Fox Letters*, 9.

5. Neidhardt, *Fox Letters*, 9.

6. Wendy Neidhardt to Mom, March 14, 1973, in Neidhardt, *Fox Letters*, 13.

7. Neidhardt, *Fox Letters*, 13.

8. Neidhardt, *Fox Letters*, 14.

9. Wendy Neidhardt to Mom, March 22, 1973, in Neidhardt, *Fox Letters,* 15.

10. Bill and Anne Williams, questionnaire returned to author. See the next chapter for a fuller discussion of the relationship between native Ozarkers and the hipbillies.

11. Anne Williams Diary, March–April 1, 1976. Ozark In-Migration Files, Shiloh Museum of Ozark History. "Bill and Anne Williams" is an alias given to preserve anonymity.

12. Anne Williams Diary, April 1–15, 1976. Ozark In-Migration Files, Shiloh Museum of Ozark History.

13. Rodger Streitmatter, *Voices of Revolution: The Dissident Press in America* (New York: Columbia University Press, 2001), xii.

14. For some of the best work on the counterculture press, see also John Birmingham, *Our Time Is Now: Notes from the High School Underground* (Santa Barbara: Praeger, 1970); Roger Lewis, *Outlaws in America: The Underground Press and Its Context* (New York: Penguin Books, 1973); John McMillian, *Smoking Typewriters: The Sixties Underground Press and the Rise of Alternative Media in America* (New York: Oxford University Press, 2014); Laurence Leamer, *The Paper Revolutionaries* (New York: Touchstone, 1972); Abe Peck, *Uncovering the Sixties: The Life and Times of the Underground Press* (New York: Citadel Press, 1991); and Sean Stewart, *On the Ground: An Illustrated Anecdotal History of the Sixties Underground Press* (Oakland: PM Press, 2011).

15. Streitmatter, Voices, 201; George Kaplan, ed., Power to the People: The Graphic Design of the Radical Press and the Rise of the Counter-Culture, 1964–1974, (Chicago: University of Chicago Press, 2013), i.

16. Kaplan, *Power to the People*, i.

17. Streitmatter, *Voices*, 201.

18. Gwen Allen, "Design as a Social Movement," in *Power to the People*, 80, 95.

19. Fuller was best known in the 1960s and 1970s for his work on sustainability and his idea of "Spaceship Earth," best discussed in his 1968 work, *Operating Manual for Spaceship Earth.* The idea was picked up by other iconic writers of the day, notably E. F. Schumacher in his seminal *Small Is Beautiful* (1973).

20. There are several versions of this story. See: Bob Ostertag, *People's Movements, People's Press: The Journalism of Social Justice Movements* (Boston: Beacon Press, 2006), 167; Walter Isaacson, *The Innovators: How a Group of Hackers, Geniuses, and Geeks Created the Digital Revolution* (New York: Simon & Schuster, 2014), 271.

21. Isaacson, *Innovators*, 272.

22. Sam Binkley, "The Seers of Menlo Park: The Discourse of Heroic Consumption in the 'Whole Earth Catalog,'" *Journal of Consumer Culture*, 3, no. 3, November 2003: 295.

23. Dennis and Linda Sanders, interview with the author, n.d.

24. Binkley, "Seers of Menlo Park," 295. The readership figures are quoted in Binkley as well.

25. Stewart Brand, *Whole Earth Catalog*, 1968, 2.

26. Brand, *Whole Earth Catalog*, 2.

27. Brand, *Whole Earth Catalog*, 15.

28. David Pride, conversations with author, April–May 2015. Name withheld for privacy.

29. Lloyd Kahn, *Domebook 2* (Bolinas: Pacific Domes, 1971).

30. John Shuttleworth, "The Plowboy Interview," reprinted in *Mother Earth News*, January/February 1975, http://www.motherearthnews.com/nature-and-environment/interview-with-the-mother-earth-news-founder.aspx.

31. Paul Durand, "Advice on Ozarks Homesteading," *Mother Earth News*, May/June 1975, http://www.motherearthnews.com/nature-and-environment/ozarks-homesteading-zmaz75mjzgoe.aspx.

32. Durand, "Advice on Ozarks Homesteading."

33. See, for example, Sharon Kruse, "Up on the Ozarks Mountain Farm," *Mother Earth News* September/October 1974, http://www.motherearthnews.com/homesteading-and-livestock/mountain-farm-zmaz74sozraw?pageid=5#PageContent5.

34. Mary Jo Frolick to *Living in the Ozarks Newsletter* (LION), August 1975.

35. Frolick to *Living in the Ozarks Newsletter* (LION).

36. Frolick to *Living in the Ozarks Newsletter* (LION).

37. Frolick to, *Living in the Ozarks Newsletter* (LION).

38. Myrtle Cress, "Letter from Arkansas: Homesteading Tips," *Mother Earth News* September/October 1973, http://www.motherearthnews.com/homesteading-and-livestock/homesteading-tips-zmaz73sozraw.aspx?PageId=2.

39. Monte Burch, "How to Till the Land: Rototiller Advice, Tips and Tricks," *Mother Earth News* March/April 1975, http://www.motherearthnews.com/organic-gardening/till-the-land-zmaz75mazgoe.aspx?PageId=2. One back to the lander (with considerable humor) in Newton County noted that you could chart the progression of the hippies by how fast they abandoned the tillers and either went to tractors, horses, or permaculture-type systems. Anonymous, conversation with author, June 5, 2015.

40. B. Touchstone Hardaway, "The Beauty of a Cookstove," *Mother Earth News*, January/February 1971, http://www.motherearthnews.com/homesteading-and-livestock/beauty-of-a-cookstove-zmaz71jfzsea.aspx.

41. Hardaway, "The Beauty of a Cookstove."

42. Tom Hodges, "Homemade Maple Syrup in the Ozarks," *Mother Earth News* January/February 1979, http://www.motherearthnews.com/real-food/homemade-maple-syrup-zmaz79jfzraw.aspx.

43. For a brief discussion of *Kudzu* and the other more commonly known guerilla publications in the South, see "Kudzu," Wake Atlanta (website), accessed February 24, 2018, http://www.wakeatlanta.com/KUDZU1_0.html. My thanks to Thomas Kersen for engaging discussions about *Kudzu* and the counterculture in the South in general.

44. Streitmatter, *Voices*, 208. It should also be noted that Arkansas's counterculture was not exclusively made up of back to the landers or other hippies. There was a long-standing and continually evolving LGBTQ community in the state, one that availed itself to many of the same strategies as the BTLs. See Brock Thompson, *The Un-Natural State: Arkansas and the Queer South* (Fayetteville: University of Arkansas Press, 2010) for an excellent and unique discussion of Arkansas's (and the Ozarks) queer history.

45. This should not be confused with *OACC*, the Ozark Area Community Congress. The *OACC*, centered primarily in Missouri in and around West Plains, is an outgrowth of many of the activities of the back to the land movement. See "About," Ozark Area Community Congress (website), accessed December 14, 2017, http://ozarkareacommunitycongress.org/about/.

46. *Ozark Access Catalog*, April 1973, 3. University of Arkansas Special Collections.

47. Undated note on the *Ozark Access Catalog*. Ozark Institute Files, box 1, folder 6, Ozark Futures Forums, August 10, 1976–May/June 1977. University of Arkansas Special Collections.

48. *Ozark Access Catalog*, April 1973, 3. University of Arkansas Special Collections.

49. *Ozark Access Catalog*, 3.

50. *Ozark Access Catalog*, 4.

51. "Land Acquisition," *OAC*, April 1973, 4, University of Arkansas Special Collections.

52. "Land Acquisition," 4.

53. Cindy Arsaga, author questionnaire, in possession of author. See also, Marie Demeroukas, "Back to the Land," *The Back-Stay* (blog), August 7, 2013, http://shilohmuseum.org/wordpress/back-to-the-land/; Cindy Arsaga Oral History (conducted by Susan Young), July 3, 2013, Shiloh Museum of Ozark History, Springdale, AR.

54. Arsaga Oral History.

55. Arsaga Oral History. Winter weather was indeed a factor for many, reflecting the general colder period Arkansas found itself in from 1958 to a record low in 1979. See "Climate of Arkansas," Office of the Arkansas State Climatologist (website), accessed November 3, 2016, http://www.climate.ar.gov/Climate%20Intro.pdf.

56. "Letters from Our Readers," *OAC*, July 1973, 36–37.

57. Riley V. Richard to *Ozark Access Catalog*, *OAC*, August 1973, 30.

58. Lydia L. Holland to *Ozark Access Catalog*, *OAC*, August 1973, 30.

59. Joel Davidson to *Ozark Access Catalog*, *OAC*, August 1973, 30.

60. John Fitzmaurice to *Ozark Access Catalog*, *OAC*, November 1973, 26.

61. Richard and Marlene to *Ozark Access Catalog*, *OAC*, November 1973, 27. This is one of the few examples of a potential "burning out" of a hippie in the Ozarks despite popular mythology. Potentially another example occurred in Madison County, Arkansas; and one person in Newton County has had several attempts at burning him out occur, though according to back to the landers and others asked about this, the Newton County case is separate from any potential problems with hipbillies.

62. Richard and Marlene to *Ozark Access Catalog*, *OAC*, 27.

63. Richard and Marlene to *Ozark Access Catalog*, *OAC*, 27.

64. Richard and Marlene to *Ozark Access Catalog*, *OAC*, 27.

65. Richard and Marlene to *Ozark Access Catalog*, *OAC*, 27.

66. Alongside *LION* were, to name just a few, *Down Home*, *The Grapevine*, *Ozark Feminist Press*, *The Ozarks Digest*, *The Ozark Communicator* (though this and the *Digest* and *Total Lifestyle* quickly operated as more "establishment" type publications).

67. Joel Davidson, *Living in the Ozarks Newsletter* (*LION*), January 1974. University of Arkansas Special Collections.

68. Joel Davidson, *Living in the Ozarks Newsletter* (*LION*), January 1974, 2. University of Arkansas Special Collections.

69. Joel Davidson, *Living in the Ozarks Newsletter* (*LION*), January 1974, 2. University of Arkansas Special Collections.

70. Joel Davidson, *Living in the Ozarks Newsletter* (*LION*), October 1974, 1. University of Arkansas Special Collections.

71. The states were: California, Texas, Louisiana, West Virginia, Oklahoma, New Mexico, Georgia, and Kansas. Joel Davidson, *Living in the Ozarks Newsletter* (*LION*),

October 1974. University of Arkansas Special Collections. The newsletter remained under the leadership of the Davidsons until the late 1970s, when it transferred to Cary Carpenter and his wife in Harrison, Boone County. Once this transition occurred, *LION*'s trajectory slowly turned from a more stereotypical counterculture voice to one more libertarian in outlook.

72. There were many, many more like this, as well as books written during previous back to the land movements, like old copies of *Five Acres and Independence*, that were picked up from used bookstores or reprinted. For example, see Briarpatch Community, *The Briarpatch Book: Experiences in Right Livelihood and Simple Living* (San Francisco: A New Glide/Reed Book, 1978) or Alicia Bay Laurel's classic *Living on the Earth: Celebrations, Storm Warnings, Formulas, Recipes, Rumors, and Country Dances* (Berkeley: Bookworks, 1970; reprinted by Vintage Books in 1971).

73. Helen Nearing and Scott Nearing, *The Good Life: Helen and Scott Nearing's Sixty Years of Self-Sufficient Living* (New York: Schocken Books, 1989) 209; chap. 2–4.

74. See Eliot Coleman, *The New Organic Grower: A Master's Manual of Tools and Techniques for the Home and Market Gardener*, 2nd ed. (White River Junction, VT: Chelsea Green Publishing, 1995); Eliot Coleman, *The Winter Harvest Handbook: Year Round Vegetable Production Using Deep-Organic Techniques and Unheated Greenhouses* (White River Junction, VT: Chelsea Green Publishing, 2009).

75. Nearing and Nearing, *Good Life*, 274.

76. Nearing and Nearing, *Good Life*, 278.

77. Nearing and Nearing, *Good Life*, 323–33.

78. Nearing and Nearing, *Good Life*, 358–59. They estimated that by 1971 and 1972 between 2,000 and 2,500 people were coming to visit them each year. See Nearing and Nearing, 361.

79. Coleman started his career as a BTL in 1968 when he moved to Maine, establishing his farm on land purchased from Helen and Scott Nearing, and has become a globally recognized expert on various methods for small-scale, organic vegetable production and has written, most notably, *The New Organic Grower* (1989) and *Four Season Harvest* (1992), essential reading for beginning organic farmers.

80. Agnew, *Back from the Land*, 123.

81. The Nearings sought to divide each day into two four-hour blocks, morning and afternoon, or "bread labor" and "personally determined activities." Nearing and Nearing, *Good Life*, 51.

82. It should also be noted that the majority of the money that came in from the Nearings' work did not go directly to them. Rather, most of it went to their study center, the Social Science Institute. See Vivien Ellen Rose, "Homesteading as a Social Protest: Gender and Continuity in the Back to the land Movement in the United States, 1890–1980." (PhD diss., Binghamton University, SUNY, 1997), 288.

83. Cindy Arsaga, author questionnaire, in possession of author. See also Demeroukas, "Back to the Land."

84. James Bohlen, *The New Pioneer's Handbook: Getting Back to the Land in an Energy-Scarce World* (New York: Schocken Books, 1975).

85. William Grimes, "Jim Bohlen, 84, a Leader in Greenpeace, Is Dead," *New York Times*, July 9, 2010, B9.

86. Sam Binkley, "The Seers of Menlo Park," 290.

87. Thomas Frank, *The Conquest of Cool: Business Culture, Counterculture, and the Rise of Hip Consumerism* (Chicago: University of Chicago Press, 1997), 9.

88. Frank, *Conquest of Cool*, 26.

89. Bohlen, *New Pioneers Handbook*, 4–5.

90. Bohlen, *New Pioneers Handbook*, 5, 8.

91. Bohlen, *New Pioneers Handbook*, 27–91.

92. Bohlen, *New Pioneers Handbook*, chap. 4, 5. Bohlen also provided for his readers the basics for utilizing passive solar construction, a topic not far from the mind of Ozark counterculture members in the Ozarks.

93. See Carter Taylor Seaton, *Hippie Homesteaders: Arts, Crafts, Music, and Living on the Land in West Virginia* (Morgantown: West Virginia University Press, 2014); and Turman "Appalachian Alter-Natives," for excellent discussions of how the back-to-the-land community did this in Appalachia.

94. Tom Wolfe, "The 'Me' Decade and the Third Great Awakening," *New York Magazine*, August 23, 1976. I am grateful for Robert McMath and Blake Perkins for highlighting this.

95. This is counter to the "New Ozarks" that emerges as a result of the more immediately powerful tourist and retiree economy that is growing at the same time. See Perkins, *Hillbilly Hellraisers*, chap. 6, 7.

CHAPTER 3

1. See Perkins, *Hillbilly Hellraisers*, chap. 6, 7 for the most complete discussion of the development the "New Ozarks." For a recent example of how this plays out elsewhere in the Upland South, see Turman, "Appalachian Alter-Natives."

2. By contrast, in some texts the back to the land community is not addressed. The magisterial *Arkansas: A Narrative History* has virtually no discussion of the counterculture in the Ozarks or Arkansas writ large. See Jeannie M. Whayne et al., *Arkansas: A Narrative History*, 2nd ed. (Fayetteville: University of Arkansas Press, 2013). Ben Johnson's *Arkansas in Modern America* is similar in its omission of the counterculture in the Ozarks. See Ben F. Johnson, *Arkansas in Modern America, 1930–1999* (Fayetteville: University of Arkansas Press, 2000).

3. Milton Rafferty, *The Ozarks: Land and Life*, 2nd ed. (Fayetteville: University of Arkansas Press, 2001), 247–248. It should be noted that counterculture in-migrants did often know more about these programs, and others like VISTA, than many locals. This is largely the result of a combination of things ranging from urban activism during the establishment of the Great Society to higher education rates.

4. Rafferty, *Ozarks*, 71.

5. Blevins, *Hill Folks*, 200.

6. Blevins, *Hill Folks*, 200.

7. Blevins has noted this as well, basing his interpretation on his own anecdotal evidence. To be fair, though, it must be noted that the back to the land community was in no way the focus of Blevins's work. Brooks Blevins, email conversation with the author, May 23, 2014.

8. The Ozark Folk Fair should not be confused with the Ozark Folk Festival that had been in Eureka before, and remained after, the Folk Fair.

9. Sheila Daniels, "Ecology Being Emphasized in Folkfair Site Preparations," *Times-Echo*, April 19, 1973, 16.

10. Daniels, "Ecology Being Emphasized in Folkfair Site Preparations," 16.

11. Daniels, "Ecology Being Emphasized in Folkfair Site Preparations," 16.

12. Daniels, "Ecology Being Emphasized in Folkfair Site Preparations," 16.

13. Daniels, "Ecology Being Emphasized in Folkfair Site Preparations," 16. Acts included The Earl Scruggs Revue, Nitty Gritty Dirt Band, Ozark Mountain Daredevils, Big Mama Thornton, Jimmy Driftwood, Mason Profit, and John Lee Hooker. Daniels, "Opry Stars to Headline, Ozark Mountain Folkfair," Time-Echo, April 12, 1973, 1, 4. Approximately twenty thousand people came to the Folkfair despite the inclement weather. See Steve Vanhook, "Music, Drugs and Mud Mix at Folkfair," Times-Echo, May 31, 1973, 1, 8. While Jeffords and others believed the Folkfair was a success and economic benefit to the community, some differed in their interpretation. An anonymous letter to the editor of the Times-Echo argued that the Folkfair was populated by "parasites" who were subsidized by the "solid citizens" of Eureka, ending the short letter with a plea that "our fair city never again be so disgraced." Anonymous, "Folkfair 'Wernt' Great," Times-Echo, June 21, 1973, 5.

14. Daniel, "Opry Stars to Headline," 1, 4.

15. John Fuller Cross to Joel Bunch, September 14, 2016. (Emphasis in original.) Letter in possession of author.

16. John Fuller Cross to Joel Bunch, September 14, 2016. Letter in possession of author. It should be noted that the fears of Cross and others in the Eureka establishment about the Folk Fair were increased by the memory of the riots and property damage at Rockaway Beach in Taney County, Missouri, over the July 4 weekend of 1965. There the AP reported that "thousands of beer-drinking youths battled officers and smashed windows," resulting in the arrests of 175 people out of the eight thousand young folks in attendance. Nine businesses had their windows shattered, and bashing cars, the group also overturned one police car. Police estimated that by the time it was all over, after three young men were arrested for motor vehicle violations, some two thousand people had been involved in the riots. With this as the context, Cross's concerns make sense. It should be noted, however, that what set off the riots had nothing to do with what the hipbillies were doing in the Arkansas Ozarks. John Fuller Cross to Joel Bunch, September 14, 2016. See also "Holiday Youth Riots Erupt at Rockaway Beach, Four Other Resorts," Northwest Arkansas Times, July 5, 1965, 1; and "Ready for Trouble," Northwest Arkansas Times, September 6, 1965, 4.

17. Michael Niman, People of the Rainbow: A Nomadic Utopia, 2nd ed. (Knoxville: University of Tennessee Press, 2014), 18.

18. See "The Rainbow Family's Fourth Annual Spiritual Gathering," Mother Earth News May/June 1975, Accessed June 30, 2017, http://www.motherearthnews.com/nature-and-environment/spiritual-gathering-zmaz75mjzgoe.

19. Rainbow Atma to LION, October 1975.

20. Atma to LION, October 1975.

21. Letter quoted in "Rainbow Family Visiting Ozarks," Ozark Digest, June 1975, 13.

22. Blevins, Hill Folk, 193–200.

23. Blevins, 193–4; Perkins, Hillbilly Hellraisers, chap. 5, 6.

24. Blevins, Hill Folk, 193–200.

25. John Fuller Cross, Oral History Interview by Tom Dillard, September 2, 2011, 46–47, Vertical File, Special Collections, University of Arkansas Libraries.

26. See various editorials in the Eureka Springs Times-Echo over the course of

1972, such as "Let's Take Our City Seriously," from April 13, 1972; or "Voting Is Your Privilege," from May 11, 1972, which offered such warnings as "We don't want Eureka Springs taken over by a deviate sub-culture." "What Sort of Future Do You Want," *The Times-Echo*, May 25, 1972.

27. Editorial, "What Sort of Future Do You Want," *The Times-Echo*, May 25, 1972.

28. Editorial, "What Sort of Future Do You Want."

29. Editorial, "What Sort of Future Do You Want."

30. Glen Jeansonne, conversation with author, August 2, 2014.

31. Blevins, *Hill Folks*, 241; Glen Jeansonne, *Gerald L. K. Smith: Minister of Hate* (New Haven: Yale University Press, 1988) 200–201; Glen Jeansonne, conversation with author, August 2, 2014.

32. Editorial from the *Times Echo*, quoted in *Down Home*, June 15–July 15, 1972, 2. Only one member—Gary Eagen—of the Eureka counterculture would win a seat on city council, but that would be later, in 1976. Three others ran but handily lost to longtime Eureka establishment figures. Frank Egan, email conversation with author, November 4, 2014.

33. Editorial from the *Times Echo*, quoted in *Down Home*, June 15–July 15, 1972, 2. See "Let's Take Our City Seriously," *Times Echo*, April 13, 1972, 6.

34. "Let's Take Our City Seriously," *Times Echo*, April 13, 1972, 6.

35. "Let's Take Our City Seriously," 6.

36. "Let's Take Our City Seriously," 6.

37. Folks like Cross were not universally in favor of the type of growth coming to the region. Indeed, Cross noted in his oral history for the University of Arkansas that he was opposed to some development near a spring that serviced his house. For Cross, the impact of building shopping centers and tourist attractions needed to be balanced with the whole need of the community, something he has worked to preserve throughout his tenure in the city. See John Fuller Cross, interview with Tom Dillard, September 2, 2011, Vertical File, Special Collections, University of Arkansas Libraries, Fayetteville.

38. Blevins, *Hill Folks*, 241–44. The establishment of the Folk Center was not without its own culture battles, thanks in large part to the idiosyncratic nature of Harold Sherman, or even Jimmy Driftwood, and the contentious reputations they achieved in the county.

39. W. K. McNeil, *Ozark Country* (Jackson: University Press of Mississippi, 1995), 168.

40. McNeil, *Ozark Country*, 170–71.

41. Blevins, *Hill Folk*, 251.

42. Bill Royce, "An Evaluation of the Ozark In-migration" (speech), from "Proceedings of the Ozarks In-Migration Conference, 14–15 May 1976," Ozark Institute Files, box 1, folder 1, p. 5, University of Arkansas Special Collections. In some cases the reports of nudity were greatly over-exaggerated. In Washington County, for example, rumors had spread that the Dome People were in favor of a more nudist lifestyle, and while people there and elsewhere in the region did at times work naked, this was not always the norm. Indeed, one member of the community there remembered they had a visitor come through looking for a place to settle and, after visiting them for a week, was disappointed there was not all that much nudity. David Pride, conversation with author, April 15, 2015.

43. Royce, "Ozark In-migration."

44. Blevins, *Hill Folks*, 247–51.

45. Glen Ohrlin, interviewed by Brooks Blevins, June 23, 2003, "The Creation and Development of the Arkansas Folk Festival and the Ozark Folk Center: An Oral History Project," Lyon College (website), accessed November 3, 2014, web.lyon.edu/groups/mslibrary/rcol/oralhistory.htm.

46. Blevins, *Hill Folks*, 251.

47. Glen Branscum, interviewed by Brooks Blevins, June 18, 2003, "The Creation and Development of the Arkansas Folk Festival and the Ozark Folk Center: An Oral History," Lyon College (website), accessed November 3, 2014, web.lyon.edu/groups/mslibrary/rcol/oralhistory.htm.

48. Leo Rainey, interviewed by Brooks Blevins, July 2, 2003, "The Creation and Development of the Arkansas Folk Festival and the Ozark Folk Center: An Oral History," Lyon College (website), accessed November 3, 2014, web.lyon.edu/groups/mslibrary/rcol/oralhistory.htm.

49. David Pride, conversation with author, March 15, 2015.

50. Pride.

51. Brenda Moosey, interview with Dan Kelley, August 20, 2007, in possession of author.

52. Moosey, interview.

53. Moosey, interview.

54. Unattributed excerpt in *LION*, May 1974, 1.

55. See chapter 2 for a larger discussion of the philosophy behind the hipbillies' move to the woods.

56. *LION*, for the majority of its life under the Davidsons, functioned as a connecting tool—a message board—where people posted letters and reprinted articles in order to better understand and deal with the particular problems associated with the back to the land life.

57. Jenkin Lloyd Jones, "The Children of Nature," *Tulsa Tribune*, March 10, 1973.

58. Jones, "The Children of Nature."

59. Edd Jeffords to Jenkin Lloyd Jones, July 1973, *Ozark Access Catalog*, 2.

60. Jeffords to Jones, 2.

61. Edd Jeffords, "Folklore and Customs," *Ozark Access Catalog*, April 1973, 10.

62. Vance Randolph, *Ozark Magic and Folklore* (New York: Dover, 1947), quoted Jeffords, "Folklore and Customs," 10. In this passage in the full book, Randolph goes on to describe Ozarkers as a group that has "retained certain ancient notions which have been discarded and forgotten in more progressive sections of the United States," notions that, for Randolph, came not from African Americans or Native Americans but the old country (England or Scotland). See Randolph, *Ozark Magic and Folklore*.

63. Jeffords, "Folklore and Customs," 10.

64. Jeffords, "Folklore and Customs," 10.

65. Anonymous back to the lander, conversation with author, January 24, 2018. This person is part of a movement, bioregionalism, that prefers to maintain a collective identity and eschews personal recognition (despite his efforts to organize and push forward bioregional ideals).

66. Crescent Dragonwagon, "If You're Going to Come, Come Gently," *Ozark Access Catalog*, April 1973, 22.

67. Guy Ames, conversation with author, March 18, 2015.

68. Interview with Dennis and Linda Sanders, May 22, 2014, Fayetteville, AR. Name changed for privacy.

69. Group of back to the landers, interview with author, June 8, 2014, Pettigrew, AR. Names withheld for privacy. This was a grouping of six BTL settlers, two married couples, and two individuals. The six of them arrived between 1972 and 1980, and as of 2015, all are still on the land and employed either by successful arts or agricultural careers (or a combination).

70. Group of BTL's, interview with author.

71. Group of BTL's, interview with author.

72. Ruth McShane Weinstein, "A Force for Social Change: Ozark Back to the land Settlements, 1970–1995" (unpublished manuscript, no date), 10.

73. Sarah (no last name), "A Square Checks Out a Happening," *Down Home*, August 1972, 13.

74. Sarah (no last name), "A Square Checks Out a Happening," 13.

75. Sarah (no last name), "A Square Checks Out a Happening," 13.

76. "How to Build a Molehill into a Mountain," *Down Home*, June 15–July 1, 1972, 2.

77. Editorial, "How to Build a Molehill into a Mountain," *Down Home*, June 15–July 1, 1972, 2. Underlining in original.

78. "Molehill into a Mountain," *Down Home*.

79. Arkansas Family of 4 Wins $10,000 In 'Food Self-Sufficiency' Contest," *Arkansas Gazette*, April 27, 1977. See also "Mother's Self-Sufficient Competition," *Mother Earth News*, May/June 1977 and "Food Self-Sufficiency Tips," *Mother Earth News*, May/June 1977.

80. "Family of 4 Wins $10,000," *Arkansas Gazette*.

81. "Family of 4 Wins $10,000," *Arkansas Gazette*, April 27, 1977. The Taylor family's good fortune was reported on in mainstream news outlets across the country as well, including in a piece by CBS. It should be noted, though, that this all drew unwanted attention to the Taylors—Dan noted later that the television interview had made them out to be more than they were. See Donald Katz, "Good Times Comin' to Arkansas," *GEO*, June 1980, 35–56. Reprinted in *The Valley of the Fallen and Other Places* (New York: AtRandom, 2001), 152–73.

82. Hazel Smith, interview with author, June 25, 2014, Fayetteville, AR.

83. For those acquainted with modern haying operations, this may be unclear. Prior to the development and widespread application of round balers or square bale accumulators and grapples used by tractors to move the bales, small square bales, each about fifty-five pounds, were moved by hand from the field to the barn. For perspective, a moderate production per acre of hay is about fifty bales per acre in the Ozarks. Such labor, in the heat of the summer, quickly becomes taxing even for the most hardened farm hand.

84. Hazel Smith, interview with author, June 25, 2014, Fayetteville, AR.

85. Smith, interview with author.

86. Smith, interview with author.

87. Cindy Arsaga, interview with Susan Young, July 3, 2013, the Shiloh Museum of Ozark History. Interview accessible at the Shiloh Museum of Ozark History (hereafter Shiloh Museum).

88. Arsaga, interview.

89. Haught was not necessarily a "true" Ozark native, but operated in much of the same cultural frame as old-time Ozarkers.

90. Cindy Arsaga, interview with Susan Young.

91. Arsaga, interview.

92. Dennis Sanders and Linda Sanders, interview with author, May 22, 2014.

93. Sanders and Sanders, interview.

94. Sanders and Sanders, interview.

95. Sanders and Sanders, interview.

96. Jim Babineaux and Patty Jackson, interview with author, June 4, 2014. Names withheld for privacy.

97. Babineaux and Jackson, interview.

98. Babineaux and Jackson, interview.

99. For an outsider's perspective on this, see Katz, "Good Times Comin'."

100. Weinstein, *Force for Social Change*, 77.

101. Weinstein, *Force for Social Change*, 76–77.

102. Weinstein, *Force for Social Change*, 75.

103. Weinstein, *Force for Social Change*, 74.

104. Neidhardt, *Fox Letters,* 15.

105. Neidhardt, Fox Letters, 15. It should be noted that this superior position in not offending "simple" hill folk does not extend across the Ozarks. Indeed, most back to the landers relationships with the local community were rooted in a notion of student (BTL) to teacher (local).

106. Katz, "Good Times Comin'."

107. Katz, Good Times Comin'."

108. This is perhaps best seen in the contest surrounding the creation of a community college in Baxter County during 1973. The college, supported by State Representative Veda Shied and local groups, was defeated at the polls in part due to opposition from retirees who had moved into the area and were unsure of an institution that might bring in blacks, longhairs, and hippies, while also imposing a small tax to help fund the community college.

109. Blevins, *Hill Folks*, 199.

CHAPTER 4

1. Margaret C. McGrade, letter to the editor, *National Observer*, August 10, 1976, Ozark Institute Files (MC 252), box 1, folder 6, notebook: Ozark Futures Forums, Aug 10, 1976–May/June 1977). Special Collections, University of Arkansas Libraries. (Hereafter, Ozark Institute Files from the University of Arkansas Special Collections will be noted simply as OIF.) A quick note on sources here is in order. The Ozark Institute Files, maintained by the University of Arkansas Special Collections, are an insightful resource for those interested in how community organizations in the upland South functioned during the period. That being said, the files are somewhat incomplete—portions of the narrative regarding certain programs is limited as a result.

2. See Perkins, *Hillbilly Hellraisers*, chap. 6, 7.

3. While Edd Jeffords was focused improving relations between hippies and non-counterculture groups, not all in the region's counterculture appreciated his

efforts. In the process of gathering materials for this work, opinions were encountered within the back to the land movement about Jeffords that ranged from seeing him as a genius and indefatigable visionary to a con artist intent only on self-promotion. Based on interviews, archival work, and news reports, it appears that Jeffords was not a con artist, but that he certainly had a personal style that irked some in Eureka, and ultimately, Little Rock.

4. Mike Luster, "Looking for the Center of the Universe: Edd Jeffords and Ozark In-migration" (memorial speech), 2006, research file category and sub-category: Population / Migration; folder: Back to the land; Shiloh Museum of Ozark History, Springdale, Arkansas.

5. Luster. See also April Griffith, "Ozark Mountain Folk Fair: History in our Backyard," The Back-Stay (blog), June 7, 2013, http://shilohmuseum.org/wordpress/ozark-mountain-folk-fair/. This was only marginally successful. See previous chapter for a fuller discussion of the Folk Fair.

6. Ozark In-Migration Conference Program, May 14–15, 1976. OIF, box 1, folder 1.

7. Edd Jeffords, Ozarks In-Migration Flyer, "Introduction to Ozarks In-Migration: The Full Effect Hasn't Been Felt Yet," reprint from Arkansas Gazette, 1. OIF, box 1, folder 1.

8. Historians have remarkable access to this event—Jeffords and the conference organizers put together a complete set of the speeches and information handed out and used for the conference. See OIF, box 1, folder 2.

9. Editorial, Springdale News, April 25, 1976.

10. Gale Baldwin, "Migrants to Ozarks Blamed for Problems: Impact of Population Growth Discussed" Springfield News-Leader, March 27, 1977.

11. The data available only record those living out of state in 1975, but population increases related to in-migration across the Ozarks were occurring between 1970 and 1975 as well. Thus, the total number of people in the area who lived in a different state prior to 1971 is likely higher than the 19 percent reflected here.

12. For the data presented in this paragraph, see A Changing Arkansas as Reflected by Population and Related Data, 1970–1980, prepared by the Demographic Research Division, University of Arkansas at Little Rock; USDA Agriculture Census 1950–1982. For a more complete breakdown of the data analyzed here, see Appendix A.

13. A Changing Arkansas. Farmers here do not necessarily correspond to landowning farmers.

14. A Changing Arkansas. This data is flawed, however. Urban population data is only reported for Baxter, Benton, Boone, and Washington Counties in 1970. In 1980 Carroll, Fulton, and Sharp Counties are included. As one familiar with the Arkansas Ozarks might surmise, the greatest numerical increases occurred in the Springfield Plain counties of Benton and Washington Counties.

15. Thanks go out to Robert McMath and Blake Perkins for a lively discussion about this issue that helped me better understand what such a change might mean in rural communities.

16. See Jesse Ray Sims, "Beyond Coattails: Explaining John Paul Hammerschmidt's Victory in 1966" (master's thesis, University of Arkansas, 2017) for the most recent discussion of Hammerschmidt and his context.

17. As Blevins notes, this was not abnormal in the broad range of the upland South in the 1960s. Winthrop Rockefeller, a Republican, won the Governor's House in 1966 as well. Blevins also points out that this surge in Republican voters also

corresponds closely to the changing demographics of the state's uplands, in particular, the in-migration of middle class retirees that seem to have leaned toward the growing conservative movement in the wake of the Civil Rights and counterculture emergence. See Blevins, *Hill Folk*, 297n51.

18. See Dave Leip's Atlas of US Presidential Elections (website), access date January 15, 2018, uselectionatlas.org; Arkansas Secretary of State Paul Riviere, *A Compilation of Primary, Run-Off, and General Election Results for State and District Offices, 1976, 1978, 1980* https://www.sos.arkansas.gov/elections/research/election-results.

19. Ernie Deane, "Ozarks Country," *Springdale News*, May 19, 1976.

20. "Growth Alternatives Forum," Arkansas Humanities Project, no. 038–41–76. OIF, box 1, folder 6: Ozark Futures Forums, Aug 10, 1976–May/June 1977.

21. Press Release, October 7, 1976, Marshall (Stone County). OIF, box 1, folder 6: Ozark Futures Forums, Aug 10, 1976–May/June 1977. Meetings were held in Carroll, Madison, Newton, Marion, Searcy, Stone, and Izard Counties; surveys were conducted in Boone, Benton, Carroll, Madison, Newton, and Washington Counties. The survey conducted prior to the meetings is reprinted in Ralph Desmarais and Edd Jeffords, eds., *Uncertain Harvest: The Family Farm in Arkansas* (Eureka Springs: Ozark Institute, 1980).

22. Press Release, October 7, 1976, Marshall (Stone County). OIF, box 1, folder 6: Ozark Futures Forums, Aug 10, 1976–May/June 1977. See also Perkins, *Hillbilly Hellraisers*, 190–92.

23. Jerry Rephan, "Ozarks Future Forum," *Grapevine*, October 4, 1976.

24. "Newton Countians Discuss Growth, Related Problems," *Harrison Daily Times/Boone County Headlight*, October 6, 1976; "Forum Meeting Well Attended— Lots of Protest," *Jasper Informer*, October 7, 1976. OIF, box 1, folder 6: Ozark Futures Forums, Aug 10, 1976–May/June 1977. The concerns about 2,4D in Newton County were echoed in Madison County as well, and in the early creation of the Ozark Institute as Gary Turner, a leader of CEASE took park in the initial brainstorming about the purpose of the OI. OIF, box 1, folder 4, "Sourcebook: Conference on Ozark In-Migration, Proceedings and Papers, February 1974–May 15, 1979.

25. Editorial, "Lakeview May Have a Choice" *Baxter Bulletin*, Mountain Home, November 10, 1976. OIF, box 1, folder 6: Ozark Futures Forums, Aug 10, 1976–May/June 1977.

26. Janet Nelson, "What's in the Future," *Baxter Bulletin*, November 11, 1976 OIF, box 1 folder 6: Ozark Futures Forums, Aug 10, 1976–May/June 1977.

27. Nelson, "What's in the Future."

28. Perkins, *Hillbilly Hellraisers*, 192.

29. Frank Reuter, "Family Farms in Northwest Arkansas," report on Ozark Futures Forums, in Jeffords, *Uncertain Harvest,* 54.

30. Reuter, "Family Farms in Northwest Arkansas," 54.

31. See Perkins, *Hillbilly Hellraisers,* chap. 7 for a fuller discussion of this, as well as the reaction to AmeriCorps and VISTA workers throughout the region. See also Marvin Schwartz, *In Service to America: A History of VISTA in Arkansas, 1965–1985* (Fayetteville: University of Arkansas Press, 1988).

32. The beginning date for the Ozark Institute is somewhat disputed. One former member, Craig Fuller, remembers the Institute as having started before the In-Migration conference, while some papers in the OIF present it as having begun somewhat later. Craig Fuller, conversation with author, February 28, 2018.

33. "Proposal to Executive Board," April 20, 1977, OIF, box 1, folder 3, Sourcebook: Conference on Ozark In-migration, Proceedings and Papers, February 1974–May 15, 1979.

34. "The Ozark Institute Proposal," undated, OIF, box 1, folder 3, Sourcebook: Conference on Ozark In-migration, Proceedings and Papers, February 1974–May 15, 1979.

35. Wallace E. Smith to Unknown, September 13, 1976. OIF, box 1, folder 4, Sourcebook: Conference on Ozark In-Migration, Proceedings and Papers, February 1974–May 15, 1979.

36. Joel Davidson, "Notes from New Beginnings Community," *Ozark Communicator*, Harrison, November 1976. OIF, box 1, folder 6, Sourcebook: Ozark Futures Forums, August 10, 1976–May/June 1977. For more on Ozark bioregionalism, see chap. 6.

37. NCAT Grant Application, "Proposal for Regional Newsletter," May 1977, 1–5. OIF, box 1, folder 3, Sourcebook: Conference on Ozark In-Migration, Proceedings and Papers, February 1974–May 15, 1979; Craig Fuller, conversation with author, February 28, 2018.

The application highlighted many of the problems that would ultimately bring down the Institute, namely too large a focus area and community partners with little relationship to the Ozarks. The OI noted in its paperwork here that it was seeking to work not just in the Arkansas Ozarks but also in Missouri, Kansas, and Oklahoma. NCAT was relatively new at the time the OI submitted its grant application. Formed in 1976, NCAT focused on programs to aid those at the bottom rungs of the economic ladder in society, especially in rural communities. See "The History of NCAT," National Center for Appropriate Technology (website), accessed February 9, 2018, https://www.ncat.org/history/.

38. Minutes of the Ozark Institute Board of Director, May 14, 1977. OIF, box 1, folder 3, Sourcebook: Conference on Ozark In-Migration, Proceedings and Papers, February 1974–May 15, 1979. The project was funded via a National Center for Community Action grant of $1,075.

39. CETA Grant Proposal, "Community Nutrition," April 11, 1977. OIF, box 1, folder 4, Sourcebook: Conference on Ozark In-Migration, Proceedings and Papers, February 1974–May 15, 1979. The grant application was for $46,845, enough to pay the salary for five staff members to implement the program.

40. R. Robin McDonald, "Ozark CAO Sponsors Successful Food Co-op and Community Cannery," *National Center Reporter*, January 1978. OIF, box 1, folder 3, Sourcebook: Conference on Ozark In-migration, Proceedings and Papers, February 1974–May 15, 1979.

41. McDonald "Ozark CAO Sponsors Successful Food Co-op and Community Cannery." See also Wallace Smith to Mary Rodgers, January 26, 1978. OIF, box 3, folder 6, Correspondence-Ozark Producer-Consumer Alliance, January 6, 1978–April 30, 1979. Craig Fuller, conversation with author, February 28, 2018.

42. Craig Fuller remembered that the whole idea of the OPCA emerged from Jeffords's and his own desire to "only do what people wanted to do." Craig Fuller, conversation with author, February 28, 2018.

43. Edd Jeffords to Jerry McMahon, October 24, 1978. OIF, box 3, folder 6, Correspondence-Ozark Producer-Consumer Alliance, January 6, 1978–April 30, 1979.

44. Flyer, Madison County Community Cannery, OIF, box 3, folder 6,

Correspondence-Ozark Producer-Consumer Alliance, January 6, 1978–April 30, 1979. Bill and Anne Williams questionnaire (name changed for privacy); in author's possession. The cost for using the facility was fifteen cents a quart and ten cents a pint if you brought your own jars.

45. See, for example, Wallace Smith to Mary Rodgers, January 26, 1978. OIF, box 3, folder 6, Correspondence-Ozark Producer-Consumer Alliance, January 6, 1978–April 30, 1979.

46. Craig Fuller to OPCA Board, July 20, 1978. OIF, box 3, folder 6, Correspondence-Ozark Producer-Consumer Alliance, January 6, 1978–April 30, 1979.

47. Craig Fuller to OPCA Board.

48. Craig Fuller to OPCA Board.

49. Edd Jeffords to Jerry McMahon, October 24, 1978. OIF box 3, folder 6: Correspondence-Ozark Producer-Consumer Alliance, January 6, 1978–April 30, 1979.

50. Edd Jeffords to Jerry McMahon.

51. "Ozark Producer-Consumer Alliance Review of 1979," OIF box 7, folder 6: Little Rock File no. 210–711, 1977–1980.

52. Press Release, "FFDS—The Cutting Edge / Lead," June 18, 1980. OIF, box 2, folder 5: News Releases, June 18, 1980–April 2, 1981.

53. Press Release, "FFDS—The Cutting Edge / Lead."

54. Press Release, "FFDS—The Cutting Edge / Lead."

55. Press Release, "FFDS—The Cutting Edge / Lead."

56. Press Release, "FFDS—The Cutting Edge / Lead."

57. Press Release, "FFDS—The Cutting Edge / Lead."

58. "Ozark Institute CETA Audit Report, October 1, 1979–September 30, 1980," OIF, box 5, folder 3: Frank White Suit, July 26, 1980–October 24, 1981.

59. CETA Program Review, April 1981. OIF, box 5, folder 3: Frank White Suit, July 26, 1980–October 24, 1981.

60. "Family Seed Bank Press Release," June 23, 1980. OIF, box 2, folder 5: News Releases, June 18, 1980–April 2, 1981; See also "Community Seed Bank Project Description," OIF, box 7, folder 5: Little Rock file no. 210A-28(1B2), 1980.

61. "Family Seed Bank Press Release," June 23, 1980. OIF, box 2, folder 5: News Releases, June 18, 1980–April 2, 1981.

62. "Family Seed Bank Press Release." Note Jeffords' choice in language here. As mentioned before, the Ozarks were experiencing—like the rest of the nation—a surge in antifederal sentiment commensurate with the Reagan revolution. As such, anything that smacked of a government handout had to be carefully avoided—and in the case of the Institute, even that would not be enough to provide a buffer from political ill will. Indeed, the FFDS had originally been named the Rural Employment Develop Service—REDS—which was scrapped in favor of FFDS once a friend in Little Rock reminded Jeffords and the OI to pay attention to their constituency. An acronym like REDS, associated as it could be with communism, would probably not go over all that well in the region during the 1970s. Craig Fuller, conversation with author, February 28, 2018.

63. "Community Seed Bank Project Description," OIF, box 7, folder 5: Little Rock file no. 210A-28(1B2), 1980.

64. The Ozark Institute Files have no record of who these seeds were distributed to (as far as were they back to the landers or locals). "Family Seed Bank Press

Release," June 23, 1980. OIF, box 2, folder 5: News Releases, June 18, 1980–April 2, 1981; "Community Seed Bank Project Description," OIF, box 7, folder 5: Little Rock file no. 210A-28(1B2), 1980. The OI estimated that seed cost per family gave a "realistic potential return to the family of produce harvest valued at $456.70 in addition to providing seed stock for replenishment of Community Seed Banks," which allowed the program an increased measure of stability while also being able to expand. "Community Seed Bank Project Description," OIF, box 7, folder 5: Little Rock file no. 210A-28(1B2), 1980.

65. Edd Jeffords to Harold Daricek, September 22, 1980, OIF, box 7, folder 5: Little Rock File no. 210A–28(1B2), 1980.

66. Edd Jeffords to Frank J. Iuen III, May 12, 1980. OIF, box 7, folder 5: Little Rock file no. 210A-28(1B2), 1980. See also, Craig Fuller to Edd Jeffords, undated memo, OIF, box 6, folder 4: OI Investigation Papers, March 26, 1980–1982.

67. John Fuller Cross noted, however, that Jeffords was put onto the Eureka Springs Centennial Commission largely due to his grant-writing expertise—and the fact that he had "mellowed" a bit. John Fuller Cross, conversation with author, February 28, 2018.

68. Edd Jeffords to OI BOD, August 19, 1980. OIF, box 2, folder 4: OI Board of Directors—Misc. Business and Papers, Winter 1977–April 20, 1982. That fall, Jeffords and Craig Fuller travelled to Little Rock for a preliminary meeting about their new CETA grant, only to be told that their "success rate was too high" and they "were making everybody look bad." In particular, their cost per participant was much lower than other CETA awardees, which apparently was a problem. Fuller recalled looking over at Jeffords after the meeting and telling him, "I think we're being set up." Craig Fuller, conversation with author, February 28, 2018.

69. Oakley became noted for her opposition to the Clintons, in particular with the publication of her 1994 book, *On the Make: The Rise of Bill Clinton* (Washington DC: Regnery Publishing, 1994).

70. There are few in-depth discussions of Clinton's gubernatorial career. See Diane D. Blair, "Fortieth and Forty-Second Governor: William Jefferson Clinton, 1979–1981; 1983–1992," in *The Governors of Arkansas: Essay in Political Biography*, ed. Timothy Donovan et al., (Fayetteville: University of Arkansas Press, 1995). For a more critical view of the Clinton years in Little Rock, see Oakley, *On the Make*.

71. "Richard Nixon, Statement on Signing the Comprehensive Employment and Training Act of 1973, December 28, 1973," The American Presidency Project (website), accessed February 6, 2018, http://www.presidency.ucsb.edu/ws/index.php?pid=4088.

72. "Richard Nixon, Statement on Signing the Comprehensive Employment and Training Act of 1973."

73. The development of conservatism and anti-New Deal efforts in the 1970s and 1980s has received a great deal of attention in the last several years. Some informative works include, but are not limited to, Cowie, *Stayin' Alive*; Darren Dochuk, *From Bible Belt to Sun Belt: Plain Folk Religion, Grassroots Politics, and the Rise of Evangelical Conservatism* (New York: W. W. Norton, 2011); Kim Phillips-Fein, *Invisible Hands: The Businessmen's Crusade Against the New Deal* (New York: W. W. Norton, 2009); Swartz, *Moral Minority*; William Berman, *America's Right Turn: From Nixon to Clinton*, 2nd ed. (Baltimore: Johns Hopkins University Press, 1998); Borstelmann, *The 1970s*; David T.

Courtwright, *No Right Turn: Conservative Politics in Liberal America* (Cambridge: Harvard University Press, 2010); Godfrey Hodgson, *The World Turned Right Side Up: A History of the Conservative Ascendancy in America* (Boston: Houghton Mifflin, 1996); Philip Jenkins, *A Decade of Nightmares: The End of the Sixties and the Making of the Eighties* (Oxford: Oxford University Press, 2006); Lisa McGirr, *Suburban Warriors: The Origins of the New American Right* (Princeton: Princeton University Press, 2001); Justin Vaisse, *Neoconservatism: A Biography of a Movement*, trans. Arthur Goldhammer (Cambridge: Belknap Press, 2010); and James T. Patterson, *Restless Giant: The United States from Watergate to Bush v. Gore* (Oxford: Oxford University Press, 2005).

74. Jim Lair, "Reflections of an Outlander," *Carroll County Tribune*, June 13, 1980.

75. Jim Lair, "Reflections of an Outlander," *Carroll County Tribune*, August 11, 1980; Jim Lair, "Reflections of an Outlander," *Carroll County Tribune*, July 25, 1980.

76. See Jim Lair, *An Outlander's History of Carroll County, Arkansas* (Marceline: Walsworth Publishing Company, 1983), vii. Lair's history of Carroll County is notable for its omissions, particularly the problematic past of other "adopted sons" like Gerald L. K. Smith. See Lair, *Outlander's History*, 241.

77. Damon Thompson and Andrew Polin, "Jeffords seeks $2 million in suit against White," *Arkansas Democrat*, September 18, 1980.

78. "Jeffords Response to Frank White Lawyers," OIF, box 5, folder 3: Frank White Suit, July 26, 1980–October 24, 1981. The charge was reduced later in August by the municipal court to a charge of carrying a prohibited weapon in his vehicle.

79. Edd Jeffords, "Statement," July 25, 1980. OIF, box 5, folder 3: Frank White Suit, July 26, 1980–October 24, 1981.

80. Jeffords, "Statement."

81. Jeffords, "Statement."

82. Michael Mager, "Statement," date unknown. OIF, box 5, folder 3: Frank White Suit, July 26, 1980–October 24, 1981.

83. Edd Jeffords, Response to Frank White's Lawyers, undated, OIF, box 5, folder 3: Frank White Suit, July 26, 1980–October 24, 1981.

84. Frank White Deposition Transcript, June 1, 1981. OIF, box 5, folder 4: Frank White Suite, July 26, 1980–October 29, 1981. Presumably, Cross noted his own difficulties with Jeffords in the conversation.

85. Meredith Oakley, "Jeffords Blames Publisher for Inquiry," *Arkansas Democrat*, September 17, 1980.

86. Oakley, "Jeffords Blames Publisher for Inquiry,"

87. Oakley, "Jeffords Blames Publisher for Inquiry,"

88. Deposition of John Tyson, July 1, 1980. OIF, box 5, folder 4, Frank White Suite, July 26, 1980–October 29, 1981; "Assault Charges Brought Against Eureka Man," *Carroll County Tribune*, July 30, 1980.

89. Wallace Smith to Editor and Jim Lair, September 18, 1980. OIF, box 6, folder 6: FBI Papers—Little Rock file no. 210-A-28(1A), 1976–1980.

90. Smith to Editor and Jim Lair.

91. Billy Rojas of Eureka Springs and OI, contract for consulting services, July 1, 1980. OIF, box 2, folder 10: Contracts for Consumer Services, September 21–January 30, 1981. The contract was renewed at the end of July for another few weeks.

92. Billy Rojas to Ted Larimer, October 2, 1980. OIF, box 5, folder 2: News Clippings, April 26, 1980–October 20, 1982.

93. Rojas.

94. Edd Jeffords to Jim Costilow, October 9, 1980, *Times-Echo*. For a draft of the letter, see also OIF, box 5, folder 2: News Clippings, April 26, 1980–October 20, 1982.

95. "State Senator to Enter Institute Investigation," *Carroll County Tribune*, September 24, 1980; See Jeffords's response to Farwell in "White Criticizes Clinton Approval of Training Plan," *Arkansas Democrat*, August 26, 1980. Jeffords was quoted as saying that" the institute's cost for training and placing the participants in jobs is about $17,000, well below the $25,000 to $40,000 state average. He said the institute has about a 75 percent placement average compared to the 45–50 percent average in comparable CETA programs." This is not quite true, as a later CETA audit showed a 69 percent placement rate, still above the state average but not as high as Jeffords wanted everyone to think. For Farwell's concerns, see Wayne Farwell, letter to the editor, *Carroll County Tribune*, September 12, 1980.

96. Meredith Oakley "Senator's Rising Anger over the Ozark Institute Not Triggered by Politics" *Arkansas Democrat*, September 28, 1980. Not all readers found her perspective on the issue, which at times seemed to favor White and Hendren, helpful. Responding to some of her earlier pieces, a reader wrote in to note, "I have been amused and annoyed by her many inaccuracies." See letter to the editor, *Arkansas Democrat*, September 28, 1980.

97. Jim Lair, "Public Meeting on Institute Grant Changes Little," *Carroll County Tribune,* October 1, 1980.

98. Lair, "Public Meeting on Institute Grant Changes Little."

99. Lair, "Public Meeting on Institute Grant Changes Little."

100. Desmarais and Jeffords, *Uncertain Harvest*, vii.

101. Desmarais and Jeffords, *Uncertain Harvest*, vii. The Arkansas state nickname from 1953 until 1995 was "Land of Opportunity." In 1995, after a concentrated state park promotion campaign, the state legislature changed the nickname to "The Natural State." See David Ware, "State Nicknames," The Encyclopedia of Arkansas History and Culture (website), accessed April 28, 2017, http://www.encyclopedia ofarkansas.net/encyclopedia/entry-detail.aspx?entryID=3150.

102. "Statement to Family Farm Symposium," Winrock Farms, June 15, 1979. Thomas Chipman McRae IV Papers (MC 1325), Series II, Subseries III: Agriculture— Family Farm Symposium, box 5, folder 36, Special Collections, University of Arkansas. Hereafter TCM Papers.

103. "Statement to Family Farm Symposium."

104. Tom Hamburger, "Thousands Forced to Leave Farming," in Desmarais and Jeffords, *Uncertain Harvest*, 40.

105. National Rural Coalition, "Policy Recommendations," in Desmarais and Jeffords, *Uncertain Harvest*, 92.

106. Douglas Wilson to Larry McCord, October 9, 1980. OIF, box 6, folder 6: FBI Papers-Little Rock file no. 210-A-28(1A), 1976–1980.

107. Wilson to McCord.

108. Wilson to McCord.

109. "Investigation of Ozark Institute is nearing completion, FBI says," *Arkansas Democrat*, October 23, 1980.

110. Edd Jeffords, public statement RE: FBI Investigation, November 12, 1980. OIF, box 6, folder 6: FBI Papers-Little Rock file no. 210-A-28(1A), 1976–1980.

111. Jeffords, public statement.

112. Press Release: Ozark Institute CETA Program Ceases, April 2, 1981, OIF, box 2, folder 5: News Releases, June 18, 1980–April 2, 1981.

113. Edd Jeffords to John Lisle, March 26, 1982. OIF, box 2, folder 4: OI Board of Directors-Misc. Business and Papers, Winter 1977–April 20, 1982.

114. Edd Jeffords to Institute BOD, July 28, 1981. OIF, box 2, folder 4: OI Board of Directors-Misc. Business and Papers, Winter 1977–April 20, 1982.

115. Jeffords to unknown, October 18, 1982. OIF, box 6, folder 3: OI Financial and Bank Information (Misc.) Audits, 1974–November 15.

CHAPTER 5

1. Rachel Carson, *Silent Spring*, (Boston: Houghton Mifflin, 1962). For a new look at where Carson fits in the broad story of American environmentalism, see Chad Montrie, *The Myth of Silent Spring: Rethinking the Origins of American Environmentalism* (Berkeley: University of California Press, 2018).

2. "F" to Ruth Weinstein, *Force for Social Change*, 89. Emphasis in original.

3. Sidney Bell to *LION*, November 1974, 5.

4. Gary Turner to *LION*, November 1974, 9.

5. See Kathryn Newfont, *Blue Ridge Commons: Environmental Activism and Forest History in Western North Carolina* (Athens: University of Georgia Press, 2012), esp. 130–60, for a discussion of clear-cutting. For other perspectives on environmental struggles in the American South during the 1960s, 1970s, and 1980s, see Albert Way, *Conserving Southern Longleaf: Herbert Stoddard and the Rise of Ecological Land Management* (Athens: University of Georgia Press, 2011); Craig Colton's *Southern Waters: The Limits to Abundance* (Baton Rouge: Louisiana State University Press, 2014); and Chad Montrie's *To Save the Land and People: A History of Opposition to Surface Coal Mining in Appalachia* (Chapel Hill: University of North Carolina Press, 2003). For the USFS's approach to herbicides in the Ozarks, see Larry Henson, *Vegetation Management with Herbicides: Final Environmental Statement* (Russellville: United States Forest Service, 1975).

6. Montrie illustrates this point in his examination of opposition to coal mining. See Montrie, *To Save the Land*, 3.

7. 2,4,5-T and 2,4-D, when mixed together, are the main components of Agent Orange.

8. Gary Turner to *LION*, November 1974, 9. In 1979 the EPA would issue an injunction after several miscarriages were reported in Oregon related to the creation of dioxin as a byproduct of 2,4,5 T. "EPA Halts Most Use of Herbicide 2,4,5 T: Study Finds Miscarriages Occurred Among Oregon Women Just After the Spraying Period There," *Science* 203 (March 1979): 1090–91.

9. Gary Turner to *LION*, November 1974.

10. Turner to *LION*.

11. "K" to Ruth Weinstein, in *"Force for Social Change*, 88. "K" notes that in the mid-1970s, then Governor David Pryor reorganized the state Quorum Court system, devolving power out into the counties "without really giving them the authority to do too much." See "K" in Weinstein, 88.

12. Gary Turner to *LION* November 1974, 10.

13. Arkansas State Plant Board Annual Reports, 1969–1980. Hereafter ASPB Report.

14. *ASPB Report*, 1968.

15. *ASPB Report*, 1978.

16. Editorial, "Stop the Bombing," *Ozark Digest*, June 1975, 2.

17. *ASPB Reports, 1969–1980*. This is a growth rate of only 21 percent. This statistic is not recorded in the 1979 and 1980 annual report. Manufacturing permits as well experienced only slight growth.

18. "J" to Ruth Weinstein, in *Force for Social Change*, 25. It should also be noted that the state agricultural extension agency published a pamphlet, *Arkansas Lawn Weeds* (extension circular 528, 1967) that highlighted the use of 2,4-D and 2,4,5-T in treating lawn weeds.

19. For an example of Secretary Butz's philosophy, see "Earl Butz versus Wendell Berry," *CoEvolution Quarterly* (Spring 1978): 50–59.

20. Blevins, *Hill Folk*, 149.

21. Blevins, *Hill Folk*, 174–78.

22. USDA Agriculture Census Data, 1950–1982. During this same period, the total amount of working farmland dropped by 29.89 percent (4.5 million acres to 3.37 million acres). See Appendix C for data table.

23. Blevins, *Hill Folk*, 149.

24. See "Ozark Woman Speaks Out on Aerial Spray Dangers," *Ozark Access Catalog*, June 1975, 2. It was also printed in *ACRES, USA*, an agriculture magazine founded in 1970 by Carl Wilken.

25. "Ozark Woman Speaks Out," 2.

26. "Ozark Woman Speaks Out," 2.

27. "Ozark Woman Speaks Out," 2.

28. "Ozark Woman Speaks Out," 2. Beyond this report, there is only anecdotal support for claims made about the negative impact of these chemicals.

29. "Ozark Woman Speaks Out on Aerial Spray Dangers," *The Ozark Digest*, June 1975, pg. 2.

30. "The 2,4,5 T Story That Cost a Man His Job," *Ozark Digest*, July 1975, 10.

31. "The 2,4,5 T Story," 10.

32. Brooke Ligon to Dale Bumpers, May 8, 1975, folder 19, box 6, Dale Bumpers Papers (MC1490), series 3, subseries 2, University of Arkansas Special Collections. Hereafter DBP Papers.

33. Mrs. Mary Tuttle to Dale Bumpers, June 16, 1975, folder 19, box 6, DBP, series 3, subseries 2. As far as is evident from the sources, Mrs. Tuttle was not a back to the lander.

34. M. L. Pardue to Dale Bumpers, August 25, 1975, folder 19, box 6, DBP, series 3, subseries 2. M. L. Pardue was Michael Pardue, Robbie Pardue's husband. Both were contributors to *LION*.

35. Pardue to Dale Bumpers.

36. Dale Bumpers to W. Robb Nisbet, December 19, 1975, folder 19, box 6, DBP, series 3, subseries 2. For a limited treatment of Bumpers's perspective on the issue, see Jeannie Whayne, "The Incidental Environmentalists: Dale Bumpers, George Templeton, and the Origins of the Rosen Alternative Pest Control Center at the

University of Arkansas," *Agricultural History* 89, no. 1 (Winter 2015): 3–28. For a brief discussion on the history of 2,4,-D in Arkansas, see Jama Grove, "'Unjustified Expectations of Magic': Arkansas Agricultural Specialists' Adoption of DDT and 2,4-D" (unpublished manuscript, May 2, 2014).

37. Dale Bumpers to W. Robb Nisbet, December 19, 1975, folder 19, box 6, DBP, series 3, subseries 2.

38. "Forest Service Ordered to Stop Herbicide Use," (AP) *Northwest Arkansas Times*, June 25, 1975, 29.

39. "Forest Service Ordered to Stop Herbicide Use."

40. "Forest Service Ordered to Stop Herbicide Use."

41. Aubrey Shepherd, "Outdoor Sports," *Northwest Arkansas Times*, October 12, 1975, 19.

42. Shepherd, "Outdoor Sports," 19.

43. "Animals and Trees—1; Dow Chemical Co.—0," *Ozark Digest*, July 1975, 10.

44. The first meeting of the NCWA occurred on Thomas Creek near the headwaters of the Little Buffalo in early 1975 with six people. They were quickly joined by a local, Ray Rilee, who "was starting to find deformed squirrels in the woods—just evidence of things not being right." "F" to Ruth Weinstein, in *Force for Social Change*, 89.

45. Joel Davidson, "2,4,5 T," *LION*, August 1975, 1.

46. Davidson, "2,4,5 T," 2.

47. Davidson, "2,4,5 T," 2.

48. Davidson, "2,4,5 T," 2. The "raping" of the Ozarks was a theme that Davidson discussed often, most notably in his presentation at the Ozarks In-Migration Conference the following year titled "Colonial Exploitation of the Ozarks."

49. Robbie Pardue, "Ecology Corner," reprinted in *LION* October 1975, 3.

50. It should be noted that the fight against the use of highly toxic defoliants is still under way in the Ozarks. During the 1980s and 1990s, a case filed against the USFS by several members of the NCWA brought regional attention to the issue, and currently (as of 2016), efforts in Madison, Newton, and Benton counties to combat the use of these chemicals by electrical power companies are underway. The fight during the 1980s and 1990s was chronicled in the documentary *The Natural State of America* (2011) directed by Brian Campbell.

51. See Newfont, *Blue Ridge Commons*; Montrie; *To Save the Land*; Colton, *Southern Waters*; and see other sources.

52. See Newfont, *Blue Ridge Commons* for an excellent discussion of this series of events.

53. "An Old Law Kindles Dispute," *Northwest Arkansas Times*, March 28, 1976, 17.

54. "Old Law Kindles," 17. This was part of a broader conversation throughout the region as well about forest management tactics. "Alternatives Presented for Forest Management," *Northwest Arkansas Times,* December 28, 1977, 15.

55. Jerry Ashworth to *LION*, January 1976, 12.

56. "C.E.A.S.E. Takes the Initiative (and You Can Too!)," *LION,* June 1976, 20.

57. Anne Williams remembered the first meeting, at least an informal one, of CEASE occurring in St. Paul on April 24, 1974 and then a larger picnic gathering at the end of July. Williams Diary, entries June 8–July 29th. Shiloh Museum of Ozark History.

58. Peggy Frizzell, "Eco-Logie," *Northwest Arkansas Times*, October 11, 1976. Frizzell noted that 882 people was about 20 percent of the county's population.

59. Frizzell, "Eco-Logie."

60. "T" to Ruth Weinstein, in *Force for Social Change*, 27. It should also be noted that by 1977, the NCWA was open to the USFS using 2,4-D to destroy pot found growing in the National Forest. "Herbicide Approved for Destroying Pot," *Blytheville Courier News*, July 6, 1977.

61. Frizzell, "Eco-Logie."

62. Jane See White, "2,4,5 T Herbicide Controversy Rages in Arkansas," (AP) *Blytheville Courier News*, November 27, 1978; also printed in the *Fort Walton Beach Playground Daily News* in Florida and *The Northwest Arkansas Times*.

Throughout the campaign, opposition came in varied and often comedic forms. The Stone County Cattlemen's Association, for example, placed ads in the county's papers opposing even the opinion ballot and noted as a postscript no doubt intended to appeal to native hill folk and, potentially, socially conservative in-migrants, that "2,4,5 T is harmful to marijuana weeds if applied in liberal amounts." White, "2,4,5 T Herbicide Controversy."

63. "Benefit Concert Planned," *NWA Times*, June 1, 1978.

64. Environmentalists Claim Victory," (AP) *Blytheville Courier News*, November 21, 1978.

65. "Environmentalists Claim Victory."

66. Haring was unspecific as to whether he meant nationally or in the Ozark-St. Francis region. "Environmentalists Claim Victory."

67. White, "2,4,5 T Herbicide Controversy."

68. White. Quote from the extended version of the article printed in the *Northwest Arkansas Times* on November 29. Emphasis added.

69. They were not allowed to be used in residential or recreational areas and not on food crops, save rice.

70. White, "2,4,5 T Herbicide Controversy."

71. White, "2,4,5 T Herbicide Controversy."

72. White, "2,4,5 T Herbicide Controversy."

73. "Herbicide Ban Ordered," (AP) *Benton Courier*, February 28, 1979.

74. "Herbicide Ban Ordered."

75. Since the 1980s, however, there has been an ongoing fight between residents of the Ozarks and companies using these chemicals in right of ways that cross farms and waterways in the area. See Brian Campbell, "Growing an Oak: An Ethnography of Ozark Bioregionalism," in *Environmental Anthropology Engaging Ecotopia: Bioregionalism, Permaculture, and Ecovillages*, ed. Joshua Lockyer and James R. Veteto (New York: Berghahn Books, 2013).

76. It should be noted here that a "wilderness ethic" in the spirit of John Muir, for example, is not the same as the "land ethic" discussed in chapter 2.

77. William Cronon, "The Trouble with Wilderness; or, Getting Back to the Wrong Nature," in *Uncommon Ground: Toward Reinventing Nature*, edited by William Cronon (New York: W. W. Norton, 1996), 79.

78. Cronon, 79. See, for example, conversations and actions surrounding the newly created Buffalo National River.

79. Cronon, *Uncommon Ground*, 79.

80. Pettigrew Group, interview with author, June 8, 2014. This group, and others, noted that "down low" hippies were ones who primarily lived in urban centers like Fayetteville or Eureka and only came out to the woods and farms for parties.

81. Anonymous, "His Search for Detachment," in Campbell, *Aquarian Revolution*, 57–59.

82. Anonymous (name withheld for privacy). This sentiment was expressed through most interviews conducted for this project, as well as in those collected by Weinstein and D. Campbell.

83. For an insightful discussion of how this emotional aspect functions in environmental ideology, see Kay Milton, *Loving Nature: Towards an Ecology of Emotion* (London: Routledge, 2002).

84. Newfont, *Blue Ridge Commons*.

85. This is a counter to Cronon's idea that, in general, Americans began to see wilderness and the human experience as inhabiting opposing positions. Rather than this antagonistic stance, the back to the land community argued, via lived experience, that such a bifurcation was counterproductive to the goals of the deep revolution. See Cronon, "Trouble with Wilderness," 69–90.

86. Cronon, *Uncommon Ground*, 86. Cronon also agrees, at least in part, with this idea, when he argues that we must ask wilderness to "tell us about *home*, the place where we actually live." Cronon, 87–90; emphasis in original.

87. Guy King Ames, interview with author; March 18, 2015; Anonymous, interview with author, January 24, 2018; Joel Davidson, interview with author, August 15, 2014. For further development of this idea, see Wendell Berry, in particular Berry, *Unsettling of America*; Berry, *Way of Ignorance*; and Wendell Berry, *Fidelity: Five Stories* (New York: Pantheon, 1993). This attitude should be contrasted with the flat-water tourist economy that, in part, kept the call for damming projects alive in the region.

88. Mike Carr, *Bioregionalism and Civil Society: Democratic Challenges to Corporate Globalism* (Vancouver: UBC Press, 2004), 71; Robert L. Thayer, *Lifeplace: Bioregional Thought and Practice* (Berkeley: University of California Press, 2003), 3.

89. Josh Wilson, "Another Green World/1970s-spawned Planet Drum Foundation Presages Today's Green Renaissance" *SFGate*, February 5, 2004, http://www.sfgate.com/news/article/Another-Green-World-1970s-spawned-Planet-Drum-3179914.php#item-85307-tbla-4.

Berg has stated that he sees the beginning of the bioregional movement as starting with Rachel Carson's *Silent Spring*. See Ron Chepesiuk, *Sixties Radicals, Then and Now: Candid Conversations with Those Who Shaped the Era* (Jefferson, NC: McFarland Publishing, 1995), 120.

90. It should be noted, however, that as a group, OACC members do not take principal credit for many things as they prefer to operate through group consensus and initiative. Thus, while "G" is widely accepted as a key founder of OACC, he asked that he be given a more anonymous status.

91. "G," interview with author, January 24, 2018.

92. "G," interview with author, January 24, 2018.

93. "G," interview with author, January 24, 2018.

94. "G," interview with author, January 24, 2018.

95. "G," interview with author, January 24, 2018.

96. "G," interview with author, January 24, 2018.

97. "G," interview with author, January 24, 2018.

98. Barbara Harmony, "From Resentment to Gratitude: How the Bioregional Movement Changed Me" from the unpublished memoirs of Barbara Harmony, ed.

Sasha Daucus, available at "Resources," Ozark Area Community Congress (website), December 18, 2018, http://ozarkareacommunitycongress.org/resources/; Barbara Harmony, interview with author, May 28, 2014. The issue of gender dynamics will be explored in the following chapter.

99. "G," interview with author, January 24, 2018.

100. Anonymous, quoted in Campbell, "Growing an Oak," 59.

101. "G" was a member of this community. See Campbell, "Growing an Oak," 60–62. As with "G," the founder of New Life Farm will remain anonymous.

102. The founder of New Life Farm did not necessarily purchase the land with the intention of becoming a part of bioregionalism. See Michael Fischer and Michael Swack, "New Life Farm, Drury, Missouri," Harvard Workshop on Appropriate Technology for Community Development, Department of City and Regional Planning, Harvard University, Boston, 1979.

103. Fischer and Swack, "New Life Farm."

104. "G," interview with author, January 24, 2018; Harmony, "Resentment to Gratitude;" Jacqueline Froelich, "Bioregionalism; AKA Ozark Area Community Congress," in *The Encyclopedia of Arkansas History and Culture* (website), http://www.encyclopediaofarkansas.net; Campbell, "Growing an Oak."

105. For a full treatment of OACC and its lasting impact, see Campbell's excellent ethnography, "Growing an Oak."

106. Guy King Ames, conversations with author, Spring 2015–Spring 2016. For a brief look at OOGA and ancillary organizations, see Campbell, "Growing an Oak," 58–75. This is before the creation of the National Organic Standards from the USDA.

107. Don Troop, "Group Angry About Chicken Litter Law," *Northwest Arkansas Times*, August 12, 1989; Plant Board OKs Organic Fertilizer Use," *Northwest Arkansas Times*, December 11, 1988.

108. AP, "Organic Farmers Shedding Hippie Image," *Northwest Arkansas Times*, July 30, 1989.

109. Gordon Watkins, quoted in "Organic Farmers Shedding Hippie Image," *Northwest Arkansas Times*, July 30, 1989.

110. Guy King Ames, interviews with author, Spring 2015–Spring 2016.

111. "New Directions in Ozark Farming: Conference at North Arkansas Community College Eyes Agriculture," *Northwest Arkansas Times*, October 16, 1986.

112. "New Directions in Ozark Farming." OOGA was partnered with two other organizations, FORGE (Financing Ozarks Rural Growth and Economy) and the OSFVP (Ozark Small Farm Viability Project). The OSFVP was similar in intention as the Ozark Institute's FFDS, though it prioritized small organic farms with its programming and information distribution. FORGE is still around, offering assistance and loans to residents of the Ozarks. See http://forgeonline.com, accessed July 25, 2017. See also, "As Children of the '60s, We Had Always Wanted to be Helpful to Society," *Countryside and Small Stock Journal* 77, no. 1 (Jan/Feb 1993): 72–73; Laurent Belsie, "Organic Farming Gains Ground," *Christian Science Monitor*, May 31, 1990, 6. See also the *Ozark Organic Growers Association Newsletter*, of which a partial collection is available via the University of Arkansas Special Collections; and the *Ozarks Organic Grower*, the newsletter of the OSFVP; the first nine issues are available via microfilm from the University of Arkansas Libraries.

CHAPTER 6

1. Wendy Neidhardt to Chuck, November 5, 1974, in Neidhardt, *Fox Letters*, 62–63. The names used here are aliases to protect the identities of those in the letters.

2. Wendy Neidhardt to Chuck, 63. This sentiment was expressed by Craig Fuller, hipbilly and Ozark Institute staffer, as well.

3. Wendy Neidhardt to Chuck, 63.

4. Wendy Neidhardt to Chuck, 63.

5. Peter Coyote's memoir of his days in the counterculture is enlightening, both to the excesses and problems within the movement and to its impact and attempts to sincerely change the world. Whereas most memoirs of the period come across as particularly self-indulgent, Coyote's rather brutal honesty as to the impact of the movement on individuals and communities—as well as his own personal shortcomings—is refreshing. See, Peter Coyote, *Sleeping Where I Fall: A Chronicle*, 3rd ed. (Berkeley: Counterpoint Press, 2015).

6. Coyote, *Sleeping Where I Fall,* 290.

7. Coyote, *Sleeping Where I Fall*, 290. See also the recollections of women BTLs in the Ozarks in Weinstein, *Force for Social Change*, in particular "J's" comment, saying, "[Women] have a harder time adapting—the hippie females. So many cases I've heard of where the female spouse wanted to move to town. The only reason they're hanging out is because it was the guy's cup of tea, his thing. He loved being out here, and she wasn't getting enough social interaction, she wasn't fulfilled." (Weinstein, 69). This is reflected as well in conversations by the author with groups in Madison County.

8. Robert O. Self, *All in the Family: The Realignment of American Democracy Since the 1960s* (New York: Hill and Wang, 2012), 105.

9. Brenda Moosey, interview with Dan Kelley, August 20, 2007, recording in possession of author. Laurel, *Living on the Earth.*

10. Moosey, interview with Dan Kelley.

11. Moosey, interview with Dan Kelley. For reference, $27.00 in 1971 has roughly the same buying power in 2016 as $160.46, equating to about thirty-two six-packs of Budweiser beer at 2016 prices.

12. Moosey, interview with Dan Kelley.

13. *Communities* had a sister publication, *Communitas*, which featured an article on an Arkansas group known as the Mulberry Farm in September of 1972.

14. Kate MeWhinney, "Women and Communal Societies," *Communities*, no. 1 (December 1972): 37.

15. Dianna MacLeod and Rachel Bedard, "Women in Community," *Communities*, no. 25 (March/April 1977): 8; 11–12.

16. Jeanne Tetrault and Sherry Thomas, *Country Women: A Handbook for the New Farmer* (New York: Anchor Books, 1976), xiii. See also, Jessica Louise Lynn, "Country Women: Back-to-the-Land Feminism and Radical Feminist Praxis in the Women's Liberation Movement" (master's thesis, Southern Illinois University, 2013); Laurie York and Carmen Goodyear, *Women on the Land: Creating Conscious Community*, (Albion, CA: Mendocino Coast Films, 2012).

17. Tetrault and Thomas, *Country Women*, xiv.

18. Tetrault and Thomas, *Country Women*, xiv.

19. Tetrault and Thomas, *Country Women*, xv–xvi.

20. Advertisements, *Country Women*, May 1976, 61. Ads for people to come and join various women's groups in the Ozarks occurred in almost every issue from the Spring of 1976 to the Winter of 1978. See in particular *Country Women*, nos. 19–24; 31. It should be noted that in some cases hipbilly women, as a means to integrate into local communities, adopted some of the Ozark gender norms. For example, Jane Parker, in her essay on gender in the Ozarks, tells the story of "Diana," presumably a back to the lander in the thinly-veiled Stone County, as learning to pay attention to how she interacted with men when she was out without her husband in order to ensure that she was not perceived in a negative light by the community. See Jane Parker, "Engendering Identity(s) in a Rural Arkansas Ozark Community," *Anthropological Quarterly* 65, no. 3 (July 1992): 148–55.

21. For the history of midwifery, see Helen Varney Burst et al., *A History of Midwifery in the United States: The Midwife Said Fear Not* (New York: Spring Publishing Company, 2013); Barbara Ehrenreich and Deirdre English, *Witches, Midwives, and Nurses: A History of Women Healers*, 2nd ed. (New York: Feminist Press at CUNY, 2010).

22. For a brief history of midwifery in Arkansas, see Maria Chowdhury, "Midwives," The Encyclopedia of Arkansas History and Culture (website), late updated May 23, 2017, *http://www.encyclopediaofarkansas.net/encyclopedia/entry-detail .aspx?entryID=3781#*. See also Helen Varney, *Varney's Midwifery*, 4th ed. (Sudbury, MA: Jones and Bartlett Learning, 2004), 6–8.

23. See Elaine Tyler May, *America and the Pill: A History of Promise, Peril, and Liberation* (New York: Basic Books, 2010) for a concise and engaging discussion of the history of birth control, in particular "the pill," in the 1960s and 1970s.

24. "Natural Birth Control Review," *LION*, February 1976, 11.

25. The Farm, led by Steve Gaskin and Ina May Gaskin, became a beacon of communal living alongside places like Black Bear Commune (associated with the Diggers) in California. Established in Summertown, Tennessee, in 1971, it quickly established itself as a center of learning in midwifery, holistic living, and more. See www.the farmmidwives.org; www.midwiferyworkshops.org; and www.thefarm.org, accessed August 3, 2018.

26. Ina May Gaskin, *Spiritual Midwifery*, 4th ed. (Summertown, TN: Book Publishing, 2002), 12.

27. "L" to Ruth Weinstein, in *Force for Social Change*, 66.

28. Gaskin, *Spiritual Midwifery*, 12.

29. David E. Smith and James Sternfield, "The Hippie Communal Movement: Effects on Child Birth and Development," *American Journal of Orthopsychiatry* 40, no. 3 (April 1970): 528.

30. "L" to Ruth Weinstein, in *Force for Social Change*, 65–66.

31. Smith and Sternfield, "Hippie Communal Movement," 528.

32. Barbara Katz Rothman, *A Bun in the Oven: How the Food and Birth Movements Resist Industrialization* (New York: New York University Press, 2016), 126.

33. Smith and Sternfield, "Hippie Communal Movement," 528.

34. Rothman, *Bun in the Oven*, 6–9.

35. Gaskin, *Spiritual Midwifery*, 17. Elizabeth Davis, author of textbooks for midwifery, describes the process of birth in a similar fashion: "The most potent lesson of childbirth is the revelation of essential feminine force. Giving birth calls on a woman to shed her social skin and discover her ability to cooperate with and surrender to

elemental forces." See Elizabeth Davis, *Heart and Hands: A Midwife's Guide to Pregnancy and Birth* (New York: Ten Speed Press, 2012), 7.

36. Indeed, a common saying among the midwife community is, "Peace on earth begins with birth."

37. "K" to Ruth Weinstein, in *Force for Social Change*, 65.

38. "K" to Ruth Weinstein, 65.

39. Advertisement, *LION*, September 1975, 10. The Pardues were also vocal critics of the 2,4-D policies of the USFS.

40. Pat Lurowski, *LION*, September 1975, 5.

41. Donna Hudson to *LION*, October 1975, 4–6.

42. Hudson to *LION*, 4–6. Underlining in original.

43. Hudson to *LION*, 4–6. Hudson would write back to *LION* in January 1976 describing her birth process and the various issues surrounding it. See Donna Hudson to *LION*, January 1976, 5–7. Such advocacy was not always lauded by readers of *LION*. Indeed, in response to Donna Hudson's comment about doing things right, Mau Blossom, a nurse with the Golden Light Birthing Service in Doniphan, Missouri, wrote in and stated that Ms. Hudson's comments might well be a "disaster." She continued, "I say this is comparable to advising one to memorize pictures of a lava flow as preparation for standing on the hillside of a volcano which may errupt [*sic*]." See Mau Blossom to *LION*, January 1976, 7.

44. Joe Baldwin, conversation with author, March 3, 2016.

45. Brandt, conversation. Brandt also noted, as many others have, that their experiences in Newton County, as they related to native Ozarks both independent of and with the Sassafras commune, was good—and revolved around work.

46. "AD" to *LION*, March 1975, 4. It should be noted that this was not quite true—utilizing a midwife in Arkansas had been made virtually illegal after the 1950s, save in some communities where rurality and economics prevented the establishment of an accessible medical practice by a doctor, a practice sometimes termed "permitted midwives." Race undoubtedly played a role in this: the majority of registered and unregistered midwives were black, while the majority of doctors were white and felt their practices were harmed by the persistence of traditional obstetric care. Midwifery would not be made legal again until 1983, and then only provisionally, until it was expanded to the state from 1985 to 1987. A full treatment of the history of midwifery in the Ozarks, and Arkansas, has yet to be written.

47. "AD" to *LION*, March 1975, 4.

48. See Ed Barham et al., *100 Years of Service*, (Little Rock: Arkansas Department of Health, 2013, http://www.healthy.arkansas.gov/aboutADH/100Years/Documents/100yearsBooklet.pdf), 28.

49. See USDA Census (website), accessed December 2017, https://www.census.gov/data/tables/time-series/dec/census-poverty.html.

50. Barham, *100 Years of Service*, 28. See also Michael B. Dougan, "Health and Medicine," The Encyclopedia of Arkansas History and Culture (website), late updated July 18, 2018, http://www.encyclopediaofarkansas.net/encyclopedia/entry-detail.aspx?entryID=392; Chowdhury, "Midwives." Aside from Chowdhury's brief article, there is as of yet no comprehensive history of midwifery in the state, or the Ozarks, nor of its revival in the 1980s and 1990s.

51. Suzanne McCarthy to *LION*, June 1974, 2–3.

52. Smith and Sternfield, "Hippie Communal Movement," 527.

53. Smith and Sternfield, "Hippie Communal Movement," 527.

54. Smith and Sternfield, "Hippie Communal Movement," 528. Data on breast-feeding rates during the 1970s is problematic. Despite this, the National Institute for Health estimates that between 1970 and 1975 approximately 5 percent of mothers breastfed at six months postpartum. See US Department of Health and Human Services, *The Surgeon General's Call to Action to Support Breastfeeding* (Washington, DC: US Department of Health and Human Services, Office of the Surgeon General, 2011), https://www.ncbi.nlm.nih.gov/books/NBK52681/.

55. Smith and Sternfield, "Hippie Communal Movement," 528.

56. Smith and Sternfield, "Hippie Communal Movement," 529.

57. "J" to Ruth Weinstein, in *Force for Social Change*, 67.

58. "J" to Ruth Weinstein, 67.

59. "B" to Ruth Weinstein, in *Force for Social Change*, 68. Emphasis in original.

60. "E" and "T" to Ruth Weinstein, in Or *Force for Social Change*, 100. This was true even among the native Ozarkers: during election season candidates came down to the school and gave out "whiskey and wine." ("E" and "T" to Ruth Weinstein, 101.) The story of the Headwaters School—its creation and survival through the changes Madison County has experienced is worthy of more space than can be afforded here.

61. "Children of Flower Children," *Spectrum*, April 11–24, 1990, 6.

62. Jennifer Billig, quoted in "Children of Flower Children" *Spectrum*, 7.

63. "S" to Ruth Weinstein, in *Force for Social Change*, 101.

64. "S" to Ruth Weinstein, 101.

65. Lee McCoy, "Children of Flower Children" *Spectrum* 1990, April 11–24, 1990. For other reflections on growing up as a child of back to the landers, see Alice Driver, "Not Yet Lost," *Oxford American*, May 11, 2016, http://www.oxfordamerican.org/item/855-not-yet-lost.

66. Sunshine Broder, conversation with author, August 10, 2015.

67. Sunshine was quick to note that she never told her friends at school that they ate rabbit for fear of being perceived as different. Sunshine Broder, conversation with author, August 10, 2015.

68. Broder, conversation.

69. Broder, conversation.

70. Broder, conversation.

71. Broder, conversation.

72. See Thompson, *Un-Natural State*.

73. Robert O. Self, *All in the Family*, 4, emphasis in the original. Self's discussion of the changing understanding of American manhood in particular is illuminating for scholars attempting to understand some of the nuanced impacts of the countercul-ture on American life at the end of the twentieth century.

74. See Thompson, *Un-Natural State*, beginning in particular on page 140, for an excellent discussion both of this dynamic, as well as the evolution of homosexuality in Arkansas.

75. As Thompson notes, groups shared their land availability in national publica-tions such as *Country Women*, which had advertisements from several Arkansas Ozarks places, beginning in particular with the March 1976 issue. See also Kate Ellison, "Lesbian Land: An Overview," *Alternatives*, May–June 2003, 39–41; Janelle Lavelle,

"Lesbian Land," *Southern Exposure* 16, no. 3 (1988): 36–38. For a full study on the women's movement in Northwest Arkansas, see Allyn Lord and Anna M. Zajicek, *The History of the Contemporary Grassroots Women's Movement in Northwest Arkansas, 1970– 2000* (Fayetteville: 2000). The University of Arkansas Special Collections holds a copy of the manuscript, as well as the records of the Northwest Arkansas Women's Center, which is a trove of information waiting for a more detailed examination by historians.

76. "N" to Ruth Weinstein, in *Force for Social Change*, 27.

CONCLUSION

1. Wendell E. Berry, "It All Turns on Affection," (41st Annual Jefferson Lecture in the Humanities, National Endowment for the Humanities, Washington, DC, 2012), https://www.neh.gov/about/awards/jefferson-lecture/wendell-e-berry-lecture. Emphasis added.

2. Berry, "It All Turns on Affection."

3. Berry, "It All Turns on Affection."

4. "B" to Ruth Weinstein, in *Force for Social change*, 23.

5. "J" and "B" to Ruth Weinstein, in *Force for Social Change*, 137.

6. See "Arkansas Presidential Primaries Results," Politico (website), last updated December 13, 2016, https://www.politico.com/2016-election/primary/results/map/president/arkansas/.

BIBLIOGRAPHY

PRIMARY SOURCES

Archival Collections

Shiloh Museum of Ozark History, Springdale, Arkansas

Cindy Arsaga Oral History
Cindy Rimkus Diary
Ernie Dean Papers
In-Migration Files

University of Arkansas Special Collections, Fayetteville, Arkansas

Arkansas State Plant Board Annual Reports, 1968–1980
Broadside Collection
Dale Bumpers Papers
John M. Beam Papers
Ozark Institute Files
Roy Reed Papers
Thomas McRae IV Papers
University of Arkansas Agricultural Extension Circulars
Vada Sheid Papers

Periodicals, Newsprint, and Broadcast Companies

ABC
ACORN News
ACRES, USA
Arkansas Democrat-Gazette
Arkansas Gazette
Baxter Bulletin
Benton Courier
Blytheville Courier News
CBS
Christian Science Monitor

Communities
Country Women
Down Home
Edible Ozarkansas
Grapevine
Hard Labor
Life
Living in the Ozarks Newsletter (LION)
Marshall Mountain Wave
Mother Earth News
New York Times
New York Times Magazine
Northwest Arkansas Times
Oxford American
Ozark Access Catalog
Ozark Communicator
Ozark Digest
Ozark Feminist Press
Ozark Star
Ozarka
Ozarks Organic Grower
Plowboy
Rolling Stone
Saturday Evening Post
Scribner's
SFGate
Spectrum
Springdale News
Times-Echo
Total Lifestyle
Tulsa Tribune
Whole Earth Catalog

Published Memoirs, Letters, and Interviews

Campbell, Denele, ed. *Aquarian Revolution: Back to the Land, Thirty-Two Personal Stories*. CreateSpace Independent Publishing Platform, 2013.
Neidhardt, Sarah, ed. *The Fox Letters, 1973–1980* (self-published, no date).

Federal and State Government Records

Arkansas Secretary of State. *A Compilation of Primary, Run-Off, And General Election Results for State and District Offices, 1976, 1978, 1980.*
Barham, Ed. *100 Years of Service*. Little Rock: Arkansas Department of Health, 2013.
Dailey, George H. *Age-Specific Net Migration in the Ozarks Region, 1950–1970: A Chartbook*. Columbia: University of Missouri, 1978.

Dailey, George H., Thomas E. Jokerst, Robert L. McNamara, and Rex R. Campbell. *A Quarter Century of Population Change in the Ozarks, 1950–1970: A Statistical Abstract Presented to the Ozarks Regional Commission.* Columbia: University of Missouri, 1978.

Daniels, Charlie. *Historical Report of the Secretary of State.* Fayetteville: University of Arkansas Press, 2008.

Demographic Research Division, UALR. *A Changing Arkansas As Reflected by Population and Related Data, 1970–1980.* Little Rock: UALR, 1985.

Henson, Larry. *Vegetation Management with Herbicides: Final Environmental Statement.* Russellville, AR: United States Forest Service, 1975.

United States Department of Agriculture Census, 1950–1982.

Documentaries

Commune, produced by Jonathan Berman. Five Points Media, 2005.

Gettin' Back!, produced by Ronald McCulloch, 1973.

The Natural State of America, produced by Brian Campbell. Ozarkadia Films, 2011.

The Sixties, produced by Tom Hanks and Gary Goetzman. CNN, 2014.

Women on the Land: Creating Conscious Community, produced by Laurie York and Carmen Goodyear, Albion, CA: Mendocino Coast Films, 2012.

SECONDARY SOURCES

Essays, Articles, and Book Chapters

Blair, Diane. "Fortieth and Forty-Second Governor: William Jefferson Clinton, 1979–1981; 1983–1992." In *The Governors of Arkansas: Essays in Political Biography,* edited by Timothy Donovan, Willard B. Gatewood, and Jeannie M. Whayne, 261–75. 2nd ed. Fayetteville: University of Arkansas Press, 1995.

Campbell, Brian. "Growing an Oak: An Ethnography of Ozark Bioregionalism." In *Environmental Anthropology Engaging Ecotopia: Bioregionalism, Permaculture, and Ecovillages,* edited by Joshua Lockyer and James R. Veteto, 58–75. New York: Berghahn Books, 2013.

———. "Just Eat Peas and Dance: Field Peas (Vigna unguiculata) and Food Security in the Ozark Highlands, *US Journal of Ethnobiology* 34, no. 1 (March 2014): 104–22.

———. "A Gentle Work Horse Would Come in Right Handy: Animals in Ozark Agroecology." *Anthrozoos* 22, no. 3 (2009): 239–53.

———. "In Search of Arcadia: Agrarian Values and the Homesteading Tradition in the Ozarks, USA." *Environmental Values* 25 (2016): 145–66.

———. "Confrontations on Karst: Antibiocide Activism in the Ozarks, United States." *Culture, Agriculture, Food and Environment* 37, no. 2 (2015): 96–106.

Cowie, Jefferson. "Nixon's Class Struggle: Romancing the New Right Worker, 1960–1973," *Labor History* 43, no. 3 (2002): 257–83.

Cronon, William. "The Trouble with Wilderness; or, Getting back to the Wrong

Nature." In *Uncommon Ground: Toward Reinventing Nature* ed. William Cronon, 69–90. New York: W. W. Norton, 1995.

"Earl Butz versus Wendell Berry." *CoEvolution Quarterly* (Spring 1978): 50–59.

Edgington, Ryan. "'Be Receptive to the Good Earth:' Health, Nature, and Labor in Countercultural Back-to-the-Land Settlements." *Agricultural History* 82, no. 3 (Summer, 2008): 279–308.

Ellison, Kate. "Lesbian Land: An Overview," *Alternatives*, May–June 2003, 39–41.

Ewert, Sara Dent. "Bioregional Politics: The Case for Place." *Oregon Historical Quarterly* 103, no. 4 (Winter 2002): 439–51.

Grove, Jama. "'Unjustified Expectations of Magic:' Arkansas Agricultural Specialists' Adoption of DDT and 2,4-D." Unpublished.

Hay, Amy M. "Dow Chemical vs. 'Coercive Utopians': Constructing the Contested Ground of Science and Government Regulation in 1970s America." *Business and Economic History On-Line* 9 (2011), www.thebhc.org/publications.BEHonline/2011/hay.pdf.

Holley, Donald. "Leaving the Land of Opportunity: Arkansas and the Great Migration." *Arkansas Historical Quarterly* 64, no. 3 (Autumn 2005): 245–61.

Katz, Donald. "Good Times Comin' to Arkansas." In *The Valley of the Fallen and Other Places*, 152–73. New York: AtRandom, 2001.

Lavelle, Janelle. "Lesbian Land," *Southern Exposure* 16, no. 3 (1988): 36–38.

Parker, Jane. "Engendering Identity(s) in a Rural Arkansas Ozarks Community." *Anthropological Quarterly* 65, no. 3 (July 1992): 148–55.

Perkins, J. Blake. "Growing the Hills: The Ozarks Regional Commission and the Politics of Economic Development in the Mid-American Highlands, 1960s-1970s." *Missouri Historical Review* 107, no. 3 (April 2013): 144–67.

Smith, David E., and James Sternfield. "The Hippie Communal Movement: Effects on Child Birth and Development." *American Journal of Orthopsychiatry* 40, no. 3 (April 1970): 527–30.

Whayne, Jeannie. "The Incidental Environmentalists: Dale Bumpers, George Templeton, and the Origins of the Rosen Alternative Pest Control Center at the University of Arkansas." *Agricultural History* 89, no. 1 (Winter 2015): 3–28.

Webb, Sue. "By the Sweat of the Brow: The Back-to-the-Land Movement in Depression Arkansas." *Arkansas Historical Quarterly (AHQ)* 42, no. 4 (Winter 1983): 334–35

Dissertations and Theses

Lynn, Jessica Louise. "Country Women: Back-to-the-Land Feminism and Radical Feminist Praxis in the Women's Liberation Movement." Master's thesis, Southern Illinois University, Carbondale, 2013.

Sims, Jesse Ray. "Beyond Coattails: Explaining John Paul Hammerschmidt's Victory in 1966." Master's thesis, University of Arkansas, Fayetteville, 2017.

Turman, Jinny A. "Appalachian Alter-Natives: The Back-to-the-Land Migration and Community Change in Appalachia, 1970–2000." PhD diss., West Virginia University, Morgantown, 2013.

Books and Pamphlets

Agnew, Eleanor. *Back from the Land: How Young Americans Went to Nature in the 1970s, and Why They Came Back*. Chicago: Ivan R. Dee, 2004.

Anderson, Terry. *The Movement and the Sixties: Protest in America from Greensboro to Wounded Knee*. 5th ed. New York: Oxford University Press, 1996.

Armstrong, David. *A Trumpet to Arms: Alternative Media in America*. Los Angeles: J. P Tarcher, 1981.

Bailey, Beth. *Sex in the Heartland*. Cambridge, MA: Harvard University Press, 1999.

Bailey, Beth, and David Farber, eds. *America in the Seventies*. Lawrence: University of Kansas Press, 2004.

Bartley, Numan V., and Hugh D. Graham. *Southern Elections: County and Precinct Data, 1950–1972*. Baton Rouge: Louisiana State University Press, 1978.

Becker, Jane S. *Selling Tradition: Appalachia and the Construction of an American Folk, 1930–1940*. Chapel Hill: University of North Carolina Press, 1998.

Belasco, Warren J. *Appetite for Change: How the Counterculture Took on the Food Industry*. Ithaca: Cornell University Press, 2006.

Berger, Bennett M. *The Survival of a Counterculture: Ideological Work and Everyday Life Among Rural Communards*. Berkeley: University of California Press, 1981.

Berry, Wendell. *The Unsettling of America: Culture and Agriculture*. San Francisco: Sierra Club Books, 1977.

———. *Nathan Coulter*. Rev. ed. New York: Ithaca Point Press, 1985.

———. *The Way of Ignorance and Other Essays*. Berkeley: Counterpoint Press, 2006.

———. *Fidelity: Five Stories*. New York: Pantheon, 1993.

Blevins, Brooks. *Arkansaw/Arkansas: How Bear Hunters, Hillbillies, and Good Ol' Boys Defined a State*. Fayetteville: University of Arkansas Press, 2009.

———. *Hill Folks: A History of Arkansas Ozarkers and Their Image*. Chapel Hill: University of North Carolina Press, 2002.

Bohlen, James. *The New Pioneer's Handbook: Getting Back to the Land in an Energy-Scarce World*. New York: Schocken Books, 1975.

Borsodi, Ralph. *This Ugly Civilization*. New York: Simon and Schuster, 1929.

———. *Flight from the City: An Experiment in Living on the Land*. New York: Harper and Brothers, 1933.

———. *Prosperity and Security: A Study in Realistic Economics*. New York: Harper, 1938.

Borstelmann, Thomas. *The 1970s: A New Global History from Civil Rights to Economic Inequality*. Princeton: Princeton University Press, 2013.

———. *The Cold War and the Color Line: American Race Relations in the Global Arena*. Cambridge, MA: Harvard University Press, 2003.

Braunstein, Peter, and Michael William Doyle, eds. *Imagine Nation: The American Counterculture of the 1960s and '70s*. New York: Routledge, 2002.

Briarpatch Community. *The Briarpatch Book: Experiences in Right Livelihood and Simple Living*. San Francisco: A New Glide/Reed Book, 1978.

Brown, Dona. *Back to the Land: The Enduring Dream of Self-Sufficiency in Modern America*. Madison: The University of Wisconsin Press, 2011.

Burst, Helen Varney, and Joyce Thompson. *A History of Midwifery in the United States: The Midwife Said Fear Not*. New York: Spring Publishing Company, 2013.

Carr, Mike. *Bioregionalism and Civil Society: Democratic Challenges to Corporate Globalism*. Vancouver: UBC Press, 2004.

Carson, Allan. *The New Agrarian Mind: The Movement Toward Decentralist Thought in Twentieth Century America*. New Brunswick: Transaction Publishers, 2000.

Chepesiuk, Ron. *Sixties Radicals, Then and Now: Candid Conversations with Those Who Shaped the Era*. Jefferson, NC: McFarland Publishing, 1995.

Cochrane, Willard W. *The Development of American Agriculture: A Historical Analysis*. Minneapolis: University of Minnesota Press, 1979.

Cohan, Ray. *How to Make It on the Land*. New York: Galahad Books, 1972.

Cohen, Lizabeth. *A Consumer's Republic: The Politics of Mass Consumption in Postwar America*. New York: Vintage Books, 2003.

Coleman, Eliot. *The New Organic Grower: A Master's Manual of Tools and Techniques for the Home and Market Gardener*. 2nd ed. White River Junction, VT: Chelsea Green Publishing, 1995.

———. *The Winter Harvest Handbook: Year Round Vegetable Production Using Deep-Organic Techniques and Unheated Greenhouses*. White River Junction: Chelsea Green, 2009.

Colton, Craig. *Southern Waters: The Limits to Abundance*. Baton Rouge: Louisiana State University Press, 2014.

Compton, Neil. *The Battle for the Buffalo River: The Story of America's First National River*. Fayetteville: University of Arkansas Press, 2010.

Conkin, Paul Keith. *The Southern Agrarians*. Knoxville: University of Tennessee Press, 1988.

Cowie, Jefferson R. *Stayin' Alive: The 1970s and the Last Days of the Working Class*. New York: New Press 2012.

Cox, Craig. *Storefront Revolution: Food Co-ops and the Counterculture*. New Brunswick: Rutgers University Press, 1996.

Coyote, Peter. *Sleeping Where I Fall: A Chronicle*. 3rd ed. Berkeley: Counterpoint Press, 2015.

Daniel, Pete. *Dispossession: Discrimination Against African American Farmers in the Age of Civil Rights*. Chapel Hill: University of North Carolina Press, 2013.

Davis, Elizabeth. *Heart and Hands: A Midwife's Guide to Pregnancy and Birth*. New York: Ten Speed Press, 2012.

DeKoven, Marianne. *Utopia Limited: The Sixties and the Emergence of the Postmodern*. Durham: Duke University Press, 2004.

Dochuk, Darren. *From Bible Belt to Sunbelt: Plain-Folk Religion, Grassroots Politics, and the Rise of Evangelical Conservatism*. New York: W. W. Norton, 2012.

Ehrenreich, Barbara, and Deirdre English. *Witches, Midwives, and Nurses: A History of Women Healers*. 2nd ed. New York: Feminist Press at CUNY, 2010.

Flader, Susan L., and J. Baird Callicott, eds. *The River of the Mother God and Other Essays*. Madison: University of Wisconsin Press, 1991.

Flamm, Michael W. *Law and Order: Street Crime, Civil Unrest, and the Crisis of Liberalism in the 1960s*. New York: Columbia University Press, 2005.

Frank, Thomas. *The Conquest of Cool: Business Culture, Counterculture, and the Rise of Hip Consumerism*. Chicago: University of Chicago Press, 1997.

Fuller, R. Buckminster. *Operating Manual for Spaceship Earth*. New York: Simon and Schuster, 1969.

Gaddis, John Lewis. *The Cold War: A New History*. New York: Penguin Books, 2006.

Ginsberg, Allen. *Collected Poems, 1947–1980*. New York: Harper Perennial, 1988.

Gitlin, Todd. *Sixties: Years of Hope, Days of Rage.* New York: Bantam Books, 1993.

Gould, Rebecca Kneale. *At Home in Nature: Modern Homesteading and Spiritual Practice in America.* Berkeley: University of California Press, 2005.

Hale, Grace Elizabeth. *A Nation of Outsiders: How the White Middle Class Fell in Love with Rebellion in Postwar America.* Oxford: Oxford University Press, 2011.

Harkins, Anthony. *Hillbilly: A Cultural History of an American Icon.* Oxford: Oxford University Press, 2004.

Harington, Donald. *The Architecture of the Arkansas Ozarks.* Boston: Little, Brown, 1975.

———. *Let Us Now Build a City: Eleven Lost Towns.* San Diego: Harcourt Brace Jovanovich, 1986.

Hamilton, Shane. *Trucking Country: The Road to America's Wal-Mart Economy.* Princeton: Princeton University Press, 2008.

Hedgepeth, William. *The Alternative: Communal Life in America.* London: Macmillan, 1970.

Hogue, Wayman. *Back Yonder: An Ozark Chronicle,* edited by Brooks Blevins. Fayetteville: University of Arkansas Press, 2016.

Holmes, John Clellon. *Go.* New York: Scribner, 1952.

Houriet, Robert. *Getting Back Together.* New York: Coward, McCann, and Geoghegan, 1971.

Hurt, R. Douglas. *American Agriculture: A Brief History.* West Lafayette: Purdue University Press, 2002.

Hyman, Louis. *Debtor Nation: The History of America in Red Ink.* Princeton: Princeton University Press, 2012.

Isaacson, Walter. *The Innovators: How a Group of Hackers, Geniuses, and Geeks Created the Digital Revolution.* New York: Simon and Schuster, 2014.

Jacob, Jeffrey. *New Pioneers: The Back-to-the-Land Movement and the Search for a Sustainable Future.* University Park: Pennsylvania State University Press, 1997.

Jeansonne, Glen. *Gerald L. K. Smith: Minister of Hate.* New Haven: Yale University Press, 1988.

Jeffords, Edd, and Ralph Desmarais. *Uncertain Harvest: The Family Farm in Arkansas.* Eureka Springs: Ozark Institute, 1980.

Johnson, Ben F. *Arkansas in Modern America, 1930–1999.* Fayetteville: University of Arkansas Press, 2000.

Kahn, Lloyd. *Domebook 2.* Bolinas, CA: Pacific Domes, 1971.

Kaplan, George, ed. *Power to the People: The Graphic Design of the Radical Press and the Rise of the Counter-Culture, 1964–1974.* Chicago: University of Chicago Press, 2013.

Katz, Donald. *The Valley of the Fallen and Other Stories.* New York: AtRandom Books, 2001.

Kerouac, Jack. *The Dharma Bums.* New York: Penguin Books, 2006.

Klatch, Rebecca E. *A Generation Divided: The New Left, the New Right, and the 1960s.* Berkeley: University of California Press, 1999.

Knobloch, Frieda. *The Culture of Wilderness: Agriculture as Colonization in the American West.* Chapel Hill: University of North Carolina Press, 1996.

Lair, Jim. *An Outlander's History of Carroll County.* Marceline, MO: Walsworth, 1983.

Laurel, Alicia Bay. *Living on the Earth: Celebrations, Storm Warnings, Formulas, Recipes, Rumors, and Country Dances.* Berkeley: Bookworks, 1970.

Lecther, Andy. *Shroom: A Cultural History of the Magic Mushroom*. New York: Ecco, 2007.

Lee, Martin A., and Bruce Shlain. *Acid Dreams: The Complete History of LSD; The CIA, the Sixties, and Beyond*. New York: Grove Press, 1992.

Leopold, Aldo. *A Sand County Almanac with Essays on Conservation from Round River*. New York: Sierra Club/Ballantine Books, 1970.

Liensech, Michael. *In the Beginning: Fundamentalism, the Scopes Trial, and the Making of the Antievolution Movement*. Charlotte: University of North Carolina Press, 2009.

Lighton, William. *Happy Hollow Farm*. New York: George H. Doran, 1915.

Lockyer, Joshua, and James R. Veteto, eds. *Environmental Anthropology Engaging Ecotopia: Bioregionalism, Permaculture, and Ecovillages*. New York: Berghahn Books, 2013.

Lord, Allyn, and Anna M. Zajicek. *The History of the Contemporary Grassroots Women's Movement in Northwest Arkansas, 1970–2000*. Fayetteville: 2000.

Marchand, Roland. *Advertising the American Dream: Making Way for Modernity, 1920–1940*. Berkeley: University of California Press, 1986.

Marcuse, Herbert. *One-Dimensional Man: Studies in the Ideology of Advanced Industrial Society*. 2nd ed. London: Routledge, 1991.

Marling, Karal Ann. *As Seen on TV: The Visual Culture of Everyday Life in the 1950s*. Cambridge, MA: Harvard University Press, 1998.

Massey, Elaine. *Bittersweet Country*. Norman: University of Oklahoma Press, 1986.

May, Elaine Tyler. *Homeward Bound: American Families in the Cold War Era*. New York: Basic Books, 2008.

———. *America and the Pill: A History of Promise, Peril, and Liberation*. New York: Basic Books, 2010.

McGirr, Lisa. *Suburban Warriors: The Origins of the New American Right*. Updated ed. Princeton: Princeton University Press, 2015.

McNeil, W. K. *Ozark Country*. Jackson: University Press of Mississippi, 1995.

Miller, Timothy. *The 1960s Communes Hippies and Beyond*. Syracuse: Syracuse University Press, 1999.

Milton, Kay. *Loving Nature: Towards an Ecology of Emotion*. London: Routledge, 2002.

Montrie, Chad. *The Myth of Silent Spring: Rethinking the Origins of American Environmentalism*. Berkeley: University of California Press, 2018.

———. *To Save the Land and People: A History of Opposition to Surface Coal Mining in Appalachia*. Chapel Hill: University of North Carolina Press, 2003.

Murphy, Paul. *The Rebuke of History: The Southern Agrarian and American Conservative Thought*. Chapel Hill: University of North Carolina Press, 2001.

Nearing, Helen, and Scott Nearing. *Living the Good Life: How to Live Sanely and Simply in a Troubled World*. New York: Schoken Books, 1970.

———. *The Good Life: Helen and Scott Nearing's Sixty Years of Self-Sufficient Living*. New York: Schocken Books, 1989.

Nearing, Scott. *The Making of a Radical: A Political Autobiography*. New York: Harper and Row, 1972.

Newfont, Kathryn. *Blue Ridge Commons: Environmental Activism and Forest History in Western North Carolina*. Athens: University of Georgia Press, 2012.

Niman, Michael. *People of the Rainbow: A Nomadic Utopia*. 2nd ed. Knoxville: University of Tennessee Press, 2014.

Oelschlaeger, Max. *The Idea of Wilderness: From Prehistory to the Age of Ecology*. New Haven: Yale University Press, 1991.

Oldfield, J. E. *Five Acres and Independence: A Handbook for Small Farm Management*. New York: Dover Publications, 1973.

Ostertag, Bob. *People's Movements, People's Press: The Journalism of Social Justice Movements*. Boston: Beacon Press, 2006.

Perkins, Blake. *Hillbilly Hellraisers: Federal Power and Populist Defiance in the Ozarks*. Urbana: University of Illinois Press, 2017.

Pitcaithley, Dwight. *Let the River Be: A History of the Ozark's Buffalo River*. Santa Fe, NM: Southwest Cultural Resources Center, 1997.

Rafferty, Milton. *The Ozarks: Land and Life*. 2nd ed. Fayetteville: University of Arkansas Press, 2001.

Randolph, Vance. *Ozark Magic and Folklore*. New York: Dover Publications, 1947.

Robinson, David E. *The Complete Homesteading Book: Proven Methods for Self-Sufficient Living*. Charlotte: Garden Way Publishing, 1974.

Robbins, Paul. *Lawn People: How Grasses, Weeds, and Chemicals Make Us Who We Are*. Philadelphia: Temple University Press, 2007.

Roszak, Theodore. *The Making of a Counter Culture: Reflections on the Technocratic Society and its Youthful Opposition*. Berkeley: University of California Press, 1995.

Rothman, Barbara Katz. *A Bun in the Oven: How the Food and Birth Movements Resist Industrialization*. New York: New York University Press, 2016.

Rubin, Louis D. *I'll Take My Stand: The South and the Agrarian Tradition, by Twelve Southerners*. New York: Harper and Brothers, 1930.

Saltmarsh, John A. *Scott Nearing: The Making of a Homesteader*. White River Junction, VT: Chelsea Green, 1991.

Schulman, Bruce J. *The Seventies: The Great Shift in American Culture, Society, and Politics*. Boston: Da Capo, 2002.

Schumacher, E. F. *Small Is Beautiful: Economics as if People Mattered*. New York: Schocken Books, 1975.

Schwartz, Marvin. *In Service to America: A History of VISTA in Arkansas*. Fayetteville: University of Arkansas Press, 1988.

Self, Robert O. *All in the Family: The Realignment of American Democracy Since the 1960s*. New York: Hill and Wang, 2013.

Selvin, Joel. *Altamont: The Rolling Stones, the Hells Angels, and the Inside Story of Rock's Darkest Day*. New York: Dey Street Books, 2016.

Sherman, Jory. *My Heart is in the Ozarks*. Harrison: First Ozark Press, 1982.

Shi, David. *The Simple Life: Plain Living and High Thinking in American Culture*. Athens: University of Georgia Press, 2007.

Slocum-Schaffer, Stephanie A. *America in the Seventies*. Syracuse: Syracuse University Press, 2003.

Smith, Sherry L. *Hippies, Indians, and the Fight for Red Power*. Oxford: Oxford University Press, 2012.

Snyder, Gary. *Turtle Island*. New York: New Directions Books, 1974.

———. *Riprap and Cold Mountain Poems*. 1959. Reprint. Berkeley: Counterpoint Press, 2009.

Stearn, Steve. *The Angel of Forgetfulness*. New York: Viking Penguin, 2005.

Streitmatter, Rodger. *Voices of Revolution: The Dissident Press in America*. New York: Columbia University Press, 2001.

Suri, Jeremi. *Power and Protest: Global Revolution and the Power of Protest.* Cambridge, MA: Harvard University Press, 2005.

Sutton, Leslie, Parr Sutton, and Maribeth Lynes. *Visits with Ozark Country Women.* Little Rock, AR: August House, 1979.

Swartz, David R. *Moral Minority: The Evangelical Left in an Age of Conservatism.* Philadelphia: University of Philadelphia Press, 2012.

Teale, Edwin Way. *Wandering Through Winter.* New York: Dodd, Mead, 1965.

Tetrault, Jeanne, and Sherry Thomas. *Country Women: A Handbook for the New Farmer.* New York: Anchor Press, 1976.

Thayer, Robert L. *Lifeplace: Bioregional Thought and Practice.* Berkeley: University of California Press, 2003.

Thompson, Brock. *The Un-Natural State: Arkansas and the Queer South.* Fayetteville: University of Arkansas Press, 2010.

Thoreau, Henry David. *Walden and Civil Disobedience.* New York: Barnes and Noble Books, 2003.

Turner, James Morton. *The Promise of the Wilderness: American Environmental Politics Since 1964.* Seattle: University of Washington Press, 2012.

Turner, Jeffery A. *Sitting In and Speaking Out: Student Movements in the American South, 1960–1970.* Athens: University of Georgia Press, 2010.

Way, Albert. *Conserving Southern Longleaf: Herbert Stoddard and the Rise of Ecological Land Management.* Athens: University of Georgia Press, 2011.

Weinstein, Ruth. *A Force for Social Change: Ozark Back-to-the-Land Settlements, 1970–1975.* Little Rock: Arkansas Humanities Council, 1996.

West, Don. *Broadside to the Sun.* New York: W. W. Norton, 1946.

Whayne, Jeannie M., Thomas A. DeBlack, George Sabo III, and Morris S. Arnold. *Arkansas: A Narrative History.* 2nd ed. Fayetteville: University of Arkansas Press, 2013.

Whitfield, Stephen J. *Scott Nearing: Apostle of American Radicalism.* New York: Columbia University Press, 1974.

———. *The Culture of the Cold War.* Baltimore: Johns Hopkins University Press, 1996.

Woods, Randall. *Quest for Identity: America Since 1945.* Cambridge: Cambridge University Press, 2005.

Wright, Harold Bell. *The Shepherd of the Hills.* Branson: Shepherd of the Hills Historical Society, 1987.

Wrigglesworth, Chad, ed. *Distant Neighbors: The Selected Letters of Wendell Berry and Gary Snyder.* Berkeley: Counterpoint Press, 2014.

Wulf, Andrea. *The Invention of Nature: Alexander von Humbolt's New World.* New York: Knopf, 2015.

INDEX